JOHN SMAILES is a journalist, motorsport commentator and publicist, and until recently proprietor of a specialised communications agency. He was the managing editor of the 60th-anniversary history of the Confederation of Australian Motor Sport, now Motorsport Australia, the governing body of Australian motor racing. For Allen & Unwin he has written *Climbing the Mountain*, the autobiography of Australian motorsport legend Allan Moffat OBE; *Race Across the World*, the incredible story of the 1968 London–Sydney Marathon and a sequel to *The Bright Eyes of Danger*, written with the first Australian Touring Car Champion David McKay; and *Mount Panorama*, the full history of Australia's most revered motor-racing circuit for cars and motorcycles. *Speed Kings* fulfils a lifetime ambition to chronicle attempts by Australians and New Zealanders to conquer the greatest speedway of all.

www.johnsmailes.com.au

JOHN SMAILES

SPEED KINGS

Australia and New Zealand's quest to win the Indy 500,
the world's greatest motor race

ALLEN&UNWIN
SYDNEY•MELBOURNE•AUCKLAND•LONDON

First published in 2020

Allen & Unwin
83 Alexander Street
Crows Nest NSW 2065
Australia
Phone: (61 2) 8425 0100
Email: info@allenandunwin.com
Web: www.allenandunwin.com

A catalogue record for this
book is available from the
National Library of Australia

ISBN 978 1 76052 939 0

Internal design by Midland Typesetters, Australia
Index by Puddingburn
Set in 12.5/17.5 pt Minion Pro by Midland Typesetters, Australia
Printed and bound in Australia by Griffin Press, part of Ovato

10 9 8 7 6 5 4 3 2 1

In appreciation of my grandfather, Charles,
and my father, John Arthur Henry,
who, in the basement of Woolgar's Garage
at Circular Quay, ignited my enthusiasm
for motor racing in the round

And, as always, JJS

Contents

Introduction

My name is Rupert Jeffkins and I am Australia's original speed king.

I damn near won the Indianapolis 500 in 1912 and I could have finished in the top ten the year before, the first time the world's most important car race was ever held, if my co-driver hadn't been on drugs.

I was the first Australian—ever—to chance my arm on going overseas to race cars and I won wherever I went, on the Continent and in the US. I made my name on the wooden-planked ovals of California, the cinder tracks of the Midwest but mainly on the bricks of the mighty 2.5-mile (4-kilometre) Indianapolis quadrangle, the biggest and best racetrack the world has ever known.

People called me a barnstormer, a stuntman, a gun for hire. They also called me a drifter, a chancer, and a person of questionable moral fibre. There's some truth to all of that. But at a time when the motorcar was changing the world, I was there on the front-line, working with the car makers and factories to make speed the essence of their success.

I was hired by Serpollet, Velie, Mercer and Mercedes to develop and race their cars. Truth be known, I talked my way into a lot of those situations. People said I was full of BS and there's some truth to that, too. But true grit and determination bring their own reward and if you're a boy from Maitland, New South Wales, born to a family without prospects, then you make your own good fortune.

Half my career was forged overseas, the rest when I returned to Australia.

I promoted motor races and I fixed them as well. I was backed by cash from less-than-legitimate sources. I built my own car, fulfilling my own dream to become a car maker.

I was the master of mass media. For twenty years I toured the cinemas and public halls of Australia and New Zealand with a moving picture show called The Death Toll of the Speedway. *People flocked to hear me speak while jerky, lurid, black-and-white pictures of crashes, many fatal, filled the screen.*

At the very core of my presentation was the Indianapolis Motor Speedway—the greatest racetrack that's ever been.

I couldn't have done any of it without the Indianapolis 500.

Seventeen Australian and New Zealander race car drivers have attempted to win the most important superspeedway race of all time. Only two have succeeded—in 2008, New Zealander Scott Dixon, and in 2018, Australian Will Power.

Another 80—mechanics, engineers, designers, managers, strategists, team owners, promoters and star-struck dreamers— have made the Indianapolis 500 their holy grail. One such, Barry Green, a boy from rural Western Australia, won in his first full year as a team owner, with Jacques Villeneuve at the wheel. Villeneuve would later become F1 World Champion.

Paul 'Ziggy' Harcus waited three decades for his Indy win. The 64-year-old team strategist was the voice of reason, talking constantly into the ear pods of his driver, the kamikaze-like rocket ship that was Takuma Sato. Ziggy was like a second brain for Sato. His average speed over 200 laps—the 500 miles (804 kilometres) that defines the Indy 500—was 155.39 mph (250.02 km/h). The only Japanese ever to win Indy claimed the chequered flag just 0.2011 seconds clear of second place.

Speed at Indianapolis is a relative concept. Racing at 7 metres per second is blindingly quick by any standard, but by Indy measurements, Sato's win was the slowest race average of the decade.

'The Indianapolis 500 magnifies everything,' says Leigh Diffey. 'It's as if every race expands to fill the track's own unique reputation.' Diffey was talking to me from behind the wheel of his typically American pick-up—larger perhaps than necessary— driving to the fortress-like studios of NBC Sports, just half an hour from his home in Ridgefield, Connecticut, a mile north of the New York state border.

Diffey was a Down Under success, the first Australian and the first non–US-born citizen to anchor Indy 500's TV commentary. He had recently accepted US residency status—the better to expand his horizons—and he had been appointed to call play-by-play action for track and field at the Tokyo Olympics.

But his delivery remained true to his Aussie roots. The boy from Brisbane forged his skill in Supercars, Australia's premier sedan car championship, where his accurate and exciting commentary defined laconic: never a wasted word and yet intuitively using the right one.

His arrival at Indy, to take up the plum job in US motorsport, was more rewarding for the mere fact that he didn't speak like they did.

The Indy 500 is as ingrained in the American psyche as the Super Bowl. Americans rule Indy—that's a fact. But that they dominate the event is a myth. In 104 races since 1911, 30 have been won by non-Americans. Twenty-one foreigners from eleven countries have had their names engraved on the Indy's Borg-Warner Trophy, the most revered of all motorsport prizes.

The United Kingdom and Brazil top the list of non-American winners with seven victories each. Three multiple Formula One world champions figure in the results: Jim Clark and Graham Hill from Britain, and Emerson Fittipaldi from Brazil.

France has claimed four wins. In 2019, Simon Pagenaud ended a 99-year drought for his nation. It was in 1920 that Gaston Chevrolet, one of three Swiss-French–born car-making brothers, had previously won the race for France. He died just six months later, on the timber-board track of the Beverly Hills Speedway. Chevrolet had applied for US citizenship in 1914, but his acceptance is in doubt. If he had won Indy as an American, then the gap for French winners extends 105 years back to René Thomas in a Delage, in 1914.

Anomalies of nationality cloud the Indy record books.

Three Italians are credited with victory, but only one stands up to scrutiny. Mario Andretti, the name synonymous with speed, took US citizenship in 1964 and won at Indy in 1969. Dario Resta, 1916 winner, was born in Italy but raised in the United Kingdom and raced under the British flag. Only Ralph De Palma was an Italian citizen when he won in 1915. He became a US citizen five years later. De Palma would figure strongly in the career of Rupert Jeffkins.

Will Power now holds dual citizenship, and the Americans have appropriated Scott Dixon. In 2018 the mayor of Indianapolis proclaimed 24 September Scott Dixon Day.

There were 42 consecutive races—the Golden Years—when an American etched his name on the trophy. In the minds of all Americans—and in the eyes of the world—Indy became the United States' own motor race. That legend continues.

In 1961 Australia's Jack Brabham raced a rear-engine Cooper Climax at Indianapolis and came ninth. He upset the status quo and started an avalanche. In 1965 Jim Clark used a spindly rear-engine Lotus adapted from Formula One to beat the big brutish front-engine Indy roadsters that even now evoke the spirit of Indy. Graham Hill repeated the rear-engine rout the following year. After those two victories, the roadsters were doomed but American drivers were not. They quickly adapted and embraced the new cars and for 22 years they wrested back control of their race.

The dam broke again in 1989. Emerson 'Emo' Fittipaldi of Brazil won Indy for American team owner Ueal 'Pat' Patrick. Since Emo's victory through to 2020, 22 Indys have been won by foreign drivers.

It's a paradox. Indianapolis—of all the motor races in the world—is regaled as the great American bastion. Even though it's not.

1

The Laying of the Bricks

Carl G. Fisher was an early Elon Musk. He could see seismic change coming and he wanted to lead it. For Fisher it wasn't enough to create the Indianapolis Motor Speedway, which he did—all the better to showcase the world's greatest invention, the motorcar—but he built a city alongside it, which he called 'Speedway'.

His town of Speedway would be the world's first city without horses, where people would commute in cars and on bicycles. The residents of Speedway would live in real houses, not shanties, serviced by electricity, and they would dedicate their lives to building automobiles in nearby factories. Indianapolis would become a hub of the United States motor industry, maybe the equal of Detroit.

Fisher built roads. Not just trunk roads, but major freeways. In 1912 he was instrumental in constructing the Lincoln Highway, the first car-carrying road to traverse the entire United States. Cars couldn't flourish without roads. Infrastructure was a term yet to be invented. But the need was there.

He built destinations. Out of swampland, Fisher created Miami Beach. The great American humorist Will Rogers said, 'Fisher was the first man to discover there was sand under the water, sand that could hold up a real estate sign. He made the dredge the national emblem of Florida.'

And then his run came to an end. Fisher lost his pile in the great stock market crash of '29. He lived out his days through the kindness of friends and died, aged 65, in 1939.

Fisher had opened his first bicycle shop in 1891 when he was just seventeen. He had two brothers in the business, both younger. The bike shop was not Carl's first venture. There was no money in the Fisher household; their alcoholic dad had decamped, and Carl had been working odd jobs to support the family since the age of twelve.

The United States in the 1890s was in the grip of a bicycle craze, and Fisher caught the wave. The first bicycles were expensive; at A\$150 (more than A\$4000 now), about one-third the average annual wage, they were the playthings of foppish youths. But technical advancements made them safer and more comfortable, and a genuine alternative to the horse. Pedal power liberated middle-class Americans. More than four million mounted up in that decade alone.

By the mid-1890s, Albert Augustus Pope, the father of the American pushbike industry, was making a quarter of a million Columbia-brand bikes a year—and earning a massive royalty from many other brands for each bike they sold using his patents. Mass production made them cheaper and accessible. Suddenly, you could buy a bicycle for as little as A$22.

It hadn't been easy. As late as 1880 the city of New York banned bicycle riding in Central Park, perceiving a threat to pedestrians and horses alike. Pope had been a fearless captain in the American Civil War, for the Union Army, just a decade and a half earlier. He took the city on full frontal, paying the legal fees of riders he encouraged to ride into the park. His style was confrontational, but he most certainly wasn't a promoter. He left that to others.

The teenage Carl G. Fisher knew how to promote. From his small bicycle store in downtown Indianapolis, he organised a troupe of stunt and high-speed riders—he called them the 'speed kings'. They barnstormed the state, racing on board tracks, match-racing each other. The races, usually, were rigged—all the better to excite. Fisher rode as well. It was never only about the money. His ex-wife Jane (he had three) wrote in her biography: 'He often said—he just liked to see the dirt fly.'

In 1898 at Fisher's urging, the League of American Wheelmen conducted their national racing championship in Indianapolis on a purpose-built quarter-mile board track, Newby Oval. It was hugely ambitious, with capacity for 15,000 spectators, and brought massive cachet to the city. Fisher backed it and made money out of it.

But he could also see the wave peaking. There was too much competition in the bike business; profit margins were being slashed. Fisher had longed to be a manufacturer but now he counted his good fortune that he'd stayed out of the big-risk end of the craze, content to remain a retailer and become a supplier of specialty parts from workshops he'd set up downtown. He watched while the smaller makers went broke, consumed by the big manufacturers like Pope.

Besides, there was something bigger coming.

Before the turn of the century Fisher became Indianapolis's first motorist. He'd imported a 2.5-horsepower (1.8-kilowatt) De Dion-Bouton tricycle; powered by a single cylinder four-stroke engine, it was a hybrid of car and bike. This would be the next big thing—Fisher was sure of it.

On 3 November 1900, with just 4500 committed automobilists in the entire United States, the first New York Motor Show opened at Madison Square Garden. Sixty-nine exhibitors showed off 160 vehicles. It's estimated that 50,000 people paid 50 cents apiece to be there.

Fisher paid a bit more. The 26-year-old arrived in style by steam train from Indianapolis, and he went home as the first multi-franchised car dealer in the entire country. His big brand was Oldsmobile. Ransom E. Olds was America's first mass producer—even before Henry Ford. In his first year, 1901, Olds turned out 425 of his Curved Dash Runabouts for a recommended retail price of US$650. The automobile craze expanded so fast that four years later he had made 19,000 of them.

Fisher also secured the Winton franchise. He'd known Scotsman Alexander Winton through his Winton Bicycle Company and liked the quality of his manufacturing. Winton hand-built his cars—in 1899 he made 100 of them and, incredibly, that made him the United States' largest manufacturer. Winton branded his cars emotively—Flyer and Bullet—and they lived up to their names.

4

Fisher took his Winton barnstorming to new heights that left his bicycle promotions in the shade.

The dawn of mechanisation was the talk of the new century. The aeroplane had not yet been invented. Wilbur and Orville Wright wouldn't fly at Kitty Hawk until 1903. People racing automobiles, setting records and performing stunts was as exciting as it got. The automobile craze needed entrepreneurs like Fisher. He went on the county fair circuit—charging promoters US$500 to make an appearance and punters US$10 for a high-speed ride.

In Indianapolis they called him 'Crazy Carl'. He jumped a car off a two-storey building to prove it could be driven away. He built a 50-metre ski ramp on the side of his dealership and drove a car up it in less than ten seconds. He flew a huge gas-filled balloon across downtown Indianapolis with a car suspended beneath (involving a bit of subterfuge because the car had had its engine removed to lighten the burden). Like any switched-on car dealer, he ran showroom promotions—guess the number of live bees in a bottle and win a set of tyres—and if he got lucky with his sales spiel, he'd send his customers home in a new car.

Simultaneously he became part of the fabric of the city of Indianapolis and a man of considerable influence. The shakers and movers gravitated to him. Together, they ran a think-tank in a private room at the back of a restaurant near his original bike shop, enthusiastically seeking opportunity.

Fisher brought Prest-O-Lite to the table. Young inventor P.C. Avery had approached him with a failsafe way of making an automobile headlight seven times brighter than anything before. Fisher passed it on to one of his customers, Jim Allison, who was a member of the inner circle, and took a bit of the company for himself. The Concentrated Acetylene Company, owned by Fisher, Allison and Avery, would go on to supply headlights to pretty much the entire automotive market and make them a fortune. Union Carbide bought the company in 1917 for US$9 million. (Prest-O-Lite still exists but its batteries are now branded Exide and its spark plugs are Autolite and owned by Ford.)

Another member of the circle, Frank Wheeler, made carburettors. The Wheeler-Schebler Carburetor Company would one day become BorgWarner. Almost from its outset it was a first-tier supplier to more than fifteen car companies, all of them major.

Completing the circle, Arthur Newby was already a car maker—he called his car the National. Nationals had initially been electric vehicles but with the urging of the think-tank he'd turned to gasoline and embraced motor racing as his promotional tool. Newby trusted Fisher. He'd built the Newby Oval on Fisher's say-so. He'd torn it down, too, when Fisher warned him that crowd support for bicycle races was wearing thin. He snuck out with his capital intact.

The rapid growth of the car industry was stunning, exponential and without peer.

Detroit, just 270 miles (434 kilometres) to the north-east of Indianapolis and blessed by easy access to the geographically significant Great Lakes, which guaranteed a parts supply trade route even in the dead of winter, was seizing the automotive-making ascendancy. Henry Ford built his first plant there.

But Indianapolis wasn't far behind. By the end of the first decade of the new century, it would boast more than twenty car makers, and ultimately it would be home to almost 60, many building their vehicles within a ten-block radius.

The think-tank could smell opportunity. At the turn of the century, there was less than 500 miles (804 kilometres) of sealed road in the whole country, most in metropolitan areas. So they came up with a big idea: a test track to both develop and showcase automobiles that would be an industry first.

It was a much better idea than road racing. If you wanted to promote, you needed to keep the cars in view of the spectators. In 1904 millionaire William K. Vanderbilt Jnr ('Willie K.' to his friends) ran the first serious road race on Long Island over 30 miles (48 kilometres) of public roads. Fisher went to Long Island to witness it. It only served to convince him that motor racing in the round was the way to go.

He responded by repurposing a racetrack around the Indiana Fairgrounds to run a 100-mile (160-kilometre) event in 1905. Arthur Newby's National won it, then went on to set a world-first 24-hour record, driving 1096 miles (1763 kilometres), its path lit by Prest-O-Lite lanterns placed around the track.

But Fisher's bid to build the world's first superspeedway was beaten by the British. In 1907 Hugh F. Locke King, son of the seventh Baron King of Ockham, built Brooklands Motor Circuit on his own estate outside London. It cost him £150,000 (£15.8 million today) and he did it because he believed, like Fisher, that his national motor industry needed a test and development centre if it was to compete with European makers.

Locke King's 2.75-mile (4.42-kilometre) 30-degree banked concrete oval opened with a 24-hour record run. Selwyn Edge drove his British-built Napier solo to cover 1581 miles (2543 kilometres)—almost 50 per cent more than the Indianapolis Fairground record.

Fisher took the news—the disgrace—to his think-tank and urged immediate action.

He'd found 130 hectares of farmland just west of the city for the asking price of US$72,000 (US$2 million today). Fisher put it to Newby, Wheeler and Allison and to his bank manager. The bank declined, spooked by the risk, but the four amigos remained committed. On 8 February 1909 they inaugurated the Indianapolis Motor Speedway Company. Fisher was its president, Newby and Wheeler vice-presidents, and Allison secretary treasurer. The documentation was not filed until 20 March.

On Thursday 19 August, the first car race on the Indianapolis Motor Speedway—a two-lap, 5-mile (8-kilometre) dash—was run. It was won by Austrian-born Louis Schwitzer on a Stoddard-Dayton. It had been a remarkably quick construction program, despite being hampered by late-winter rains and snowstorms: a green field had been transformed into a finished speedway in just five months. And the speedway had already hosted two previous meetings—a balloon race in June to keep interest alive, and in the week before cars first used the track, a motorcycle race was held. The 10-mile (16-kilometre) amateur motorcycle championship was won by Indianapolis's Erwin G. Baker, later to be dubbed Cannonball Baker by the media in recognition of his long-distance speed attempts. The Cannonball Baker Sea to Shining Sea road race across the US, named in his memory, remains to this day the best-known, unofficial, undercover, totally illegal but completely deniable high-speed event of all time.

The first Indianapolis speedway track was surfaced with crushed earth and rock. Riders who crashed suffered not just gravel rash but cuts and contusions, and their wounds filled with tar. The first car meeting commenced despite the warnings from injured motorcyclists, and five people were killed—three competitors and two spectators. On Day One, driving in the 250-mile (402-kilometre) Prest-O-Lite Trophy, Wilfred 'Billy' Bourque and his riding mechanic Harry Holcomb spun out of Turn Four, hit a rut and flipped several times, then struck a fence post. Both died.

In the face of official sanction, Fisher galvanised a 300-person overnight work crew to repack the surface. Next morning the track was in a shape good enough to convince officials to start the 300-mile (482-kilometre) Wheeler-Schebler Trophy Race. The trophy was more than two metres tall, made of silver, and was said to have cost Frank Wheeler US$10,000 (US$280,000 today) to have made.

Charlie Merz was a works driver for Arthur Newby's National team. He was just seventeen when he first drove for National. At the 175-mile (281-kilometre) mark, just after halfway, Merz's front right tyre let go on Turn One and his car cannoned off the track through the outer fencing. Mercifully, only a few of the 37,000-strong crowd were standing there. Two were killed, along with Merz's riding mechanic Claude Kellum. Merz survived, crawling out from under the car to hit the engine kill switch and avoid an explosion. Almost simultaneously Bruce Keen's Marmon hit a spectator bridge at the other end of the track—this time without death, although riding mechanic

James Schiller suffered serious head injuries. Fisher's partners called for an early halt to the race. Instead of ending in triumph, the first race meeting at the Indianapolis Motor Speedway had become a killing field.

With outrage, Indiana Lieutenant Governor Frank J. Hall lobbied Governor Thomas Marshall to propose and pass a law prohibiting motorsport. People went to motor races as they did to bullfights, in anticipation of bloodletting, he asserted. But bullfights didn't put spectators' lives at risk.

Commercial expediency shut down his protest. Indianapolis's motor industry didn't want its most valuable new asset closed; in fact, neither did the entire United States. The car industry was too important to its economy. Fisher would simply have to find a solution.

It came from the Wabash Clay Company, a proud Indiana firm. The Indianapolis Motor Speedway partners had considered all alternatives, even concreting the surface as they had at Brooklands. But already the Brooklands surface was breaking up under extremes of weather. The strong advice was to use bricks—3.2 million of them, each weighing just under 10 pounds (4.5 kilograms). Bricks, the engineers said, would provide more traction than any other surface and would increase potential average speeds by up to 2 mph (3.2 km/h). The bricks began arriving by rail car from Veedersburg, 64 miles (103 kilometres) to the west, each to be laid by hand. Concrete walls 9 inches (22 centimetres) thick and 33 inches (83 centimetres) high would rim the track corners to contain the cars and ensure spectator safety.

Brick laying was an artform. The existing surface provided a sound base, overlaid with sand into which the bricks were pressed with a roller. Equal parts sand and cement held them together. Surface variation was limited to just 1.2 centimetres in every 4 metres of track. It took just 63 days to complete the job, and an average of more than 50,000 bricks were laid each day. At their peak, some crews were laying 140,000 bricks in a nine-hour shift. In a clever publicity stunt, the speedway claimed that the key brick was made out of solid gold. It was there for Governor Marshall to lay on 17 December 1909. It wasn't gold: it was a Wheeler-Schebler carburettor made from bronze and brass that had been melted down and poured into a Wabash brick-shaped cast. Nobody minded. It was the thought that counted.

In front of the governor, in freezing conditions, Lewis Strang's 200-horsepower (150 kilowatt) Fiat rattled off a 10-mile (16-kilometre) average speed of 73.58 mph (118.39 km/h). The next day, without the fuss of celebrities, it set a new American speedway 5-mile (8-kilometre) record of 91.8 mph (147.7 km/h). Comparatively, the abandoned Wheeler-Schebler Trophy Race, which had been held on the unsealed surface, had been run at an average speed of 55.61 mph (89.47 km/h).

News media was quick to give the speedway a new name—the Brickyard. With a rush of smaller speedways being constructed across the country, its brick surface was Indianapolis's point of difference. The others were made of clay or boards. Only the Indy speedway was made of bricks. That's the way it would remain for half a century until 1961, when they paved over the lot, except for one strip across the finish line, known forever as the Yard of Bricks. Like the Blarney Stone, it's there to be kissed.

Carl Fisher threw everything at the 1910 season.

He scheduled three race meetings throughout the summer and a Festival of Aviation featuring the Wright Brothers. Orville Wright flew Carl Fisher on a low-level pass of the speedway. One of the Wright biplane pilots, 21-year-old Walter Brooking, set a new altitude record, just on 5000 feet (1500 metres), launched from a sled near Turn Two of the speedway. It commanded national attention.

Fisher promoted his 1910 race meetings as largely injury-free, justification for the new surface. The daring and somewhat accident-prone Herb Lytle spoiled a perfect record. Herb broke his leg when his American overturned and pinned him on the north-east turn. But there'd been a fatality in private practice. Local National works driver Tommy Kincaid, 23, had won the Memorial Day Prest-O-Lite race at the end of May but did not return for the Labor Day meeting in September. Official records offered no explanation. Yet there's a photograph of his headstone showing a date of death of 7 July 1910. And a small story in the *Indianapolis Star* on the same date. It's the first rule of deniable public relations. Like a tree falling in the forest, or without social media coverage, if there wasn't a crowd or a camera there to see it happen, perhaps it didn't. Fisher thought so, anyway.

The 1910 season had been a watershed for US motorsport. In pursuit of sales promotion, works teams had joined a national circuit, starting at Los Angeles's Ascot track, moving to the new steeply banked 1-mile (1.6-kilometre) board track at Los Angeles Motordrome and then up to the Atlanta Speedway.

Indianapolis was the grand finale. But crowds hadn't met the organisers' expectations. They'd not been down, but they'd not been terrific either. Fisher and Newby had experienced waning crowd support before. They'd shut the Newby Oval bicycle velodrome just in time. Could there, they reasoned, already be too much motor racing going on? Had they saturated Indianapolis with three grand race meetings over the summer? They needed a big idea, something to guarantee the Brickyard a stand-alone look of greatness.

They needed an event to test cars to their limit and provide a platform for industry promotion that the whole world, not only the US, would notice. They considered a 24-hour race—but on their racetrack, over that distance, with cars being so fragile, the likelihood of anyone finishing would be slim and, besides, who'd stay up all night to watch it? They needed something that would occur in an economic, time-efficient manner, so that non-committed racegoers could watch the start, stay for the finish and still be home for supper.

No—they would promote the longest, highest speed sprint-marathon race the world had ever seen, a race where the distance was achievable only if car, driver and team were the very best. They would run the Indianapolis 500.

And if it didn't work, they reasoned, they could always try something else.

2

The Speed King

Rupert Jeffkins couldn't believe it. He'd clung to the wooden-framed seat of the works Mercedes for almost 199 laps of the 1912 Indianapolis 500 and he was less than 4 miles (6.4 kilometres) from the finish line and victory. This was to be the turning point of his career—the big boast he could carry with him for the rest of his life. He was going to win the World's Greatest Motor Race. He was going to be Australia's Speed King.

Okay, so he was the riding mechanic. The driver was the imperious Italian Ralph De Palma. But the riding mechanic was a vital part of the team. He wasn't just along for the ride. His job was to pump fuel from the tank to the engine. There was a brass plunger at his feet—a bit like a bicycle pump—and he'd work it like crazy to keep the fuel flowing. Then there was the oil.

These babies chewed through oil at a rate of almost a litre every 10 miles (16 kilometres). The oil reservoir was almost as big as the fuel tank and he had to keep pumping that too.

The riding mechanic was the eyes and ears of the car.

De Palma, the Italian, only had to look forward. Rupert needed to keep an eye on all that was going on around them—not that there was much need for him to look behind. They'd been the class of the field. From the time they assumed the lead on lap three, they'd sprinted away. No one was catching them. They were, incredibly, five and a half laps ahead of the locally built National driven by 22-year-old Indianapolis resident Joe Dawson. They had eleven minutes up their sleeve. But they had paid a heavy price for their pace. The much-vaunted brick surface was physically demanding on the cars and their crews. They were being pummelled. De Palma's hands and forearms were so cramped and sore from hanging on that Rupert had to reach across and help steer the car. It was hard for them to see, hard to think.

Maybe that's why he missed it. On lap 196 of 200, the big Mercedes (it would be another fourteen years before Benz joined the party) started to slow. It was almost imperceptible at first and De Palma pressed on. But then smoke started to billow. Damn. Jeffkins was in charge of engine management. The spirit level gauge on the wooden dash in front of him told him how much oil he had to pump into this monster of a motor. Why had he not seen it? Or was it something else?

Slowly—but with enough margin for them to reach the finish ahead of the other competitors—they crept on, with cars passing them now, including Dawson unlapping himself. Surely, though, they'd be okay. *Don't accelerate. Coast. Use the throttle as little as possible. Let momentum do its work*, Rupert told himself.

They had been averaging better than 80 mph (128 km/h) and before this major problem they had been expecting to make it to the chequered flag in just a tad over six hours. They could afford to extend that time; they had the margin.

And then, *bang*. Coming into Turn Four, a conrod snapped, blowing a hole in the crankcase. All Rupert's remaining pure mineral oil, with its heady, intoxicating aroma, spewed onto the bricks, accompanied by heavy metal shrapnel ricocheting down the track. The massive Mercedes came to a halt.

They weren't sure whether they were on their last or their penultimate lap. All they knew was that halfway down the five-eighth mile (1-kilometre) main straight, a chequered flag was beckoning. By now both occupants had jumped out of the car and had begun to push. Jeffkins was at the rear of the car, shoving with all his might. De Palma walked alongside, guiding the steering wheel and perhaps applying some degree of forward motion.

There were 80,000 people at Indianapolis Motor Speedway that day. Some had already begun to leave, certain that victory was going to the big, grey Number Four and that the local car and driver would be vanquished. Suddenly, they rose to their feet. They may not have come to the racetrack that day to cheer the Merc home, but they were damned sure they were going to applaud this heroic effort. Their ovation started as a small rumble and grew to become a roar of approval and support.

Joe Dawson and riding mechanic Harry Martin ploughed ahead. They, too, weren't certain of their situation so they completed two additional laps, just to be certain. There was no disputing the result. The rules stipulated that a car had to finish under its own power and it had to complete the full 500 miles. The Mercedes had done neither. There was one more lap to go, and in their wildest dreams they couldn't push the car that far.

Dawson and Martin won in 6 hours 21 minutes 6 seconds, at an average of 78.71 mph (126.64 km/h).

The 500-mile rule created quite an anomaly. Even as Dawson was accepting his accolades, and the US$20,000 winner's prize, others raced on. The last car to finish, Ralph Mulford's Knox, rolled across the line 8 hours 53 minutes after the start at an average speed of 56.28 mph (90.55 km/h), officially to this day the slowest finishing time ever recorded at the Indy 500. Mulford took his time—stopping to fit softer shock absorbers because he was hurting badly, and sending out for a chicken dinner and ice cream because he needed his strength. His efforts netted him US$1200. De Palma and Jeffkins were classified eleventh, the first non-finisher, and out of the money.

Winner Joe Dawson went home to his mother, enjoyed a quiet meal then caught a trolley car to the YMCA for a long, hot steam bath. He allowed himself a celebratory cigar. Jeffkins, meanwhile, checked himself into the newly opened Methodist Hospital, his nerves and his body jarred beyond his ability to cope. He claimed that De Palma joined him, but there's no record of this and it's unlikely to have happened. Jeffkins' version of any event, it turned out, was always open to question.

It's disillusioning when your hero doesn't live up to your expectation. Rupert had been the first Australian at Indy. He never made

the Motorsport Hall of Fame—not even close. But he was the first Australian to race cars internationally and for a while he knocked on the door of deserved rather than simply contrived fame. Seen through the prism of a century of changing social standards you'd probably give him a break. To get to where he was, he had to be a big-talking self-believing self-promoter, but he was not necessarily kosher on the fact-check scale. The facts seldom got in his way.

Rupert Jeffkins was a love rat. He married three times and never, it seems, divorced. He left his first wife in Australia to seek his fortune overseas and when he returned after twelve years, he did not reunite with her. He left another wife behind in Indianapolis. Jeffkins and his third wife had five children and one of them was responsible for the simple plaque laid years after his death in 1954, atop his pauper's grave.

Rupert was born on 20 October 1881 in Maitland, New South Wales, third child of eleven. His father was a prison warder at the jail named for the inland city at the head of the Hunter River. They hanged sixteen people inside the jail's stone walls and flogged many more.

Rupert's surname was Jiffkins. He changed the vowel when he entered the United States, a simple foil to reinvent himself. His father William and mother Clara had emigrated from England only four years before his birth. They'd already had two daughters before Rupert. William had been a career military man, a staff sergeant in the NSW Military Service—rigid, upright, respectful, and because of his unbending principles, ultimately the subject of a clash of wills of such magnitude that he was summarily dismissed from his prison job. His story made headlines. *The Sydney Truth*, a scandal sheet owned by William Nicholas Willis who straddled the salacious dual occupations of newspaper proprietor and politician, took up William's case: 'Wrongfully Accused, Illegally Dismissed, He is now Kept Down by a Villainous Slander—His Influential Friends Alienated and His Family Suffering Want.'

The paper claimed that 'Jiffkins' persecution dated from the time some gaudy popinjay of a country officer reported him for discourtesy'. *The Sydney Truth*, eager for circulation, its proprietor keen to score political points against the military, went on the attack but nothing changed.

William, two years short of his 60th birthday, remained unemployed, relying on an Imperial Services pension. The family relocated to Annandale, a working-class inner Sydney suburb. They lived in a weatherboard two-up-two-down in Young Street, one of the area's first subdivisions. Rupert, the eldest son, was under pressure to be another breadwinner for the family. When he was married, at nineteen, to seventeen-year-old Violet Mary Walsh from nearby Albion Street, he listed his occupation as carter. A year later he was gone.

It's unlikely Rupert imagined himself as a race car driver. When he was born, the world's first petrol-powered production automobile, Karl Benz's three-wheeled Patent-Motorwagen, was still five years away from launch. Even when Rupert abandoned Violet and sailed for Europe at age twenty, there were at best a handful of cars on Australian roads. There were 1.7 million horses, though, useful for a carter, one for a little more than every two people, in the whole country. In comparison, in the United States just 4192 cars were registered at the turn of the twentieth century. (Australian motor vehicle registrations would not begin until 1909, so exact figures aren't known.)

When Rupert skipped town, Australia's first motor race was still three years in the future. But it's conceivable that he'd caught the automotive bug. Already, no fewer than twenty Australian entrepreneurs were trying to build cars, mainly steamers, and their efforts made front-page news. The first imported car, a De Dion-Bouton, arrived in New South Wales in 1900, closely followed by three Benz.

Rupert set out for England and the Continent. Some young Australians were signing up to represent their newly federated country in the Boer War. Rupert wasn't one of them. In 1901 you could either board a ship that went around the Cape of Good Hope, mighty close to the war zone, or you could sail through the Suez Canal and up into the Mediterranean Sea. The ships that went via the Mediterranean sometimes stopped off in Marseille. And France was the home of the world's motor industry. Rupert's eyes would have popped. The French were on their way to turning out almost 30,000 new vehicles a year, about three times the production of the United States. If he wasn't a car enthusiast before, he quickly became one.

The motor car represented the future and he wanted to be part of it.

Rupert's account of his grand European adventure is likely a work of fiction. He claimed to have worked for the now long-defunct Serpollet car company and that may be true. Léon Serpollet's eponymous brand was kicking serious goals. In the year Rupert arrived in France, the company's workforce more than doubled—from 60 to 140—to meet demand and Serpollet, a self-promoter, was leading from the front. In 1902 he drove his dramatically streamlined car—dubbed the Easter Egg for its shape—to a new world land speed record of 75.06 mph (120.77 km/h). Soon after, he entered the 1903 Paris–Madrid, an ambitious 812-mile (1307-kilometre) trans-continental dash, abandoned at Bordeaux after nine deaths on its first day. One of those fatalities was Marcel Renault, scion of the major car maker. The French government ordered the cars shut down and towed to the railway station by horse to return to Paris. It was quickly dubbed the Race of Death and it brought an end to open-road racing in France.

Léon Serpollet may well have warmed to Rupert Jeffkins, the Australian youngster 25 years his junior. Car manu-facturers needed sales staff—demonstrators—and with clientele as demanding as the Shah of Persia and several Indian maha-rajahs, a polite, intelligent and, importantly, English-speaking chauffeur-mechanic could have found gainful employment. Car owners seldom drove or fettled their own cars.

Jeffkins, by his own account, moved on to England, only 31 miles (50 kilometres) from Boulogne-sur-Mer, the seaside car race venue in northern France where he said he last worked for Serpollet. His claim to have been next employed by British Daimler is most likely true.

English-born but Hamburg-educated engineer Frederick Simms acquired the rights to the Daimler name in Great Britain from his good friend Gottlieb Daimler, one of the industry's pioneers. Simms was a true promoter. He is said to have brought the word 'petrol' into common parlance and he was the first to use the term 'motorcar'. He also started Britain's first motorist's club, which later became the Royal Automobile Club. By the time Rupert arrived at Daimler headquarters at Coventry, the company was already a supplier by royal warrant to the king and his family. Rupert's experience with Serpollet would have carried some weight in getting a job. But did he race? Probably not.

These were heady times in the automotive industry: just to be close to the flame was enough to ignite the soul. It was easy for Jeffkins to talk up his own involvement, especially when exaggeration or falsehood was unlikely to be discovered. And he was learning from masters. No one in this new industry was shy.

When he returned to Australia in late 1912, a hero of his own making, Jeffkins gave interviews that now simply don't stand up to serious scrutiny. In his version, the period 1903–09, a turbulent time in the development of the motor industry, had him criss-crossing the Atlantic: representing the US motor industry in Europe and racing on both continents. He raced, he said, in the United States in 1904 at the 'birthplace of speed', Ormond Beach, Florida, just up the coast from Daytona, now the spiritual home of stock-car racing. Rupert said he took a wire-wheeled Daimler to the speed trials on Ormond Beach's hard-packed golden sands, but when the world record for the flying mile was broken three times in half an hour by three different drivers, Rupert wasn't one of them.

Rupert raced, he said, in the Milwaukee 24 Hour. Two were held in 1907 and 1908, part of a plethora of long-distance endurance races that sprang up across the US. On the still-unsealed Milwaukee Mile oval, the world's oldest speedway, older even than Indianapolis, and illuminated by backlit lanterns, Fred Leiser and Bobby Drake won both. In 1908 they drove their 40-horsepower (30-kilowatt) Locomobile around in left-hand circles 1195 times at an average speed of 49.79 mph (80.11 km/h). There was no sign of Rupert Jeffkins.

In 1910, however, he hit the headlines of the *Waterloo Evening Courier*, 9 July, Webster City, Iowa:

'ATTEMPT TO GET REVENGE'—Discharged Employee Ruins Parts of Automobiles
R.F. Jeffkins, a discharged mechanic at the Hanson and Tyler auto garage in this city is under arrest for malicious mischief and has been placed under $1,000 bond. It is charged that to wreak vengeance on his former employers he poured sulphuric acid into the engines and copper platings of three big automobiles belonging to the company. The crime was discovered soon after and Jeffkins placed under arrest after a dramatic chase of four miles into the country.

The case was dismissed, unproved, after 23 hours of jury deliberation.

Jeffkins had already had a run-in with the law earlier that year. In January in the district court of Chicago, he pleaded guilty to a charge of sending an improper letter to a young woman who had jilted him. He was fined one cent.

But he was, demonstrably, motor racing.

Horseracing tracks across the nation were doing double duty with cars—and pulling big crowds. On 4 July, just five days before his arrest, Jeffkins attacked the unsealed half-mile oval of the Webster City Driving Park, Iowa, the first time it had been used for cars, and won the 10-mile (16-kilometre) preliminary race by two laps. He was driving a stripped-down Willys-Overland. In the main feature, he was in the lead when his carburettor malfunctioned. He stopped to fix it and still finished second. Later in the day he drove a 5-mile (8-kilometre) exhibition against the clock and covered the distance in just over six minutes, at an average of 55 mph (88 km/h). The following day, the same newspaper that a week later would thunder his arrest compared him to Barney Oldfield, the cigar-chewing hero of early American motor racing.

It gave him some incentive. Being a racing driver was one level; being a race promoter was another thing entirely. Rupert set out to take the leap.

Marion, a city within the greater Cedar Rapids metropolitan area, is about 120 miles (193 kilometres) south-east of Webster City, and Jeffkins determined he would both promote and race in an event held in the local fairgrounds. He convinced the city council to let him replicate the success of the Webster City motor races. On 8 September, the *Marion Sentinel* reported:

AUTO RACES NO GOOD.
The least said about the auto races on Monday is the best way to forget them, perhaps. It was a financial success, to be sure, for the promoter Mr R. Jeffkins, who was never heard of in Marion until a couple of weeks ago, and who doubtless will never be heard of again. As far as being entertaining to the 4000 or 5000 people in attendance it was a dismal failure. The two motorcycle races were quite exciting, there being ten starters in the

first race. There was nothing to the auto races on account of a lack of participants. In the first auto race there was but four starters [*sic*] and this was finally narrowed down to two and in the great (?) free-for-all 20-mile race there were two starters, Jeffkins being one of them, and he was apparently defeated before he threw a tyre which completely put him out.

By the way, the fair association had nothing to do with the races. They received a stipulated rental and that was all.

Jeffkins had found a lucrative new calling as a race promoter, one he'd pursue as a career when he returned to Australia. He raced once more in 1910 at the Carroll County Fairgrounds in Iowa, but his Overland, little more than an open-wheeled buckboard upon which he precariously perched, failed to finish.

His next race would be the inaugural Indianapolis 500, and miraculously he was part of a works team.

The Indianapolis 500 was grand on every scale. The track was so vast that the cars become dots in the distance at the course extremities. Its inaugural race, held on 30 May 1911, attracted more entries than any other single American motor race before it. Forty-six entrants each paid US$500 to secure a place in the field. That was a massive amount—but nobody baulked. Forty-four cars turned up.

The race conceived by Hoosiers (the epithet for Indiana residents), for Hoosiers, was living up to expectation. Of the 24 brands entered, ten were from the state of Indiana. Fifteen of the field came from a radius no more than 130 miles

(209 kilometres) around the superspeedway and four were from the city of Indianapolis itself. Tellingly, there was only one entry from Detroit—the Buick to be driven by Louis Chevrolet.

Rupert Jeffkins found his Indy ride close to his own home base. The giant John Deere farm machinery conglomerate operated out of Moline, Illinois. Willard Lamb Velie, grandson of Deere's founder, had set up his self-named car company there as well. You could almost see Rupert drawing back his arrow and aiming it directly at the heart of Velie's business.

Velie had been doing very well without Rupert's help. Their cars were cheap and cheerful, comparatively low cost, easy to use and maintain. By the time of the Indy 500, the company had already sold more than 1000 of them, and was moving on to start a truck line as well. Perhaps that's what persuaded Velie to enter the race. Brand promotion would flow from the massive exposure the event provided.

Willard Velie and his wife Annie lived extravagantly. As their team prepared for Indy, they were already planning their new, palatial home on a 200-hectare estate on the south side of Moline. Inspired by Italian homes they'd visited on their Continental jaunts, Villa Velie would have 46 rooms, fourteen bedrooms, twelve bathrooms and marble floors, and the grounds would be planted with 21 grape varieties and feature not only a conservatory that housed banana trees, but also a ski run for the winter. (They would live in their dream villa right up to the Great Depression.)

Velie entered two cars for Indianapolis. Jeffkins, extraordinarily, would drive one. Howard Hall, an all-rounder with a lot more form than Rupert, would drive the other. Hall had been a mechanic for the Chevrolet team and in 1910 he'd ridden shotgun on land speed record-holder Bob Burman's Marquette Buick when they came home third in the Automobile Club of America's American Grand Prize race; it was contested over 415 miles (667 kilometres) on a 17.2-mile (27.7-kilometre) course through the streets of Savannah, Georgia. Race deaths in those barnstorming days were commonplace and Hall had known tragedy. He had been a driver in the 1909 Portola Road Race in San Francisco—an event conceived to celebrate San Francisco's rebirth after the earthquake of 1906. A retaining nut came off Hall's wheel and fatally struck a spectator in the head.

The Velies' entrants would be amongst the smallest cars in the Indy field: just 5.5 litres putting out 40 horsepower (30 kilowatts) compared to the imported Mercedes at 9.5 litres and almost double the power. Their chance of outright victory was slim.

Organiser Carl Fisher was overwhelmed with entries and, with companies clamouring to find out for themselves what it would take to win on this bold new track, he threw the super-speedway open to testing from 1 May. It was the start of an Indy tradition—the Month of May, in which the city turns its attention to its most prominent attraction.

Major controversy surrounded one of the local cars. The Marmon Wasp would be the only single-seat race car to enter the 1911 Indianapolis 500. Its driver would be Ray Harroun, who in 1910 claimed both the 200-mile (321-kilometre) Wheeler-Schebler Trophy and the 50-mile (80-kilometre) Remy Grand Brassard Race on the Indianapolis quadrangle. It had been a sensational year for Harroun. (Much later when the American Automobile Association retrospectively applied a points table to races held in those early years, Harroun was demonstrably the 1910 champion.) He had retired at the end of the 1910 season, aged 31, and was happily working in Marmon's design office in downtown Indianapolis, when the owner Howard Marmon approached him with a big idea—design a car to win the Indianapolis 500 and drive it yourself.

Marmon was a huge supporter of the new 500-mile race. 'I believe the appetite of the public is whetted to a keen taste for automobile speed battles,' he told *The Automobile* magazine at the beginning of 1911. 'The 500-mile race proposed at the Indianapolis Motor Speedway promises to attract a great field and will be perhaps the greatest race ever held.'

The car Harroun designed, the Marmon Wasp, wasn't strictly within the spirit of the Indy rules. It had just one seat—which meant no room for a riding mechanic. Carl Fisher had planned the race as a showcase for production cars, stripped down, lightened and fit for purpose: not purpose built. But the rules did not strictly ban a single-seater either. Howard Marmon was chairman of the General Rules Committee and vice-president of the Manufacturers' Contest Association. He had some idea how far he could push his plans within the rules.

Harroun designed two cars—a four cylinder, with a similar engine to those in the Marmon road cars, and a six cylinder, which was simply a four with two extra cylinders grafted on to give the car a capacity of 7.8 litres. The race cars were painted bright yellow; their streamlined bodywork with big disc wheels and a pointed high tail were an outstanding contrast to most of the cut-down specials.

Marmon placed Harroun in the faster six cylinder, and young Joe Dawson, another Hoosier, in the four. He secured a single relief driver, Cyrus Patschke of Pennsylvania, not so much a racer as a long-distance endurance specialist who'd set several 24-hour records. Patschke relieved both works drivers in the 500 and is in the record books as having co-won the inaugural 500 and having come fifth.

The Month of May elevated Rupert Jeffkins to new heights. Suddenly he was in the big time, part of a field of superstars. Pretty much everyone, except Barney Oldfield, was at Indy. (Big-talking Oldfield, perhaps the best-known racer of them all, and one of the original barnstormers, was under licence suspension. He'd become a race reporter instead for *The Indianapolis Star*.)

It helped to be wealthy if you wanted to race. Wealth and contacts counted. Being a graduate of an Ivy League university, having the sense of being on the inside looking out, also meant a lot. Blond-haired Spencer Wishart, son of a millionaire Wall Street financier, was in the Mercedes his father had bought him. Boyishly handsome David Bruce-Brown, related to the Roosevelts and known as 'the college boy', was in an imported Grand Prix Fiat along with Yale graduate Caleb Bragg. Washington Roebling II, whose grandfather designed the Brooklyn Bridge, had recently formed the Mercer Automobile Company and had installed British driver Hughie Hughes in his car for the 500.

Within five years all but Bragg would perish. Roebling went down with the *Titanic*. His heroism on the night of 15 April 1912, when he guided women and children to the lifeboats, is etched in his family's history. Bruce-Brown and his riding mechanic Tony Scudellari died in trials for the 1912 American

Grand Prize in Milwaukee. Wishart, racing side by side with Bob Burman in works Mercers in the 1914 Elgin Illinois road race, was killed when their wheels touched, and he slammed into a tree. Hughie Hughes was an innocent bystander, hit by an out-of-control race car right beneath the press box at Uniontown, Pennsylvania, in 1916.

Jeffkins couldn't compete in the old-school-tie stakes. His claim to fame, reported by Indy 500 starter Fred Wagner in an op-ed in the prestigious *New York Times*, was that 'He was born in the country where wild men throw boomerangs. As a mere boy he carried mail on horseback for the New South Wales Government, during which time he had some hairbreadth escapes.' Pure Rupert. But he was an international competitor and that in itself brought prestige.

A pity, then, that he was out of the Indy 500 before it even started. Forty-six cars had been entered. Forty-four arrived at the track and 40 would face the starter. Only one of the four non-starters had been be forced out due to mechanical problems, and it was Rupert. Desperate, the Australian moved to another team. The Cole Motor Car Company, from downtown Indianapolis, had entered one of its four-cylinder 'Flyers'. It was a handy piece of work. In the hands of its lead driver 'Farmer' Bill Endicott, the Cole Flyer had been a race winner. Its engineer Charles S. Crawford would later move to the renowned Stutz Motor Car Company, another Indianapolis success story.

The Cole Company brought up a spare car from the city, 3.7 miles (6 kilometres) away, for Rupert to drive, but he failed to qualify it. Right from the first Indy 500, Carl Fisher had been concerned about the potential speed disparity between competitors, and for good reason: there's nothing more dangerous than mixing fast and slow cars on a racetrack. Three days before the race, every competitor was made to undertake a qualifying run—to average 75 mph (120 km/h) from a flying start down a quarter-mile section of the front straight. That meant cars had to flash through the quarter mile (400 metres) in twelve seconds or less. To be fair, they were given three attempts. Rupert didn't make it.

An interview he gave two years later in the Australian media put his desperation on display:

> In training I was overhauling Endicott [likely they were travelling in convoy so 'Farmer Bill' could show him the way around] and as we pay no regard to rules in training I went to pass him on the inside. At that moment he looked around and in doing so steered his car down and blocked my way. There was only one thing to do—I turned my car off the track. Seeing a big hole ahead where the stump of a tree had been removed, I knew that if I slowed down my wheels would drop into the hole and I would capsize. I therefore opened the car out to its full extent, jumped the hole, passed between the trees and regained the track. Had I dropped into the hole or struck one of the trees both my mechanician [the term they used for riding mechanics] and myself would have been killed.

As consolation, the Velie factory nominated Rupert as relief driver in Howard Hall's car.

Ray Harroun's controversial Marmon Wasp raised protests from competitors: why should they have to carry riding mechanics when he didn't? Surely it was dangerous, they complained. One of the tenets of a riding mechanic was to act as a second pair of eyes, especially to look out for faster cars coming from behind. Why? Because in 1911 the rear-view mirror had not yet been invented. Harroun did just that. He fashioned a substantial mirror and placed it across the cowl of his car, held firm by two triangular stanchions. The world's first rear-vision device, now mandatory on all vehicles, had its genesis in that first Indianapolis 500. The fact that the mirror vibrated so badly that it was practically useless was Harroun's secret.

At 10 a.m. on Tuesday 30 May, Memorial Day, the first ever Indianapolis 500, Carl G. Fisher established two precedents. He drove the first-known pace car—perhaps his very own Stoddard-Dayton, a sedate form of transport—and he led away the first flying-start race. Standing starts had been the norm until then, but there had not been a mass field of 40 cars before and Fisher thought it would be safer to roll them out, appropriately at 40 mph (64 km/h).

In the first fourteen laps, there were four different changes of leadership and one death.

Johnny Aitken, driving the locally built National, led the first ever lap of the Indy 500. He'd go on to win more races at the Indianapolis Motor Speedway—fifteen, to be precise—than any other driver in its history, but none of them were the 500.

By lap twelve Sam Dickson, the riding mechanic for Amplex driver Arthur Greiner, was dead. Dickson was killed instantly when they lost a front wheel in Turn Two and he was thrown into a fence. According to *The Indianapolis Star*, 'a Roman forum atmosphere prevailed'. State militia had to use their guns as clubs to force their way through the crowd to get to the stricken co-driver. 'It was distasteful in the extreme,' the paper reported. Greiner died five years later, aged 32, in the Milwaukee Sanitarium, having had a nervous breakdown.

Winner Harroun had decided to be a tortoise in a race of hares. He'd assessed that tyre wear, and lengthy stops to replace them, would likely determine the outcome. By keeping his speed down, he managed to stop just four times to change the right rear tyre, the one that takes most of the cornering load. His other three tyres went the full distance. Second placed by 1 minute 43 seconds, bow-tied Sunday school teacher Ralph Mulford changed tyres fourteen times; the last change, nineteen laps from the finish, forced him to relinquish the lead. Time in the pits cost him the race.

Barney Oldfield, covering the race for *The Indianapolis Star*, was effusive in his praise: 'The clever Arab [Harroun's ancestors were Irish, but he had been promoted as the 'Flying Bedouin'] outthought, outguessed and outdrove the other pilots in yesterday's speed and endurance classic. After the race Harroun told me he would not drive another such race for twice what he will receive for his work yesterday.'

Harroun had not driven the distance solo: 'In my estimation the limit is reached at 500 miles and is entirely too long for the endurance of the driver,' he told the *Star*. 'I was relieved from the 170th to the 250th mile [by Cyrus Patschke] and the rest was extremely refreshing.'

It had been tough. The *Star*'s coverage was descriptive:

When Harroun finally lifted his face from the car, scores of persons saw his bloodshot eyes, his parched lips, his sun blistered face and noticed the trembling of the muscles of his body. A man rushed to his car and offered the driver a drink from a bottle of water. He attempted to moisten his lips and apparently his tongue was parched. He poured a few drops into his throat and choked. The crowd, upon seeing that Harroun was suffering from physical strain resulting from the race, stepped back that he might have more room. Kodak fiends by the score took advantage of the space.

The pounding of the Brickyard had been relentless. Cars had crashed and collapsed; many made it to the finish only after makeshift repairs. The two cars in the Case team were pulled from the race with steering failure. According to the *Star* this was prompted by 'Mrs F. Lee Norton, wife of the general manager of the company [who] begged her husband not to let the men risk their lives any longer. He leapt to his feet, frantically threw his hands up and down and yelled to his repair crew men to keep the car out of the race. He also ordered the other Case car to stay out of the race.'

Rupert Jeffkins was left in no-man's land. A timing stand mix-up, perhaps triggered by a multi-car crash, meant that almost 40 laps of the first Indy 500 went officially unrecorded. Imagine the mayhem. Two days later, in order to bring some finality, Carl G. Fisher declared the results settled and ordered the scoring records destroyed.

Howard Hall's Velie was credited with seventeenth out of 26 finishers, but there's no official record that Rupert ever got to drive. His version, though, was that he had been the strength of the side. His story varied according to his audience: to *The Motor* in Australia in January 1914 he said he finished sixth:

'Had his relief driver been as efficient, he would have finished well up in the money, however he kept his car in the race, which itself is considered no small achievement.'

In a speech to a live audience in South Australia, reported in *The Adelaide Advertiser*, 'The Speed King finished tenth. He ascertained that his relief driver was addicted to drugs. But for the circumstances, he considered he would have finished third or fourth.'

Such a shame. There is a 50:50 chance Rupert did drive a stint in that historic first race, unrecorded by the timekeepers, or expunged by Carl Fisher. What might have been a fine achievement will be forever unrecognised. And Jeffkins' conflicting versions do nothing to provide clarity.

Two weeks later, on 17 June 1911, Rupert Jeffkins, professional auto racing driver, a resident of the Plaza Hotel, married Hazel Elittia Bell, cashier, of 225½ Massachusetts Avenue, Indianapolis. She was 25. He fudged his age by four years to appear to be just two months older than his bride. And in the space on the form where it asked, 'Is this your first marriage?' he answered 'yes'. Hazel was a small-town girl from Cochranton, Pennsylvania, and she lived with her mother.

There's ironclad proof that Rupert Jeffkins raced in the United States for twelve months after that first Indy 500. He was a podium finisher for the Velie factory at the big-time Elgin

National Road Races on 26 August 1911. In the Illinois Trophy race over 24 laps (203 miles/326 kilometres) he came home a determined third behind the two works Mercers of Don Herr and Charlie Merz. He trailed them by four laps and there were only four cars in the race, but he was on the podium nevertheless. Magnanimously, he gave the course a big rap: 'Driver Jeffkins, an Australian who has seen all the famous courses in Europe, declares that not one of them compares with the Elgin course,' the *Waterloo Observer* reported in the lead-up to the event.

Rupert picked up drives, without success, from the tiny Schacht car company in Ohio. He crashed in the September Cincinnati 150-mile (241-kilometre) race, and was out of the race after just eight laps of the nineteen-lap event—the car 'wrecked'. After that he headed to the board tracks of the US West Coast.

He had speed, there's no doubt. In March 1912 at the San Jose Driving Park, in a Buick owned by the Howard Automobile Company, the San Francisco dealer, he set a new mile record for the track at 55.5 seconds. But that's not why he made the head-lines: 'A general fistfight at the end of the 25-mile [40-kilometre] event in which Emile Agraz, the promoter and one of the drivers, struck at Jeffkins and bruised the nose of T.F. Holmes, the AAA referee, marked the end of the day's racing,' said the next day's *San Francisco Chronicle*. 'Agraz accused Jeffkins of running into his Maxwell during the race.'

And then, miraculously, he was in the works Mercer team—perhaps not their A-team, but in stock-chassis 35J Raceabouts stripped simply of headlights and mudguards. His teammate was one of the absolute stars of pre-war motor racing, Ralph De Palma. It didn't get much better than that. Except that

De Palma won at the Santa Monica Road Races in the elegant blue machine and Jeffkins retired after two laps with magneto failure.

Undeniably, there was a connection between them. De Palma was a self-promoter, too, on a scale way above Jeffkins' attainments. He had results and he was smart enough to have other people make claims on his behalf. De Palma was a barnstormer like Barney Oldfield. The two set up a remarkable faux-rivalry to bring in the crowds. There were stunts: in 1910 De Palma raced against Eugene Ely's Curtiss biplane in front of 10,000 people in Poughkeepsie, New York, and won three out of three. Ely was killed the following year in an aerial demonstration accident at the Georgia State Fairgrounds.

De Palma raced motorcycles on high-banked timber ovals, up to 60 degrees, so spectators could look down on the racers in the saucer. One-eighth mile (200-metre) tracks were able to be covered in lap times of eight seconds, with wood splinters flying into the crowd. People died regularly in those demonstrations, the worst incident in New Jersey when the Texas 'Cyclone', Eddie Hasha, crashed and took another rider and four spectators with him to eternity. When he went 'legit', De Palma backed away from that sort of activity, despite the fact that it had been lucrative for him. At the end of his career, claims were made that he had won 2557 races out of 2889 contested—a win rate of better than 88 per cent. Over a 27-year career, that's an average of two races a week, which is right on the margin of believability. His claims no doubt inspired Jeffkins.

De Palma offered Rupert the role of riding mechanic in the 1912 Indianapolis 500. It wasn't a drive—no matter how much Rupert later talked up his co-driver's role—but in 1912

for a journeyman to hitch his wagon to De Palma's star sig-
nified a definite career advancement opportunity. De Palma
had access to cars across the nation. Unlike most drivers
who were connected to a factory, De Palma preferred, for the
main, to be freelance. At Indianapolis he would race a 9.5-litre
90-horsepower (67-kilowatt) Mercedes for wealthy patron
Edward J. Schroeder. De Palma and Jeffkins both understood
the value of a benefactor. Just as Rupert had acted as chauffeur
for wealthy clients in France and Britain, De Palma, early in his
career, had been a driver for the well-to-do business community in New York, ferrying them to their weekend homes on
Long Island, sometimes for the speedboat races. He met New
Jersey 'lamp manufacturer' Schroeder through that channel.
Schroeder owned one of the quickest boats, Dixie, a race winner,
and De Palma occasionally drove it. It proved a most beneficial
long-term association.

Later in Australia Rupert claimed Schroeder as his own:
'Then,' said the Speed King with a smile, 'Pete [sic] Schroeder,
a New York millionaire, selected us to drive his Mercedes. Over
there the millionaires race for the sport, you see. The arrangement was that De Palma and I shared the money.' There is
some conjecture about which of Schroeder's stable of cars the
pair drove at Indy. Most likely it was a Mercedes from the 1908
French Grand Prix, upgraded with a new engine, a monster
of a machine that reached maximum power at just 1300 rpm.
It could lope along to victory without stress.

Mechanicians, or riding mechanics, had been made mandatory in 1912. Harroun's solo victory had been a step too far for
racing authorities. Marmon stayed away from the 1912 event;
they were selling all the cars they could make, and if they didn't

win, if they had a failure, they could only lose reputation not gain it. Early in his career De Palma had served his time in the jump seat. He knew what he expected from Jeffkins. Which is why what happened in those last few laps was so unusual.

Here was a team that was well drilled and experienced in each other's duties. And yet they missed, or ignored, the warning signs, and the big Merc blew. Ultimately De Palma was in charge. As a 'pedal to the metal' kind of guy, a grandstander, he was not the sort to back off. So perhaps he ignored Jeffkins' warning. Or Jeffkins may have missed a telltale quiver from the gauges, or neglected to pump the engine oil, or the car had run out of oil, or . . . or . . .

In Australia, much later, in the *Newcastle Morning Herald* in 1914, Jeffkins finally offered a realistic and professional assessment of the situation (for all his bluff and bravado, he was a professional racer): 'The car became so hot after travelling 497 miles [799 kilometres] at the rate of 82 mph [131 km/h] that the oil would not lubricate the engine.' And there lay the story—a simple breakdown of lubricating ability. 'We tried to improvise some sort of repair, but our efforts were ineffectual.'

Eddie Rickenbacker, then a competitor, soon to be a WWI fighter ace, later to run the superspeedway, was trackside for the excruciating last, dying lap of the Mercedes. The car rode around the speedway at 20 mph (32 km/h), he said, 'crawling like a hurt animal'.

Fifty years on, in 1962, a newspaper journalist from the *Tucson Daily Citizen* visited Ralph De Palma's widow, Marion (he'd died six years earlier at age 73 from cancer) and she revealed a story not before told.

'Someone in the stands passed a bucket or something amongst Ralph's admirers,' Marion said. 'They were supposed to have collected thousands of dollars but when they carried it onto the track to present to Ralph he would have no part of it. He thanked them but told them he did not earn it and would appreciate their donating it to one of the Indianapolis hospitals.'

Sometimes history rewards failure—certainly for dignity in the face of defeat. More than a century on, the push to the pits by De Palma and Jeffkins remains one of the enduring and enshrined examples of the spirit of the Indianapolis 500. It is far better remembered than Joe Dawson's win.

Ralph De Palma departed immediately after the race to take up a works Fiat drive in the French Grand Prix—his first Continental race (in which he was disqualified for refuelling outside the pits). He didn't take Jeffkins with him and they never drove together again.

Jeffkins' career took a massive tangential turn. He spliced together a film—a montage of his racing activities, including the first two Indianapolis 500s—called it *The Death Toll of the Speedway*, and instead of risking his life on the racetrack, made money at the box office. In those pre-talkie days, he was the star of the show, standing in front of an eager and willing public, showing them what it was like to be a racing driver: 'Some smashes are depicted, incidents happen in quick succession, cars dash into walls, tyres are melted by excessive friction and cars fly around steeply banked curves at the speed of an express train.'

It was brilliant. No one had done it before. Rupert Jeffkins had become the world's first virtual race driver and he had found a niche that completely suited his talents.

On 4 October 1912, Jeffkins was locked up in the Santa Clara County Jail for speeding. It was great promotion for his film. He had just successfully completed a high-speed record run down the San Francisco Bay from Oakland to San Jose—a distance of 45 miles (72 kilometres)—in 39 minutes and three-fifths of a second, he claimed, in an Indianapolis-built Stutz emblazoned with logos proclaiming 'My City Oakland'. He did it with the full support of Oakland's mayor and chamber of commerce and carried letters from them to their colleagues in San Jose. Naturally, he added a twist.

'Rupert Jeffkins, the Australian speed king, driving the Stutz racing car in which he won the Elgin road race [he didn't— he came third in a Velie] lowered the previous record of 51 minutes flat,' the *Oakland Tribune* wrote on 6 October. 'The highest speed attained was 85 mph [136 km/h]. After Jeffkins had presented official letters to Mayor Monahan and was proceeding to lunch with Joseph T. Brooks, secretary of the Chamber of Commerce, he was arrested and held for three hours in the Santa Clara County Jail. Vigilant police officers along the route on which the little Stutz flashed like a white streak telephoned ahead to San Jose to arrest the scorcher. How this will affect Jeffkins' engagement to appear next week at Idora Park [his film show] remains to be seen,' the *Oakland Tribune* speculated.

Two months later Jeffkins was back in Australia. He disembarked in Melbourne. *The Weekly Times* reporters, who, in the custom of the day, visited the ships before they docked, clambered on board up rope ladders looking for stories. They reported: 'Rupert Jeffkins, motor-racing pioneer, returned to Australia today determined to make his mark on the local scene after some impressive performances overseas. Sydney-born Jeffkins has created a big name for himself in America.'

Rupert was eager to share the wealth of his knowledge with his countrymen, inspired particularly by his experiences in the US. In 1911 Howard Marmon had said it all: 'Concerning the automotive industry in general, I am an optimist. I am positive that the public demand is steadily growing. The fact that it is steady and not a sudden fad is encouragement to me. People need automobiles now the same as the telephone or the electric light in their homes.'

3

The Speed King
and the Roo

The Speed King could sense opportunity in Australia.

He'd barely disembarked, with enough publicity to make an impression, when he met his first person of importance, impresario John Wren, and set out to make the fortune that had eluded him in the United States.

Not, though, before first firing a shot across the bows of the Indianapolis Motor Speedway. 'A letter received yesterday by the management of the Indianapolis Motor Speedway indicates that Rupert Jeffkins, the Australian racing driver who is well known in Indianapolis, will be entered in the third annual 500-mile International Sweepstakes Race as the pilot of an English Napier car,' *The Indianapolis Star* reported in March 1913. 'It is altogether probable that the car will be entered by several English and Australian sportsmen and that Jeffkins will be nominated as the driver.'

Jeffkins never entered the race, but it was good to talk up his chances. Someone might bite.

John Wren was hero and villain all in the same package. The third son of impoverished Irish migrants, he'd grown up on the mean streets of working-class Collingwood, left school at twelve and made his first pile at nineteen when Carbine won the Melbourne Cup. With his winnings he established what would become a Melbourne institution: the 'shilling totaliser' at 136 Johnston Street, Collingwood. It was the best-known illegal gaming operation in town. A tobacconist up front, with the 'tote' out the back, it had an elaborate network of fences, trapdoors and tunnels to elude police raids. The shilling tote, a product of the 1890s depression, existed to serve the working man, when a shilling was about as much as a man could afford to bet. Police raided it regularly, so young Wren employed the best of help, in the form of barrister David Gaunson MLA. Gaunson's claim to fame was that he had defended Ned Kelly in his final trial—unsuccessfully, as it turned out.

The diminutive Wren, just 5 feet 4 inches (162 cm), collected money and influence in equal proportions. He had the ear of any politician he chose to support, right up to the state premier, whose name—appropriately, his opponents said—was Bent.

Wren ruled the streets. This was not a man you crossed. It was said that he was making more money off-course than the Victorian Racing Club at its two venues, and that sparked a turf war. Wren proposed taking over Flemington, home of the Melbourne Cup and the VRC's flagship. He'd make more money for the state's coffers, he argued, and Sir Thomas Bent pretended to play along with the idea, giving the VRC apoplexy before rejecting it.

Wren had bought and rejuvenated three rundown horse-racing tracks. By the time Rupert Jeffkins arrived in town, Wren was living in a huge mansion, and had become somewhat respectable. He was now a philanthropist, a major patron of the arts and a boxing impresario (he'd go on to buy Snowy Baker's boxing empire with stadiums in three states). He was also looking for the next big idea. Rupert showed Wren his film *The Death Toll of the Speedway*. And just like that, the deal was done. They formed between them the Australian Motor Speedway Co., electing to run their first motor race meeting at Wren's Richmond Racecourse, one of his pony and trotting tracks.

The first motor race in Australia on a purpose-built track had occurred at the Aspendale Picnic Ground Park on Melbourne's outskirts in 1906. (Sydney had to wait until 1908 for a 1.1-mile (1.8-kilometre) clay-and-cinder track to open around an existing horseracing venue at Victoria Park.)

Australia had caught the motoring craze. There were now a total of 30,000 cars in Australia—not as many as the Americans were making in a year, but enough for an entrepreneur to profit by it.

The Australian Motor Speedway Co. scheduled its first event for 22 November 1913. There would be more than a dozen races on the card and Rupert would be the star of the show, billed as 'Jeffkins, the Speed King, America's Greatest Thrill Provider, Who Has Bumped More Tracks, Burst Up More Machines and Broken More Records than any other speed fiend breathing'.

Jeffkins needed someone to race. They found him in Dug Campbell. Born in Moonee Ponds and educated at Scotch

College, he'd been the winning co-driver in the 1903 Dunlop Trial from Sydney to Melbourne and had cast aside a professional career in the city to work for the Tarrant Motor Company. He'd become a star of the Melbourne motor-racing community, winning at Aspendale and the Lilydale Hill Climb. Rupert and Dug would run three match races against each other—both Mercedes-mounted (stripped down local tourers, not the grand prix cars they claimed them to be)—for a purse of £1000. Dug became 'Tearaway Campbell—the Most Daring Driver in the Commonwealth'. Public entry was set at 2 shillings and sixpence for the leger and 10 shillings for the best seats in the grandstand. The strap line for the advertising was: 'If Excitement Hurts You, Stay Away!'

Jeffkins went on a promotional tour. Armed with *The Death Toll of the Speedway*, he hit cinemas and clubs up and down the east coast. He even travelled to New Zealand. The Speed King was in his element. It's no wonder that he missed Indy that year. But no matter: *The Herald* in Melbourne reported, 'He will be a competitor at the 1914 Indianapolis 500 mile race, as some enthusiastic admirers of his have already decided to have a big special racing car built for him to pilot in that race to represent Australia there against the speed-kings of the world.'

The promoters left no stunt undone. In front of the media, Jeffkins did flying laps of the Richmond track. He'd found a race-prepped Opel and claimed it to be a European works car. His speed on the straight was below 70 mph (112 km/h), and somewhat less again on the corners. By any standard he wasn't quick. But the promoters orchestrated concerns about high speeds: 'Yesterday the Premier of Victoria, Mr Murray, conferred with the Chief Commissioner of Police with the view to determining what steps should be taken to ensure proper protection for the public at the motor car races, set down for decision on the Richmond racecourse on Saturday next,' *The Referee* reported. 'After an inspection had been made today, it was intimated to Mr John Wren that the report to be submitted would be of a favorable nature, and no official interference with holding the meeting was likely.' Wren and Jeffkins were masters of their promotional art.

On the day of the big race The American Boys Band—Melbourne based—led the pre-race procession. Estimates of between 12,000 and 15,000 spectators crammed the venue. Dug Campbell arrived at the starting line with a kangaroo emblazoned on his racing jersey. Rupert carried the stars and stripes. Their race didn't take long. Each heat was just four laps—2 miles (3.2 kilometres).

Jeffkins took the lead from inside pole in the first race and held his advantage to the last lap—when he suddenly slowed, giving Campbell the win. What had happened? Rupert explained he'd mistaken the last lap flag for the finish flag. That can happen over four laps.

He won the second heat—one-all with the decider to go, a perfect showdown—surely not contrived. And then came rain. Spectators would need to come back the next day to get a result. But there was a problem with Jeffkins' motor, resulting in another postponement until Monday. When Rupert didn't show, the referee awarded the contest, and half the prize money, to Campbell.

The Motor in Australia declared that the emperor had no clothes:

The motor race meeting drew a big crowd to witness 70 miles an hour [112 km/h] racing, promised by the promoter. To say the least of it they went away disappointed, for speedwork on such an unsuitable track was farcical. It had been proclaimed that a Government official had seen the course tested and that a circuit of the cinder track had been negotiated in 25 seconds, equal to a speed of nearly 70 miles an hour. If that official was at the meeting on Saturday, he must have felt a very foolish individual, for the fastest lap covered during the racing did not exceed a speed of much over 40 miles an hour [64 km/h]. A Ford car could travel nearly as fast as the 90 hp Mercedes used by the contestants. No sooner had a car or motorcycle got up a bit of speed down the short straights than they had to slow for the corners. It was poor racing. Even before a downpour of rain terminated the program, many visitors left the ground. The great event of the day, the Jeffkins-Campbell match proved a very tame affair.

There was no suggestion that Wren and Jeffkins didn't make a pile of money.

Dug Campbell became a trainer in the motor industry under the title of 'Daredevil Dug, Doctor of Motoring'. He'd learned something from Rupert Jeffkins.

In 1935 Dug took his own life: 'A shot was heard as his employees were opening up business for the day and later he was found with a new gun with a cartridge discharged, and he was dead,' *The Australian Motorist* reported. 'Dug had suffered severe head injuries in race crashes and the effects of those injuries took their toll on his health.'

Rupert's youngest brother, Herbert, was just seven years old when Rupert left on his grand overseas adventure. They hardly knew each other, and yet the younger man surely looked up to the Speed King. On 4 August 1914 when the United Kingdom declared war on the aggressive German alliance and Australia vowed to stand by its mother country, the younger Jiffkins signed up for World War I.

Herbert, twenty, married his sweetheart, Dorothy Carlaw, and shortly after embarked on a troopship to Gallipoli. He fought his way ashore on 25 April 1915 and seven days later took part in the assault on the strategic hill Baby 700. He died in action, one of 1000 casualties in the attack. He is buried in the Lone Pine Cemetery overlooking Anzac Cove.

Rupert was beyond distressed. He designed a placard for shops to display in their windows. He called it 'The Real Test', and he registered it with the copyright office. The placard read: 'Our solemn Promise to the Anzacs now fighting for us—To Foster Australian Industry. This business is owned, controlled, and the staff are entirely British. We DO NOT stock or sell German made goods. Show your patriotism by purchasing HERE which will help rid Australia of the Hun element.' The poster was draped in the British flag, and included a photograph of an armed soldier, his head bleeding and bandaged.

Herbert had fallen to the Turks, but Rupert's point was made.

In 1915, Rupert married, again. His bride was Winifred Lonigan, and she was a keeper. They would have four children, Una, Kathleen, Henry and Eileen. A fifth died in the year of his birth.

Rupert didn't go to war. Instead, he remained in Australia, where he promoted many schemes and self-made opportunities. Surely one would come off. Indianapolis had given him valuable contacts. In Sydney, Reginald Marcus Clark, second-generation proprietor of the Marcus Clark chain of department stores, was keen to discover if he could retail a motorcar. In Detroit, motor dealers George and Charles Grant had formed a production team, composed mainly of Indiana-trained experts, in order to build their own car—the Grant. Rupert brought Marcus Clark and George and Charles Grant together.

In late November 1916 Rupert embarked on a nonstop Sydney-to-Melbourne round trip reliability trial to showcase the car. Naturally he added a twist. The engine would be sealed by police and never switched off during the journey. The six-day run, with an observer on board, achieved the objective. Prospects looked good, but just four months later the US entered World War I. Export plans for the Grant were put on hold and that was that.

In truth, the outcome suited Jeffkins. He had conceived a much more ambitious project. Australia, he declared, needed its own car, designed and manufactured in Australia and, most importantly, built entirely from Australian materials. He was typically bullish. The war provided a measure of natural protection. High freight costs, the prohibition on body imports, the reduction in shipping and the uncertainty of the impact the US's military preparation would have on the export of US-made cars all worked to the benefit of those attempting to start an Australian motor manufacturing industry, he declared.

The idea was born in the summer of early 1917. By July the same year a company had been registered by three partners:

W.B. (Bill) Foulis, the chief engineer; T.C. (Craig) Lawson, the money man; and R.F. (Rupert) Jeffkins, designer and managing director.

They had called the car the 'Roo', and it was produced by their Roo Motor Car Manufacturing Company. The name was whimsical but for Rupert it aptly described the pride of national ownership and evoked images of a lightweight, go-anywhere vehicle that could skip across the surface of the wretched Australian roads. And it was a name unlikely to be forgotten. The Roo was to be a runabout, to sell at a price point of just £195 (about $10,000 now). It would be a light car, built for two people, with a 1600cc two-cylinder horizontally opposed engine (like half a VW Beetle), developing 22 horsepower (16.4 kilowatts), and with a fuel economy of 50 miles per gallon (5.6 litres/100 kilometres).

The Roo Motor Car Manufacturing Company's offices were at 337 Pitt Street, Sydney, in the heart of the city. Manufacturing was to take place on a 1.2-hectare site with frontage to Parramatta Road in Burwood. It's likely the partners had funds to build a prototype, but maybe not enough to go into production. They were targeting six cars a day. Optimistically, Rupert claimed 235 advance orders. He got heaps of publicity; a lot was made of his Indy 500 record.

On Wednesday 12 September 1917, Sydney's first Labor Lord Mayor, Richard Meagher, flagged the prototype Roo away on the same inter-city run the Grant had completed the year before. Jeffkins and Foulis were at the wheel; a bonnet mascot in the form of a kangaroo, as resplendent as the Rolls-Royce Spirit of Ecstasy, guided their path. They were back in Sydney on Friday 28 September; the Australian-made Perdriau tyres 'still contained the same Sydney air with which they had started for Melbourne', the media reported. It had been a horror run for a small car and it had survived.

Coverage was extensive. Crowds in towns along the route had turned out to see the Roo pass through. On its return, the car went on display in the window of David Jones's George Street, Sydney, store. And then—nothing.

The downfall of the operation, automotive historians later said, was the attempt by the manufacturers to make every component themselves. The costs were too great, the tooling too complex. Jeffkins and Foulis had built just two Roos. A third was underway when Lawson pulled out and the money dried up.

In just a year, to the day, the partnership had dissolved and the best idea Rupert Jeffkins ever had was dead.

A decade later Bill Foulis joined aviator Charles Kingsford Smith in a project to build the Southern Cross motor car, named for Smithy's record-setting planes. Foulis's contribution was the engine—it was the Roo's twin cylinders with two more added, a direct knock-off of the Roo idea. But, like Jeffkins, Kingsford Smith also struck a financial roadblock. In 1935 he flew to England to arrange funds and was returning, his partners believed with good news, when he and his plane disappeared in the Bay of Bengal. The Southern Cross project died along with its creator.

As far as Rupert Jeffkins was concerned, Sir James Joynton Smith, KBE, Lord Mayor of Sydney in 1918, later to be the money behind *Smith's Weekly*, the newspaper that gave the Packer media empire its start, was every bit the Sydney equivalent of John Wren. Born in London as plain Jim Smith, he was as self-made as they came. He migrated to New Zealand as a ten-year-old cabin boy and, still young, was the organiser of the rough-as-guts Seamen's and Firemen's Union. When Jeffkins met him, he owned a string of hotels in New South Wales and importantly had converted lagoon and swampland just outside the city into a horse racetrack, which he turned into Sydney's first motor-racing venue. Victoria Park raceway had first run a motor race in 1908.

Jeffkins proposed they jointly promote the 'Biggest Motor Race Meeting' ever held in New South Wales. Never mind that Victoria Park had been operating for ten years, resulting in two fatalities.

The media bought it: 'Motor car races on a prepared track have not previously been held in New South Wales, but they have been held in America,' *The Sydney Morning Herald* reported, referencing the Speed King's Indianapolis experience. Rupert ramped up the advertising—'16 Hair Raising Events'—and recycled a good idea—'If Excitement Hurts You, Stay Away!'

The Referee, coincidentally owned by Joynton Smith, reported attendance at the 1919 race meeting as 18,000 but was damning of 'hoodlum' crowd behaviour. Manly's speed king A.V. Turner, in a Lexington Six, won the feature, dodging errant spectators.

The next day, Jeffkins announced that he had a better idea. He'd found an ideal site on which to stage a big road race for stock cars. It turns out that it was Sydney's Centennial Park, a place where even today people take genteel weekend strolls among the ponds. 'Is the man mad or is he merely temperamentally unable to recognise danger when he sees it?' *The Motor* in Australia trumpeted. 'We sincerely hope the park trust will jump on this proposal with all the violence it deserves.' They did.

(After World War II, Victoria Park became the manufacturing base for the British Motor Corporation—later British Leyland. Its last car of significance was the ill-fated P76, an alternative to the family cars of Holden and Ford. When Leyland closed, the site lay fallow. It later become Green Square, a massive residential and community complex.)

Just after midnight on 24 February 1922, William Jiffkins, Rupert's father, smashed the gas pipe in his family's Annandale home, sprayed kerosene about, then walked into Young Street, where he slashed his own throat and died on the footpath.

He had been living alone downstairs. According to newspapers, his wife had been away from home for some weeks, staying with friends, and a family was renting the first floor. When they heard the explosion and went to escape, they found that the bottom of the staircase had been barricaded with furniture, but they cleared the obstacle and made it outside.

One month later the city coroner found that 'Both the fire and the injuries to the deceased had been caused by the deceased while suffering from some temporary mental aberration.'

The old soldier was 84 years old.

Rupert Jeffkins once more turned his sights to Melbourne. He became managing director of the most ambitious speedway project of its time. John Wren had heeded the lesson of the makeshift speedway and determined to construct a purpose-built motordrome, along American lines. His choice of venue was the already half-completed Amateur Sports Ground on Batman Avenue on the banks of the Yarra River where building had stalled during World War I. The development was the work of Melbourne Carnivals Pty Ltd, a Wren front company.

Brilliantly, the venue would be multi-purpose, capable of hosting football games as well as car races. Speeds of between 90 and 100 mph (144 and 160 km/h) were expected within its one-third mile (536-metre) concrete oval, banked at 45 degrees. But it was immediately clear that race cars could not handle the high g-forces. Accidentally, the Motordrome had been perfectly constructed for motorcycle racing.

The Motordrome imported highly talented American riders to race the locals, putting them on consecutive month-long contracts. It was hugely successful. American motorcycle champion Ralph Hepburn was one of the stars. He would revert to cars when he returned to the States and compete in the Indianapolis 500 eleven times; the highest place he achieved was third. He died in a 1948 practice crash at the Brickyard.

Melbourne Carnivals had boasted a capacity of 100,000 for the Motordrome. But this number—more than a contemporary Olympic stadium will hold—was a wild fantasy. At their first race meeting, they claimed 30,000 spectators. Ten thousand was more likely the actual figure, but that number of people came consistently. It was good money.

Ultimately, small cars would race at the Motordrome, but their lap times were more like 60 mph (100 km/h) while the motorcycles could just touch 90 mph (144 km/h). Jeffkins delighted in promoting car versus motorcycle match races. He put the bikes down low on the bank, where their speed was handicapped, creating an even contest.

Wren invested in floodlights and ran night races—just as Jeffkins had seen in the United States. He held night football, too, the first of its kind in Australia.

But the Motordrome was killing people. In 1929 a motorcycle rode the rim and took out two young spectators. The venue gathered a reputation as a killer. Soon it became known as the 'Murderdrome', and it had to close. Wren ploughed it under, gaining publicity even out of having bulldozers smash it to the ground.

After World War II the site became the swimming venue for the 1956 Melbourne Olympic Games. It morphed into the administrative headquarters and elite training facility of Wren's beloved Collingwood Football Club. The wheel had turned full circle.

In 1940 Rupert Jeffkins bought a coalmine. It was at Parwan, 50 kilometres north-west of Melbourne. It was said to contain 190 million tonnes of coal down to 500 feet (152 metres). The previous owner had sunk a heap of investment into the mine and then died. Rupert thought he'd got a bargain but it proved not to be the case. He'd come into the market at a time of intense competition and he could not extract his coal cost-efficiently.

THE SPEED KING AND THE ROO

Then, after raising funds through shareholding, with exquisitely poor timing, he sold his own share to a local consortium just as Australia's WWII effort was creating demand.

People powered cars by any means possible during World War II, even coal. A couple of journalists with long memories approached Jeffkins while he still owned the mine to ask him about his long-abandoned Roo project. Could it be resurrected? 'No,' Jeffkins replied. There was more money to be made from Parwan coal than building Australian-made motorcars. His pioneering experience of car building in 1917, he said, had left him 'practically penniless'.

It was the last interview he ever gave.

On 18 October 1954, aged 73, the Speed King died alone in the Liverpool State Hospital and Home, in an outer south-western suburb of Sydney. The cause of his death was carcinoma of the lungs and his death certificate said that the cancer had spread. He had been living in Florence House, in Collaroy, on Sydney's Northern Beaches, an 'eventide men's retreat', effectively a refuge for the homeless. Three days later he was interred in an unmarked pauper's grave in the Anglican section of Liverpool Cemetery—E10, site 179. There is now a simple plaque on his grave. It's believed to have been paid for by his eldest daughter, Una.

4

Time Flies—
The First 50 Years

Half a century would pass before another Australian or New Zealander raced the Indianapolis 500.

They were heading in other directions. In the 1930s, during the Great Depression, dirt-track oval riders made the trek to the wealthy British speedway league where enough money was on offer to feed a family. Arthur 'Bluey' Wilkinson from Millthorpe in central New South Wales won the Speedway World Championship in 1938 at Wembley Stadium.

Bernard Rubin, son of an Australian pearl merchant, had won the Le Mans 24 Hour race in 1928 with Woolf Barnato's Bentley works team. He was living in Britain. So, too, was WWII Spitfire fighter ace Tony Gaze, who became the first

Australian to race Formula One and placed fifteenth at Circuit de Spa-Francorchamps in 1952.

But no one went to Indy.

It was not until 1961 that Jack Brabham, already a double F1 world champion and Australasia's most successful post-war motor racing export, crossed the divide. He opened a floodgate of Down Under participation.

Indy had gotten on okay without the help of the Anzacs. Ownership of the Brickyard had changed hands twice, speeds had soared, 39 drivers had won 46 races, and since 1909 52 people had been killed in its precinct, either in a quest for victory or simply observing the spectacle. One was an innocent bystander, outside the grounds. Heroes had been created.

Of the original partners from the band of four that started the speedway, Frank Wheeler, suffering from diabetes, took his own life in 1921 using both barrels of his favourite shotgun. According to *The Indianapolis Star*, Mr and Mrs Wheeler were alone at the time in their Indianapolis mansion 'with the exception of a few colored servants'.

Carl G. Fisher called it quits as president in 1923. His huge property developments at Miami Beach and Montauk, Long Island, were eating up his time and funds. He lost the bulk of his fortune in the Great Depression. Fisher handed control to James A. Allison, who surprised WWI flying ace and former competitor Eddie Rickenbacker by offering to sell him the speedway—lock, stock and barrel—in 1927. Allison was having a mid-life crisis. In that same twelve-month period he divorced his wife of many years and married his personal assistant, but one week after the nuptials in 1928 at Fisher's Montauk home, he died of pneumonia.

Arthur Newby sold the National Motor Vehicle Company to venture capitalists in 1916 and became a 'quiet philanthropist'. In perpetual poor health, he joined the upbeat Fisher and Allison in Miami real estate projects and died, unmarried, in 1933, aged 67.

Fisher was the last to go, in 1939, at 65, after a lengthy illness exacerbated by alcoholism. His last brilliant act of showmanship was to build the Caribbean Club on Key Largo, the set for the Humphrey Bogart and Lauren Bacall movie of the same name.

America's hero Eddie Rickenbacker could do no wrong. Long before Charles Lindberg, he was the country's best-known airman, with 26 confirmed WWI kills including five observation balloons he shot down. They called him the 'Balloon Buster'. He'd converted his fame into a fortune and started his own car company—building one of the first cars in the USA to incorporate four-wheel brakes—but it went bankrupt in 1927. His wealthy backers, in love with him, were undeterred and simply sent him off to find another venture. He approached his former employer Jim Allison to buy Allison Engineering Company. Instead Allison proposed the purchase of the speedway.

Rickenbacker had raced at Indy four times pre-war, and loved the sport and the racetrack, and it suited his style to be head of such a spectacular, publicly recognised entity. Initially there were several bondholders with greater shares, but over his seventeen-year tenure he cannily bought up stock.

When it came time to sell, in 1945, with the speedway in need of major renovation after its WWII hibernation, Rickenbacker passed it on for exactly what he'd paid—US$700,000. Never mind the massive improvements he'd made. It was a magnanimous gesture.

Three-time Indianapolis 500 winner Wilbur Shaw appointed himself the champion of keeping the speedway out of the hands of developers. He gave sound advice to Indianapolis businessman Anton Hulman Jnr, the owner of Clabber Girl Baking Powder products, whose father Tony had been a friend of Fisher. Hulman bought the speedway as a going concern and then appointed Shaw as president to run it.

Shaw presided over the period when low-slung, front-engine cars, with the driver offset to the right, defined the look of Indianapolis racing. They had wheels so tall that they towered over the bodywork and people joked they could be driven upside-down. Twice winner Bill Vukovich, a product of the southern California hot-rod scene, dubbed them 'roadsters', and the name stuck.

The Hulman family would enjoy the longest tenure of ownership of the speedway—74 years—right up to its purchase in late 2019 by the most masterful motorsport mogul of all, 82-year-old Roger Penske, whose team had claimed a dominant eighteen Indy 500 wins. Penske's purchase was universally acclaimed.

Speeds had gone through the roof in the first 50 years. Ray Harroun won at an average of 74.6 mph (120 km/h) in 1911; Eddie Sachs won at 138.76 mph (223.26 km/h) in 1960 and he'd qualified at 146 mph (234 km/h). It was a better than an 80 per cent improvement, but the cork was waiting to be released from its bottle. There'd soon be an exponential speed rise.

At the outset of the speedway, Fisher had passionately believed that if he built it, the manufacturers would come. Mercedes and Peugeot won in the early days. Duesenberg, an evocative, high-quality luxury manufacturer, based in

Indianapolis, with a glitterati customer base of heads of state and film stars, won four times in the 1920s. Studebaker entered a five-car team and came third in 1932.

But getting American car makers to commit to fielding works teams was an increasingly hard grind. The motor industry was sorting itself out, consolidating, and the combined strain of war and the Great Depression curtailed the public's natural enthusiasm to go racing. Instead, Indy spawned its own local motor-racing success stories.

Engineer Harry Miller built nine Indianapolis 500 winners, and cars using his engines won another three. Miller—one of the greatest minds in the history of the American racing car, although seemingly not one of its better businessmen—was so successful that between 1923 and 1928 more than 80 per cent of the Indy 500 field was made up of Millers. His engine powered the Duesenberg that won for Jimmy Murphy in 1922. At Murphy's request Miller built a front-wheel drive car—a 'puller'—in a bid to provide better traction on Indy's slick bricks. It was a grand experiment; the cost was huge, the result not so. It took six years for Billy Arnold to win in a 'puller' in 1930. Miller declared bankruptcy three years later.

Ford came to Indianapolis in 1935. It was a huge coup. Preston Tucker put the deal together. Tucker was a big talker, larger than life, somewhat replicated by John DeLorean 40 years later. Both had grand ambitions to build cars in their own names and both flamed out spectacularly. Tucker persuaded Edsel Ford that it was a no-brainer, especially as he'd secured Harry Miller as chief engineer. Miller would work as the brains of the operation, guided by the bluster of the ebullient Tucker. For Miller it was a second chance.

Edsel's dad, Henry I, wasn't so keen, and it turned out for good reason. Of the ten front-wheel drive Fords entered, only four qualified and all retired—in each case the steering box in the cramped front-wheel drive space overheated and seized, a classic engineering error. Henry ordered all ten cars destroyed. Ford was not to race at Indy for another for 30 years, well after both Henry and Edsel had passed away.

Miller died, desolate, in 1943. There was some irony that the legacy of his bankruptcy fire sale, ten years earlier, had become the bedrock of Indianapolis's success.

Fred Offenhauser had been Miller's workshop manager. When the Miller company went bust in 1933, Fred bought the rights to Miller's engine design, renamed it after himself and continued development. Offenhauser engines—known as Offys—won 27 Indy 500s between 1935 and 1976. 'Offy' and 'Indy' became synonymous. The best engine makers in the world had to beat a relatively small local shop if they wanted to win the world's greatest motor race.

The early owners continually meddled with the Indy concept, trying to get it right. In its first fifteen years, the 500 endured no fewer than five changes of engine regulations—from the heights of the fire-breathing 9.8-litre engines in the first year, to a tiny 1.5-litre motor in 1926. It was enough to drive any team mad with frustration and to steer them in the direction of financial ruin. In 1916, for one year only, the Indy 500 became the Indy 300. Carl Fisher, always niggling, incapable of leaving well enough alone, doubted the attention span of his audience. Surely, he reasoned, they'd get enough excitement from 300 miles (480 kilometres)? He was wrong. But with war clouds looming, his shortened race was interpreted as the look of leadership, a high-profile gesture to conserve precious resources.

The Indianapolis Motor Speedway closed for both world wars. It was used as an airbase for two years in World War I. Eddie Rickenbacker offered it to the US military for the same purpose in World War II but they rejected it. Maybe in a fit of pique, Rickenbacker locked the gates for almost four years—and the grand circuit deteriorated.

There's no doubting Rickenbacker's passion for Indy: there are few spaces that feel as vast as the infield of Indy when there are no races happening. Shortly after his purchase, the great airman stood in the empty infield and envisaged how it might be used year-round. An airfield surely must have been a consideration, but instead, by 1929, Indy had a golf course built—27 holes, nine inside the speed bowl. Today the course is called Brickyard Crossing, voted one of the top 100 public courses in the US, and only four holes remain inside the track. They are worth playing just for the novelty.

Riding mechanics came, went, came again, then went forever. Ray Harroun's 1911 solo win was so controversial that mechanicians were made compulsory and remained that way until 1923. A rule change made them optional again and that led to a spate of single-seat race cars, purpose-built for the task. When Rickenbacker came on board, he moved to return 'his' race to a stock formula, with greater relevance to the car makers and their customers. In 1930 he introduced back-to-the-future regulations that once more mandated two seats and he insisted someone fill the second seat.

It was unfortunate that, in the next six years, seven mechanicians died at the Brickyard. In 1937 the requirement to carry them once again became optional. The regulation banning passengers was placed in the rule books only in 1964. It was long overdue. In Europe, riding mechanics had been banned by regulation, in all competition, from 1924. It was just too dangerous.

But Indy was way ahead on helmet use. Rickenbacker made helmets compulsory in 1936. (Formula One did not mandate them until 1953, the third year of their world championship.) At Indy, skull injuries were a prevalent cause of serious injury and death, and Rickenbacker's regulations made sense.

It was nothing more than unlucky that a track, reasonably benign before his purchase, suffered a spate of crashes during his ownership. Twenty-five drivers, riding mechanics and spectators died during his seventeen-year tenure. The most bizarre death occurred just off the track. In 1931 the rear wheel and axle assembly tore out of the Miller of defending champion Billy Arnold, soared high over the perimeter fence, cleared Georgetown Road and struck eleven-year-old Billy Brink in the head. Billy was selling ice from a makeshift concession stand in the front garden of his parents' home.

Death at the speedway offered no discrimination. Speed saw to that. You could be a champion, or a novice. In 1935 Johnny Hannon, a dirt-track champion, set out on his first-ever lap of the speedway. At Indianapolis, it's best to start slow—a relative term—and build speed. Hannon, it seemed, went pedal to the metal. He hit and then cleared the wall at Turn Three and died instantly without one lap completed. Nine days later Clay Weatherly, in the same car now repaired, just squeaked out of a big crash when the throttle jammed wide open in practice. Could Hannon's throttle also have jammed? Seemingly no one connected the dots because on lap nine of the big race, Weatherly crashed and was killed. The cause was never determined.

In 1934 Rickenbacker instituted a Rookie Orientation Program, but it was waived for drivers with experience; it was considered a bit demeaning to treat them like novices. Hannon had been experienced, so he did not do the test. After his death, the program was made mandatory.

At the other end of the experience scale, Bill Vukovich had won two consecutive 500s and in 1955 was trying for a 'three-peat'. The feat has never been achieved. In a ferocious battle, he had just taken the lead at the quarter distance mark in his deep-blue Kurtis Kraft Offy roadster, the very epitome of an Indy car. He was lapping cars after just 56 laps when Rodger Ward crashed into the outside wall on Turn Two and overturned. Vukovich could not avoid the melee as two other drivers were deflected into his path. His roadster sailed high in the air, over the retaining fence, and he died instantly of a skull fracture. The news of Vukovich's death went global. If ever there was a warning of the dangers of a circuit with such high speeds and so little room for manoeuvrability, this was it.

There was a global rush of new venues in the 1920s. Le Mans, the world's oldest sports-car venue, opened in 1923, and the Monaco Grand Prix, contested around the streets of Monaco, in 1929. Together with Indianapolis they now form the Triple Crown of motorsport achievement and only one driver, the late

Graham Hill, has won all three: Indianapolis in 1966, Le Mans in 1972 and Monaco five times from 1963.

In 1922 Monza—the Autodromo Nazionale di Monza—outside Milan, was built as a combination road circuit and oval. Its oval was a concept a lot like Indianapolis and Brooklands. The three superfast ovals were hailed as the way of the future, with much promise for elite motor racing. But war got in the way. All three were mothballed in World War II and Brooklands never re-opened. Monza did, but in a revised layout. Only Indy remained true to its roots.

In 1949 the general manager of Indianapolis Motor Speedway, Theodore 'Pop' Myers, was in Europe for a meeting of the Fédération Internationale de l'Automobile (FIA), the controlling body of most motorsport in the world. Pop had been an employee of the speedway since way back in 1910. He had served three owners and, with his secretary Eloise 'Dolly' Dallenbach, was the heart and soul of the place. He carried some authority.

The FIA proposed a Formula One world championship and Pop put the speedway forward for a round. Indy's technical specifications were different, run to the rules of the American Automobile Association, but the FIA—keen to live up to the promise of a 'world' title—agreed. Amazingly, Indianapolis would remain a points-scoring round of the F1 world title for the next ten years. That meant 1950 Indy winner Johnnie Parsons would come sixth outright in the inaugural world title without ever racing on a European circuit.

In 1952 Ferrari sent five modified versions of their 1951 grand prix cars to Indianapolis. They entered their 1950 and 1951 world champions, Giuseppe Farina and Alberto Ascari, but Farina was injured in Turin and failed to arrive. Ascari found himself alone in wonderland, and he drove the only Ferrari to qualify. He started nineteenth and had worked his way up to eighth on lap 40 when his rear right wire wheel broke and sent him spinning into the infield. He went on to win his second world title anyway, without Indy points. In May 1955 he was killed testing a Ferrari 750—ironically on Curva del Vialone, one of Monza's high-banked Indy-style high-speed turns.

Five-time world champion Juan Manuel Fangio first visited Indianapolis as a spectator in 1948, then flew back in 1954 to do exploratory laps with Wilbur Shaw. The place intrigued him. In practice in 1958 he got an ill-handling Kurtis Kraft Offy up to a reasonable 142 mph (228 km/h), then tested a front-wheel drive Novi, a difficult car to drive, at 135 mph (217 km/h). But Fangio never raced at Indy—there were contractual conflicts, he said, and he could not make them work.

Stirling Moss was a non-starter, despite the ambition of Indy organisers. He never made it to the track, but his dad did. Rookie Alfred Moss drove a Fronty Ford in 1924, classified a finisher in sixteenth place. The father–son story was not to be.

Pop Myers died in 1954 but neither Indy nor the FIA gave up on the idea of crossing the streams. In 1957 and 1958 the Monza autodrome ran a 500-mile (804-kilometre) race around its newly rebuilt 2.64-mile (4.25-kilometre) banked oval. At its lip, 'Monzanapolis', as it was nicknamed, was almost a vertical 80 degrees. You could not stand on it. And it was faster even than Indianapolis. A test in an Indy car resulted in a lap average of 170 mph (273 km/h).

Monza's Race of Two Worlds did not count for world title points, but it was intended to lead to that ... except that most F1 teams failed to turn up. They had measured the mechanical stresses involved and determined it would be suicide to run their delicate cars there, even with modification. Jimmy Bryan won the first year of the Race of Two Worlds in his Kuzma-Offy. Jim Rathmann won the second in his Kurtis Kraft Offy. And then the concept was abandoned.

In the following half century there have been bold attempts in England, Germany and even Japan to emulate Indy, but each new oval serves simply to confirm the Brickyard's pre-eminent position.

5

Applying the Blackjack

Sir Jack Brabham didn't set out to change the course of Indianapolis racing—but he did. He didn't set out to create a dynasty—but over the course of 55 years three generations of his family have raced at the Brickyard. Brabham's motivation was neither of these things. It came down to a simple suggestion made by Rodger Ward, a dirt-track midget racer like himself, and an audacious attempt by Ward to win a Formula One grand prix with a speed car. He was a like mind.

Ward was, according to Brabham, a real racer. He'd been a WWII pilot, first in the twin-tailed P-38 fighter-bomber—the aircraft the Japanese called 'two planes, one pilot'—and then he'd switched to the cumbersome but iconic B-17 Flying Fortress bomber. He was good, so intuitive that the US Air Force kept him on after the war as a pilot trainer. Brabham hadn't been a pilot, he'd been an engineer, a leading aircraftman with the RAAF.

Post-war they both began racing midgets, careers on parallel paths—Brabham at the Sydney Showground and Sports Ground venues, Ward on a quarter-mile dirt track outside Wichita Falls, Texas, where he was stationed. Racing midgets was a dangerous pastime. The close confines of the bullpen quarter- and half-mile ovals, with tiny but powerful open-wheeled cars flung perpetually sideways, and giant clods of earth propelled from the drive wheels like cricket balls straight into the driver's body so hard it hurts, are not for everyone. But both Ward and Brabham found it uplifting. 'I didn't know what speed was until I hit the speedway,' Brabham once told me. Even after all his Formula One and Indy racing, he still rated the confined environment of the sub-mile as the most visceral. It was the same for Ward.

By 1948 Brabham was the New South Wales Speed Car Champion. Ward had won the San Diego Grand Prix and was well on his way to becoming a midget-racing Hall of Famer. For a decade they pursued their dreams—Brabham to Europe and Formula One, Ward to IndyCar, with a detour to become USAC Stock Car Champion. Brabham was quiet, taciturn. Ward was brazen, cocky, but Bill Vukovich's 1955 crash knocked that out of him. Ward had broken an axle, precipitating, he thought, the chain of events that sent Vukovich on his death flight. He sat high in the darkened stands that night, overlooking the speedway, and reassessed his life. He found a bit of religion and a lot of purpose.

The end of the decade—1959—was to be the best year yet for them both. On 10 May, Jack Brabham won the Monaco Grand Prix, his first grand prix victory. On 30 May, Rodger Ward won the Indianapolis 500, his first Indy win. First place in the first two events of the world championship season momentarily put them 1–2 in the title race.

Since 1951 Ward had never come close to winning Indy—his best result was an eighth. Then he joined a new team—with owner Bob Wilke and chief mechanic A.J. Watson. They were the 'three Ws' and they were the dream team. For the six years from 1959, they were first, second, third, first, fourth and second in the Indy 500.

Brabham had been with the Cooper Car Company—owned by Charles Cooper and his son John—since he arrived in England in 1955. He'd never come close to the world championship title—his best result, a 21st. Then a new 2.5-litre engine put a lot more power into the best chassis in the series and the Cooper family closed ranks around him. He won two races—Monaco and in Britain—and was consistently on the podium.

In December 1959, the Coopers and Brabham arrived at Sebring, the WWII part-concrete-paved airfield in Florida, for the final race of the title fight in a three-way battle for the championship. If they won, it would be the first ever for a rear-engine car and for a British team. It was the first US Formula One Grand Prix (there'd been one the year before for sports cars), and promoters were taking a big punt to try and draw a crowd with these little European Formula cars, so they invited a big-name drawcard—the winner of the Indianapolis 500, Rodger Ward: 'They offered me money and I was in the habit of accepting money,' he said.

Rodger didn't bring his roadster—it was designed only to turn left, and even with modification it was too heavy and far too cumbersome. In July, Ward had entered the Haybale Sports

Car Racing Championship at the tight 1.5-mile (2.4-kilometre) Lime Rock road circuit in Lakeville, Connecticut. He raced his dirt-track midget—a Kurtis Kraft Offy—against the Maserati 250 F open-wheeler of Chuck Daigh, the Maserati 300 S sports car of young Mexican Pedro Rodríguez, and even the Cooper Monaco sports car of John Fitch. And over 150 miles (241 kilometres), he had won. So, with great confidence, he brought the midget to Sebring.

'You guys have a surprise waiting for you,' Ward told John Cooper, Jack Brabham and young Cooper teammate Bruce McLaren in their Sebring hotel. His midget, he asserted, wouldn't be as fast in the straights, but it would be untouchable around corners.

In practice, they arrived at the first turn together and the Coopers sped away while Ward floundered. 'I've got to hand it to you,' Rodger said, according to Cooper's autobiography, 'Those European buggies sure take corners fast.' Cooper made him sound like a hayseed. He wasn't.

Ward watched astutely, both from his position in the race in which he was eighth and from the sideline. He watched Bruce McLaren become the youngest ever driver to win a grand prix and Jack Brabham push his out-of-fuel car for several hundred metres (shades of Rupert Jeffkins) on the last lap to be classified fourth and claim his first world title—and the more he watched, the more certain he became that the days of the Indy roadsters were as numbered as the front-engine Ferraris, which could not keep pace with the Coopers.

For no other reason than he and Brabham were like-minded, Ward spent that weekend persuading Cooper to go Stateside. Ward was a true Indy believer: 'I don't care where else you race in the world, Indy makes you a race driver.' The money helped, too.

Jack's eldest son, Geoffrey, who'd later build himself an illustrious US racing career, remains certain it was the comparatively rich purse that sealed the deal. Total prize money for the 1961 Indy 500 was US$397,910. You could make around US$3000 winning a grand prix. For the Cooper team, money was always the denominator and the cars the commodity. Wherever Brabham and Cooper raced, there was always a market price, and everything was for sale. Whenever Brabham raced Cooper cars in Australia, it was understood he would return to the Cooper factory in Surbiton minus his race car and with a bag full of cash.

Ward arranged for Brabham to test the 1960 lowline Cooper at Indianapolis. Brabham had already become a consecutive world champion and he flew into Indianapolis from Australia where he'd won a special 100-mile (160-kilometre) celebratory race, the Craven A International, at Mount Panorama and sold the car as instructed.

On his second Indy lap, Brabham achieved 128 mph (205 km/h) and was black-flagged for going too fast. He had ignored the rookie rules and, despite his world championship status, he was sanctioned by circuit officials: 'I didn't understand the fuss—I wasn't trying hard,' he said. He endured eight laps at 115 mph (185 km/h) and ten at 125 mph (201 km/h) before they let him loose. With extraordinary consistency he reeled off three laps at exactly 142.8 mph (229.7 km/h)—just 3 mph (4.8 km/h) slower than that year's pole position. The stopwatch told the tale—he was as fast as the fastest of the Indy roadsters in the corners, but slower in the straights. Ward then drove the car to give Brabham a benchmark. He confirmed the Cooper's stability as well as its lack of grunt.

Suspension tuning made some difference. By the end of the test, Brabham was up to 144.8 mph (232.9 km/h) and that would have put his 2.5-litre car eighth on the grid for that year's race in a field full of 4.2-litre specialised IndyCars.

Critically, they'd found a patron. Jim Kimberly, one-time president of the Sports Car Club of America, a gentleman racer of renown and, happily, heir to the Kleenex tissue fortune, wanted their car to run in the 1961 race as the Kimberly Special. No problem—Jack was used to branding his cars. He'd been virtually banned from racing in Australia in 1953 when he entered his first Cooper Bristol as the REDeX Special, named for an oil additive. Advertising was prohibited on race cars at the time—and still was in Europe in 1961—but Jack knew the value of a sponsorship dollar. In Australia he taped the offending name over with brown paper, which blew off before the first corner. He was a big fan of the way they did things in the States.

John Cooper built a long-wheelbase version of the Cooper, all the better to handle the 2000 corners it would need to negotiate over 500 miles, and he built a stretched 2.7-litre version of the Coventry Climax engine. It put out 25 additional horsepower (18 kilowatts), around 258 horsepower (192 kilowatts) in total, still far less than the 430-horsepower (320-kilowatt) IndyCars. Their big hope lay in less use of consumables. They had a plan. The lighter weight would mean less fuel and tyre consumption. If Jack drove conservatively to save fuel, he'd be able to synchronise tyre changes with fuel stops. Get it right and they'd need only two pit stops and be in a winning position.

Jim Kimberly had a good grasp of motor racing. He had helped put Ferrari on the map in the United States in the 1950s with a series of wins in V12 and in-line six-cylinder sports cars (his Ferrari 375 recently fetched A$13.3 million at auction). While his status was strictly amateur, he knew what it took to win. Jim established a fund of around $30,000 to build the Cooper—about three times the build cost for an F1 car of the time. When Cooper ran into scheduling challenges to make the Indy Month of May fit with its European F1 commitments, Kimberly turned on a private plane. Kimberly was an enthusiast in all that he did. He had three wives, consecutively, and his separation from the third, when he was 77 and she 35, was the talk of the Palm Beach social set. Her budget was significantly greater than that of any of his motor-racing programs.

It wasn't easy being the mouse that roared. The roadsters were so large, the Kimberly Cooper so small. They towered above the little car, making visibility difficult. The alcohol-fuel fumes from their exhaust went straight to Brabham's throat and eyes.

Danger was ever present. In practice, fourteen-time Indy veteran Tony Bettenhausen Snr was tipped to become the first driver to better 150 mph (241 km/h). In pursuit of that goal he crashed on the front straight, a victim of mechanical failure, and died upside-down on the outside wall in full view of the pits. Drivers needed to block that sort of image from their mind.

Brabham was up next in the pole-day time trials. He put the Kimberly Cooper on the thirteenth starting position, pretty much in the top third of the field, and his qualifying speed was

145.14 mph (233.53 km/h), just 2.3 mph (3.7 km/h) slower than pole-sitter Eddie Sachs.

The key to winning Indy is a well-drilled pit crew. Precision in the pits only comes from experience. The Cooper team didn't have it. In their very first pit stop, one of the crew screwed up a tyre change and cross-threaded a knock-off wheel nut. (Geoff Brabham learned from that years later—his Indy team was the best in the business. 'Although I wasn't at Dad's first Indy,' he told me. 'I didn't go to Indy until I raced there myself.' Geoff was at school in England while mum Betty and middle brother Gary, just born, were in the pits.)

Firestone tyres dominated Indy. Brabham had a British Dunlop contract and while the company designed a run of Indy-specific tyres especially for him, he got to test them only at Silverstone, hardly a left-hand oval. On the day, they didn't wear as well as hoped. Cooper's two-stop strategy became three—and if they'd planned for that Jack would have pushed harder and used more fuel. Fuel and tyre replenishment fell out of synch and the team paid the price. Brabham finished ninth, still on the winning lap, but for Jack it was four places back from where he could have been.

The tiny Cooper had, however, seized the attention of the locals.

At Indianapolis you don't ever want to turn right. The big roadsters were set up to only turn left. If they had to avoid something, they could steer down the track towards the infield or hold their station, but they didn't want to be applying opposite lock or swerve right because the big cars would bolt for the wall—like a plough horse heading for the alfalfa. It was a deadly dilemma. Sometimes a driver had no option but to aim straight for the accident unfolding directly in front, hoping like hell the other car would spin out of their way by the time they reached the scene.

When rookie Don Davis in the Dart-Kart Offy had a big moment at quarter distance, Jack, just behind, reacted instinctively. He turned right, up the track, aiming for the fast-diminishing gap between Davis and the concrete wall, and he scraped through. 'Next time round I had to pick my way through the debris of half a dozen cars that had got caught up in the accident,' Jack said. One had even flipped, adding to the melee.

Third that year, Rodger Ward watched it all. The Cooper's manoeuvrability made it safer, its lighter weight (less than 1323 pounds/600 kilograms compared to 1980 pounds/900 kilograms for the roadsters) made it far more efficient. In the hands of someone who understood the unique requirements of the Brickyard, he figured, it could be a winner. The die had been cast for major change.

Brabham earned US$7250 for his ninth-place finish. It was equivalent to two and a half grand prix wins. For that reason alone, he determined he'd be back.

Ron Tauranac AO, 95, was a resident of the latest and most technologically well-equipped retirement home in Buderim, on the edge of Queensland's Sunshine Coast. When we met there in the summer of 2020, Ron was working on a problem—more a challenge, really. His walking frame, in his opinion, was inherently inefficient. 'They make us all use them—it's a condition of living here, so we have no excuse for falling over, I guess,' he said. 'But they make you lazy; you come to rely on them.'

The fulcrum of Ron's frame was all wrong—it made the steering imprecise when he pushed down on it under full power, and that made doing laps of the home's garden path imperfect. Ron was still one of the quickest around the circuit, and fine-tuning the frame, even though he had a Computer Aided Design app on the desktop in his room, was just theoretic, something to keep the brain occupied. 'It's too late now to make money out of it,' he said wistfully, 'so I don't do it.' Above his desk was a framed Michael Turner print of Jack Brabham in action in the world championship–winning Repco Brabham.

Ron was Jack's partner in a start-up racing-car operation— Motor Racing Developments. They became one of the most powerful combinations in all motorsport. Their cars were going to be called MRDs until it was pointed out to them that the name pronounced quickly came awfully close to being a very negative description in French, so they became 'Brabhams' instead.

Jack had resigned from Cooper at the end of the 1961 season. His last race for them had been the 200-mile (321-kilometre) Riverside Grand Prix for sports cars in California, which he won, repurposing the 2.7-litre Climax engine from his Indianapolis car. At the end of the race, the engine was purchased by a promising young US driver, Roger Penske, who used it in his self-designed Zerex Special. Penske went on to be somewhat successful—ownership of the Indianapolis Motor Speedway just part of his business portfolio. The Zerex Special was pivotal, too. Two owners on, it was acquired by Bruce McLaren, who used it as the genesis of his own Can-Am sports-car program, and that development spawned the McLaren IndyCar.

Resignation from Cooper had been on Jack's mind for some time. Old Charles Cooper was stuck in his ways and that was no more evident than in 1961 when Ferrari built a lightweight V6 F1 car to comply with the new 1.5-litre formula and their driver Phil Hill blew everyone away. In the comparatively cumbersome Cooper, there was no chance Jack was going to win three world championship titles in succession. Enzo Ferrari compounded the hurt by labelling the English teams, and Cooper in particular, *garagistes*—not real race car designers.

Brabham, Tauranac and small Australian engineering firm Repco would turn that around. By 1966 they would be world champions, not once but twice—first with Jack, then with New Zealander Denny Hulme.

Tauranac, born in England, raised in Australia and proudly the recipient of the nation's second-highest civil honour, had flown to the UK to join Jack while Jack was still with Cooper. They'd worked in the second bedroom of a flat in Surbiton, designing their new car in secret until inevitably the news got out. The Brabham team could have been single-minded—intent on winning the world championship alone—but they weren't. Wherever there was a market, an opportunity to win, they were part of it. They built tiny Formula cars, sports cars and F1 cars. They even modified road cars for Rootes and Vauxhall. 'It was like a marriage,' Tauranac told me with a twinkle in his eyes, 'except with two or three wives.'

In 1964 they received a call from long-time Indianapolis 500 entrant John Zink Jnr. John Zink Snr had entered two Indys in the early 1950s as a means of promoting his engineering business. John Jnr—known as 'Jack'—had maintained the family tradition and done remarkably better than his dad. He won two years straight: with Bob Sweikert in 1955 and Pat Flaherty in 1956. Jack Zink was a smart man. In his lifetime he would register 35 patents in the field of combustion and pick up awards for his innovations. He was one of the early adopters of rear-engine technology and of alternative power sources. He tried to combine both in a turbine car at Indy but he couldn't make it work. In 1964 he turned to Brabham to build him another Indy winner. It would be called the Zink-Urschel Trackburner Special. (Urschel was an Indiana-based mechanical solutions company; in 1964 it was a sponsor, not a technology partner.) The task fell to Tauranac: 'It was just another thing to do. I liked the challenge of these things.'

Tauranac pragmatically took the space frame chassis of the customer F1 car he'd just built for the 1964 1.5-litre season, the BT11, and lengthened and strengthened it to accept a 400-horsepower (298-kilowatt) Offenhauser motor. He called it the BT12 and Zink was never the wiser. Initially the BT12 was an oversteering monster. The Offenhauser engine was not a good fit and it took a make-do fix, a massive front anti-roll bar, to partially equalise the handling.

For Tauranac the experience was frustrating: 'I was used to running the show. But I was there just to supervise. I knew what it takes to make things work.' Even with Jack: 'If he had some ideas, I'd think about them and decide what was best.' But John Zink was the team owner. He determined that softer F1 springs were the right fit for the car. It was only later, after it was all over, that they fitted harder shocks and turned a mean handling machine into a potentially race-winning weapon.

Brabham jetsetted between Indianapolis and his Formula One commitments in Europe in the Month of May before he finally qualified 25th in the field. He wasn't there to see much of what went on. It was his former Cooper teammate Masten Gregory, the 'Kansas City Flash', who gave him a warning about the most evil-handling car he'd ever experienced.

It was a low-slung rear-engine Ford built by hot-rodder and salt flat record-breaker Mickey Thompson, and Gregory, after testing it, had declined to race it. That was saying something. Brabham regarded the bespectacled, boyish Gregory as the bravest racer he'd known. Gregory's stock-in-trade was leaping from his cars moments before they crashed. It took some nerve to do that.

Now the car was two rows ahead of the Brabham on the grid, driven by rookie Dave MacDonald.

Brabham credited Gregory's warning with saving his life. 'All the way round on the rolling lap before the start I kept my eyes riveted on that red car,' Brabham said in his autobiography. 'It was visibly very unsteady.'

MacDonald passed five cars and sprayed them with grass and dirt from the track edge. He lost it on Turn Four. The car assaulted the concrete wall. Veteran Eddie Sachs, a friend of Brabham's, was directly behind MacDonald and T-boned him. Full tanks of fuel erupted in a massive explosion. Brabham braked hard, but had nowhere to go, no vision except blackness. It was instinct that got him through. He jinked left, right, then powered out the other side. His lungs were choking. Another six cars didn't make it through. Sachs died instantly, MacDonald soon after in the Methodist Hospital.

In the stands, just 400 metres away, was a young spectator at his very first Indianapolis 500. Canadian Allan Moffat, who would become one of Australia's greatest touring-car racers, had gone to Indy in the hope of meeting Team Lotus to kick-start his career. He saw the crash a different way: 'Brabham blasted through the flame, accelerating strongly so the airflow would extinguish the fire that engulfed him,' Moffat said in his auto-biography *Climbing the Mountain*.

The race was stopped for almost two hours. It was the first time the Indy 500 had been live telecast and then only to selected movie theatres throughout the country. Out of the silence came the voice of the speedway's long-term anchor Sid Collins. His impromptu eulogy remains the battle hymn of motor racing:

There's not a sound. Men are taking off their hats. People are weeping; over three hundred thousand fans here; not moving, disbelieving. Some men try to conquer life in a number of ways. These days of our outer-space attempts, some men try to conquer the universe. Race drivers are courageous men who try to conquer life and death and they calculate their risks. And in our talking with them over the years I think we know their inner thoughts in regard to racing; they take it as part of living. No one is moving on the racetrack. They're standing silently. A race driver who leaves this Earth mentally when he straps himself into the cockpit to try what for him is the biggest conquest he can make is aware of the odds; and Eddie Sachs played the odds . . . We're all speeding towards death at the rate of sixty minutes every hour. The only difference is we don't know how to speed faster, and Eddie Sachs did. Eddie Sachs exits this Earth in a race car. And knowing Eddie, I assume that's the way he would have wanted it.

The following year, the United States Auto Club mandated fuel safety cells to mitigate the risk of explosion and it changed fuel regulations, effectively, but not totally, banning gasoline. In its place it introduced alcohol-based propellant, initially methanol, which would bring its own set of challenges.

On the restart Brabham became aware of a problem. His fuel line had been fractured by the debris of the crash. It was only made apparent when his floor pan became awash with fuel. He pressed on to the first fuel stop, his driving shoes progressively wetted by fuel. At the stop, when they plugged in the refill hose under pressure, fuel gushed out. 'I thought it best to retire the car,' he understated.

The Zink Trackburner—Brabham BT12—became a blueprint for American rear-engine race cars of the future. Jack Zink employed Texan Jim McElreath to race it in the rest of the 1964 season. It endured three big crashes, the last at Turn One at Indianapolis in private practice. The car caught fire and McElreath was seriously burned. Ron Tauranac was asked to repair it: 'The racing rules had changed, so there was no point in sending it back to me in England,' he told me. Instead Zink obtained permission from Tauranac and Brabham to let him use their drawings, and the wreck, to fabricate a local copy. Incredibly, the Australians agreed. Ron truly didn't remember if money changed hands.

'I was never a money man,' Ron said in Buderim. 'I just needed enough to continue to go motor racing.' At the time, he and Brabham were fully occupied with their Repco Brabham project.

The IndyCar rebuild passed to master US fabricator Clint Brawner. He built one copy, a Moore-Offy for McElreath who raced it as the Zink Trackburner. The other, a Brawner Hawk-Ford, was for young rookie Mario Andretti. Mario brought it home third in 1965 at his first attempt. A later development of the car, the Hawk III, would carry Mario to his only Indy 500 win in 1969.

Decades later, the wrecked BT12 was discovered in the corner of Brawner's race workshop. It was restored by Australian master engineer Lou Russo and joined the collection of Melbourne enthusiast the late Nereo Dizane, whose wife Anna maintained his stable. Sir Jack Brabham drove it at the Goodwood Festival of Speed in 2004.

Indianapolis was never the Brabham team's main game: 'Other people were more specialised than me,' Ron Tauranac reflected. It was recognition, perhaps a tad late, that at the Brickyard compromise is never the path to success. It's tantalising to contemplate what might have been had the dynamic duo given Indy their full focus. 'I just liked to beat other people,' Ron said, and they did that, especially in their relatively brief time in the sun in Formula One. With their Repco project, they caught the F1 world with its pants down.

Jack's unique claim is that he is the only driver ever to have won a Formula One world championship in a car of his own manufacture. This feat was made possible by Ron's car-building genius, and by a unique engine developed by Repco. A change to a 3-litre formula in 1966 put Brabham's Oldsmobile-based Repco engine in the box seat. The immensely talented Australian engineer Phil Irving developed a comparatively straightforward V8 working from a flat in Croydon, London, near the Brabham workshop. Phil, Ron and Jack worked together to build it.

As other teams floundered, Jack won four grands prix in succession, setting up his third world title as a driver and first as a constructor. Next year Jack's New Zealand teammate and employee Denny Hulme beat the boss. Denny moved on to join Bruce McLaren in 1968, and Jack hired a young gun—the mercurial, arrogant Jochen Rindt.

By then the Repco engine was on a downward trajectory with results. They gave it more valves, more mechanical parts and far greater complexity. Jack, later, was convinced that if they'd kept it simple, they could have won the World Constructors' Championship title three times in succession. Instead they beefed up the new four-valve engine, from Formula One 3-litre to Indy-spec 4.2-litre, and took it to Indianapolis. Tauranac built a new chassis—the Brabham BT25. It was the first mono-coque chassis he'd developed. He wasn't too keen to do it: 'But I was following US regulations,' he said simply. The Indianapolis regulations mandated greater fire protection and that required a more unitary chassis than was possible with Tauranac's main-stay space frame.

Jack wasn't to drive. He was already under family pressure to step out of the cockpit—another regret he'd harbour for the rest of his long life. Instead he put Jochen in one car and Masten Gregory in another. Masten would fail to qualify. Jochen had been to Indy the year before, obsessively chasing the big money on offer. He was quite open about it: 'In Indianapolis I always feel like I am on my way to my own funeral. The track is cata-strophic. I only drive there because of the money,' he said.

In pursuit of the big bucks, Jochen had raced in 1967 in a Dan Gurney–built Eagle Ford. It wasn't a happy experience. He'd clashed with officials over the Rookie Test: 'I just don't think it was necessary for them to treat me like that. I'm not a kid.' He'd crashed when his throttle jammed open at 160 mph (257 km/h) going into Turn One. And he'd reached just half distance when his engine failed. Plus, under the rules of the day, they wouldn't let his model wife Nina into Gasoline Alley.

But when Jack asked him to go back, Jochen willingly accepted. He'd do anything for Jack. He respected him probably more than anyone else in motor racing. Brabham was his hero, and most likely something of a father figure. Both Jochen's parents had been killed in a WWII bombing raid in Hamburg when he was only one year old.

Brabham's motivation for contesting Indianapolis was akin to Rindt's. It was about the money. The Repco Brabham wasn't going to win the world championship in 1968, that was clear. But there was a chance the enlarged engine, running well, could win Indy. Brabham also had a big-time tyre contract with Goodyear and the tyre maker was eager to break Firestone's dominance of the race. They were prepared to pay pretty much any price in pursuit of just their third victory in 50 years.

Rindt returned to Indy as a dark hero. He'd bruised the sensibilities of the Brickyard's management. But his crash the year before had also given him the reputation of a superman. When the throttle stuck, he'd deliberately steered up into the Turn One wall and run along it, with the right-hand side of the car disintegrating against the concrete as it scrubbed off speed. Towards the end of the crash the fuel tank exploded; Rindt undid his seatbelts (the first time he'd worn them was at Indianapolis) and then bailed out just like Masten Gregory had. Yet when he went to the hospital for mandatory tests, his heart rate was near to normal and his blood pressure only up 6 per cent.

In the Brabham BT25, he persuaded officials to let him out on a still slightly damp track (perhaps he intimidated them) and he drove a wild, sometimes opposite lock session to qualify sixteenth at an average of 164.14 mph (264.1 km/h). Ron Tauranac, not renowned for hyperbole, exclaimed, 'Sensational.' In the race, Rindt's car lasted just five laps before the engine failed.

The Repco writing was on the wall. Rindt craved a world championship to validate his immense talent. Reluctantly he left Brabham for Lotus. In 1970 in practice at Monza he died when his car turned sharply into a track stanchion. He suffered severe throat injury when he slid down into his seatbelt.

In the Indianapolis Motor Speedway Museum there is one race car that looks completely out of place. It is a blood-red Ferrari 250 LM, still with scrutineering stickers on its windscreen. It was used by Jochen Rindt and Masten Gregory to win the 1965 Le Mans 24 Hour race. The car was outdated even then and given no chance of success. Legend has it Jochen had a hot date lined up in Paris that night and the pair agreed they would drive the car to destruction so they could leave early. But the Ferrari refused to cooperate. They flogged it for the full 24 hours and won. It was to be Ferrari's last-ever victory at Le Mans.

Jack Brabham came back in 1969. The Repco engine was gone from Formula One, replaced by a Ford Cosworth, but there was still unfinished business at Indianapolis. Jack and Ron were convinced the BT25 and the Repco engine, with a bit more development, had a chance. And the same financial incentives applied. They left their F1 driver Jacky Ickx at home. Instead they hired a rookie, Peter Revson. It's fair to assume that in his rookie year, money may have secured the Brabham drive.

Revson was generally thought to be the heir to the Revlon cosmetics fortune, but with multiple family members involved the claim may not have been totally watertight. Revson was a personality in his own right and he played with stars. He would soon race with Steve McQueen and become engaged to Indianapolis's own Miss World, Marjorie Wallace. Marjorie was stripped of her crown, while engaged to Revson, when she was caught in a tryst with singer Tom Jones.

Revson was a talented racer. His test of his will came in 1967 when his brother Doug was killed in a race crash in Denmark. He could have retreated to other pursuits but instead he raced on. At Indy he raced the Brabham from last on the grid to fifth. It was a source of immense frustration to him that Mark Donohue, two places and seven laps behind, was awarded Rookie of the Year apparently because of a stronger performance throughout the Month of May.

Revson learned a lot from Brabham. Jack extracted 163.87 mph (263.66 km/h) from his car. Revson, the last to make it into the field, did 160.85 mph (258.8 km/h) in the second car. It's likely Jack left nothing out there—so if his lap was the fastest a Repco Brabham was ever going to go, then rookie Revson did a sensational job getting so close. In the race, Brabham's locally purchased ignition system broke, and he coasted to a halt on lap 58.

Jochen Rindt watched from the sidelines. He'd been entered along with Mario Andretti and Graham Hill in a team of radical wedge-shaped four-wheel drive Lotus 64s. When a suspension component broke under load, pitching Andretti backwards into the wall, Lotus boss Colin Chapman withdrew all three cars from the field. It was an uncharacteristic admission by Chapman of the fragility of his cars. Andretti had a back-up—the Brawner Hawk III, the latter-day evolution of the Brabham BT12. It was probably the most beautiful, purposeful-looking car of its era and Andretti drove it to his first, and only, Indianapolis 500 win.

Several months before his death, I sat knee to knee with Sir Jack Brabham at his home on Australia's Gold Coast and we shouted at each other. Years of motor racing had destroyed Jack's hearing, so even with artificial aids, a high volume was required. We cleared up several mysteries—amongst them why he was called 'Black Jack'. It wasn't because of his mood or his permanent five o'clock shadow. It was because John Cooper, all those years ago, had decided that as an Australian he came from 'black fella country', highly inappropriate now. Jack was going on 88 and his career was half a lifetime behind him. He still so wished it wasn't.

'I gave up racing far too early,' he said. 'I got talked into it.' There was nothing pleasant about the way he said it, no casual old-man reminiscence. 'I could have gone on for a few more years,' he asserted. He pretty much spat the words out.

There'd been a few crashes. Formula One and Indianapolis were dangerous places to be, much more so than in later decades.

In 1969 Jack's moment of truth came in private testing at the ultra-fast Silverstone Grand Prix circuit. The left front tyre exploded from its rim at 115 mph (185 km/h) and pitched him into an earth bank. He was trapped by his legs in the car, in intense pain, and the engine had failed to switch off. It was screaming at full revs and fuel was spilling out. In private practice sessions there were no track safety marshals, no fire crew, no ambulance. Until his crew arrived, he was on his own.

'I managed to get to the kill switch to shut off the engine,' he said, matter of fact. It was nothing like as easy as he described it. He had to turn into a contortionist to reach it. 'But then I had a major debate with myself whether to activate the onboard fire extinguisher right away or wait for the car to catch fire. I'd only have one go at it.' He pushed the button and doused the hot engine and exhausts with foam. It was at that stage his crew turned up, led by a young mechanic, Ron Dennis—later to own McLaren. 'I was still trapped in the car with plenty of fuel about. Ron took a long while but did a good job to get me out without a spark.'

His wife Betty and his family were not pleased. Even his father, Tom, was against Jack continuing. By the end of the 1969 season, Jack had made the decision to sell his shares in the Brabham company to Ron Tauranac. But he'd also decided to turn 1970 into a valedictory celebration. He'd race everything he could lay his hands on: Formula One cars, sports cars, Indy. No pressure. He was now just a driver. Maybe he could win something. Maybe also he could go back on his promise . . . maybe he could extend his career.

Indianapolis was hard going. Ron had built him a new car—the Brabham BT32, an evolution of the BT25—and it had been designed specifically to accept a 2.65-litre turbocharged four-cylinder Offenhauser engine. If you can't beat them, join them.

It was putting out a theoretical 930 horsepower (693 kilowatts) in qualifying mode, but for the second year in a row the Brabham team suffered ignition problems. The engine was running at full noise only spasmodically. They tuned the chassis around what they thought the engine would give when they got the electrics fixed, but they couldn't be precise. It took Jack three full sessions of qualifying to insert himself into the grid. He snuck into the field, 26th fastest, 166.39 mph (267.72 km/h). It was a long way off Al Unser's pole of 170.22 mph (273.88 km/h).

Miraculously, in the race the engine came good. It was putting out so much horsepower that the chassis wanted to squirm around and oversteer. Jochen Rindt might have driven like that, but Jack was older, wiser, and he wanted a car that would obey his commands. He was getting warp speed down the straight—upwards of 225 mph (362 km/h)—but in the corners it took all his skill to control it. He hung on for 175 laps and then the engine called it quits. The massive torque forces of a powerful engine not in sync with its chassis meant something had to give: 'It pretty much broke in half,' he told me, deadpan. He was classified thirteenth and picked up US$20,227.

Less than three weeks later he was trapped in his F1 car again with fuel leaking. It was the Dutch Grand Prix at Zandvoort and a tyre had once more gone down. This time he was trapped in catch fencing, upside-down after multiple rollovers. He was fully conscious and kept his finger on the fire extinguisher button just in case he had to activate it. His biggest concern was what would happen after they got him out; Betty and Tom were in the pits. He knew what to expect.

But the clincher, the absolute pull-the-pin decider, came at the British Grand Prix. He was still in with a theoretical chance of winning his fourth world championship. 'All' he had to do was win to keep the title alive. It was the last corner of the last lap; he was leading, walking away from Jochen Rindt, who'd given him a huge battle all race long. And he ran out of fuel. 'That was harder to accept than any crash,' Jack said. The title was gone and with it any hope of career resurrection.

For years he blamed Ron Dennis for the fuel shortage. It was three decades before another of the team's mechanics mustered the courage to admit that he was at fault. Brabham chuckled about that. He liked the idea of holding Dennis, by then one of the biggest wigs in motorsport, accountable.

Jack Brabham, knighted for his service to motorsport and to his country, died on 19 May 2014. Rodger Ward, who got him started at Indy, had passed away a decade before, aged 83. The two of them were actively involved in supporting motorsport right to the end.

Jack's delight was in proudly following the careers of his two grandsons—Matthew, Geoffrey's boy in the United States, and Sam, David's boy in Europe. 'It's so expensive,' he said with real frustration. 'Don't know how they do it.'

Ron Tauranac, cared for by his daughter Jann, died on July 17, 2020.

6

At the Front of the Rear-End Revolution

Who would have thought it? An apprentice marine engineer from BHP's Newcastle steelworks would be the lead mechanic on Jim Clark's works Lotus when it became, heroically and historically, the first rear-engine car to win the Indianapolis 500.

Who would have thought it? The water boy who handed Clark a dixie cup on a long pole in his two pit stops would become one of Australia's most successful and revered touring-car racers.

In 1965, both happened.

Jim Smith, retired to Bondi Junction just above the golden beach, was the mechanic.

Allan Moffat, an enduring legend, was the water boy.

They were both part of the works Lotus team—Moffat a

one-off for that single Indianapolis meeting—and they shared in history.

'I took a pay cut to take that job, and I was overqualified,' said Smith, nuggety, bespectacled, with a cheeky grin and the look of someone who's never quite left the '60s behind. Son of a Wauchope dairy farmer, he'd left Australia on the last voyage of the Orient Line's *Orion*. The old girl (built 1934) was about to be decommissioned and scrapped. On her final trip, up through the Suez Canal and Greece, she was a party ship.

'With three guys I met on board, I went touring in Europe, four of us crammed in a Mini Minor,' Jim said. They got to Monaco for the grand prix. It was the first motor race Jim had seen— Graham Hill won it from Richie Ginther, both in BRM P57s, after pole man and world champion Jim Clark dropped back to eighth with gearbox problems. Monaco is like Australia's Gold Coast, just with a French accent. Beaches, bars and a permanent holiday atmosphere make it a perfect place for a motor race, so much better than the buttoned-down cities that host most street races. It's why, decades later, IndyCar enjoyed coming to its international round at Queensland's Surfers Paradise.

Smith was hooked. Back in the UK he found an advertisement in *Autosport* magazine offering a position at Lotus. 'I thought it was for the race team, but it turned out to be for the road cars,' Jim told me. 'I did it for a while but it was dead boring, so I went to sea—a couple of trips as engineer on P&O cruises out to Hong Kong.' In his short time at Lotus, Jim had made friends—with team manager and occasional driver Ray Parsons, who had been a submariner and was on a wavelength with the young marine engineer; and designer and fabricator John Joyce—both Australians.

'I was on shore leave and I walked into a Lotus pub and Ray was at the bar and said, "Wanna job with the race team?" Well, I had three months leave owing and I figured, why not.'

'When do you want me to start?' Jim said.

'How about tomorrow?' Ray replied.

They put Smith in the transporter and sent him to the frighteningly dangerous Solitude road circuit outside Stuttgart to fettle the engine and gearbox of Mike Spence, Jim Clark's Lotus 33 teammate. Spence retired from the race, Clark won, pushed all the way by motorcycle world champion John Surtees in a works Ferrari. (Spence died at Indianapolis four years later.)

Solitude for Smith was quite a debut—his first-ever motor race, working with world champions. The young Aussie was up for a few celebratory drinks in the pits when he met Lotus boss Colin Chapman. 'He wasn't impressed,' Smith recalled. 'Chunky' Chapman's bollockings were legendary but Smith didn't take it to heart.

Team Lotus first entered the Indianapolis 500 in 1963, Jim Clark's first world championship–winning year. They'd gone the previous year to a test day, straight from the US Grand Prix at Riverside, and Clark's little 1.5-litre Lotus 25 sounded like a box full of bees as it wound up and flung itself around the speedway. Chapman came to an arrangement with the Ford Motor Company and the purpose-built Lotus 29, offset to make it turn left better, almost won. Part of the reason it didn't was because the European team was hopeless at its pit stops.

Clark's one stop took 42 seconds—twice as long as the pit stop of the winner Parnelli Jones in his Watson-Offy roadster.

Lotus went back in 1964. Clark got pole, and then survived a massive suspension breakage on the front straight. Allan Moffat was there for that race, watching from the grandstand. 'The little Lotus dropped to the ground like a broken stick insect,' he said, a bit poetically. 'Jimmy worked all his magic to keep it under control at upwards of 250 km/h (155 mph) as it danced around with sparks flying from underneath. The wall was perilously close.'

Moffat was trying to infiltrate Team Lotus. The obsessive Canadian, much later to become an Australian citizen sponsored by his friend and rival Peter Brock, would spend 1964 stalking the Lotus Cortina touring-car team over half of the United States, working as a gofer where he could to try to gain their support and trust.

'The Indianapolis 500 was the first motor race I'd ever attended in the USA and I'd bought a ticket in the grandstand opposite the pits, just me and 200,000 of my closest friends,' Moffat said. 'The night before the big race I'd talked my way into the official Gasoline Alley cocktail party. For two hours I worked that room but to no avail. There wasn't much I could add to a Brickyard conversation and besides Team Lotus wasn't there—at least not that I could see. No Jimmy Clark, no Dan Gurney, no Colin Chapman. They were the faces I knew from the magazines. Anyone else would have to have been wearing a name badge.'

Ray Parsons was the common denominator for Moffat and Smith. Moffat buttonholed him at a United States Road Racing Championship round at Watkins Glen in New York state. He'd stood outside the pit, on the other side of the wire, until a mechanic took pity on him after the racing and invited him in. He got to talk to Parsons, the team manager, and Parsons gave him a chance—no money, but a job as a car cleaner and part-time truck driver as long as he paid his own way.

By the end of the season, Parsons could see that Moffat was serious and, with the help of Ford's European division in Dearborn and his father's bank balance, Moffat amazingly was sold one of the redundant works Lotus Cortinas. He brought it back to Australia, entered it in the inaugural Sandown 6 Hour race in November 1964 and won his class. It was by no means as simple as it sounds and it's a massive credit to Moffat that he parlayed that one opportunity into a stellar career. The next year he was on his way to Detroit, flying coach, to talk up his chances, when he stopped off at Indianapolis to wish 'his' team well in the 500.

'I told them I'd only build the car if I went with it to the race meeting,' Jim Smith said. He'd been assigned the task of assembling the Lotus 38 designed by Chapman and the legendary Len Terry, who'd at one stage even worked on the English Racing Automobiles (ERA) Formula cars that defined pre-war and immediate post-war British racing technology. Terry and Chapman didn't see eye to eye. They collaborated warily. Terry demanded full responsibility for the 38, but still left Lotus's employ before it raced.

Jim Smith was one of those chosen to piece together the jigsaw of the 38's design. Compared to the space frame cars that preceded it, this was Lotus's first full-monocoque tub chassis, designed so all components would neatly hang off it. They didn't. Ford had sent a 1964 engine to Lotus to use as a template for the design of the 38. The 1965 engine was different: 'We spent hours grinding bits off it to make it fit in the car,' Jim recalled.

Before they arrived at Indianapolis the team went testing at Trenton, New Jersey, the kidney-shaped semi-oval long-since closed, a victim of urban sprawl. In April, Roger McCluskey, Indy veteran and four-time national speed-car champion, was working the 38 up to speed when he hit the wall. The wreck required a whole new tub. It made the Month of May even more tense.

Jim Clark would, of course, be the lead driver. Lotus had hired Florida-born Bobby Johns, a NASCAR specialist, a good old boy who did a lot of his racing in unsanctioned events, to drive the second car. It was an unusual choice. Only the year before Johns had become the first NASCAR racer to turn a wheel on the speedway—the two disciplines just didn't mix. He'd failed to qualify that year and now here he was in the works Lotus team.

'I was standing in the pits when Colin Chapman and Jimmy Clark walked in and Colin said, "Right, you're looking after Jimmy's car,"' Jim Smith said, still a bit incredulous even after all these years. 'I was still the new boy.' But Clark and Smith had formed a bit of a bond, a trust, and Lotus was closing ranks to give their world champion what he wanted.

Moffat and Smith came together in Gasoline Alley, the team dressed in dark British-racing-green overalls, an unintentional snub to the Indianapolis tradition that regarded green as the unluckiest colour of all. 'It made us somewhat unpopular, they didn't like the British,' Smith remembered (at odds with the recollection of many Americans who recall the British invasion fondly). 'I did my best to overcome that.'

They were staying at the Holiday Inn opposite the track. Smith walked into the bar and this big bloke, a Texan, called out, 'Hey Limey.'

'No mate,' Smith replied, 'Aussie.'

The friendly Texan was A.J. Foyt and just like that Smith was in the fold. 'He bought me a drink and made me part of their month. "Hey Aussie," he'd say, "we're going out, want to come?"'

Moffat's experience was a bit different. He was more uptight— very much aware of the responsibility: 'I was there because my mates at Team Lotus had asked me. Sure, I was cleaning cars and components in a pit garage so pathetically narrow that mechanics had to take parts out into Gasoline Alley to work on them. But I especially requested to be Jim's [Clark] water-bearer and the singular honour was granted to me.'

After the fiery crash of 1964, the speedway introduced a two-pit-stop-minimum rule to prevent teams from taking huge risks with full fuel loads in order to scrape by with one time-saving stop. 'It looked like we weren't going to make it on two,' Smith said. 'In practice we sent Jimmy out to deliberately run out of fuel. When we pushed the bone-dry car to the pump to do our calculations, we found we'd be two gallons short of getting to the finish. Colin Chapman went ballistic with Ford, and demanded they do something. They said the engine was the best it was going to be, and nothing could be done. Colin turned to me and said, "Lean it out, Jim."' (The practice of 'leaning out' changes the fuel mix so less fuel is used, but it risks detonating the entire engine.)

'I did as I was told and leaned it out half a turn. Jimmy went out and two laps later he coasted back into the pits pointing his thumb over his shoulder. He'd melted all eight pistons.' For Smith it meant an all-night job to change the engine, with the issue of fuel consumption still not resolved.

'About four o'clock in the morning I heard a thump outside and I opened the door and a box was sitting there. It was a new engine with a different fuel injection system on it.' It had been shipped from Ford, a last-ditch effort to appease Chapman. 'I later found out other teams had tried that engine and couldn't make it work, but we used it and it gave us the fuel consumption we needed.'

Allan Moffat was on a steep learning curve that month. He was yet to become one of Ford's most valued test drivers, working with the renowned Kar-Kraft organisation out of Dearborn. He absorbed everything that went on and Jim Clark gave him a masterclass in tyre selection: Goodyear and Firestone were the two protagonists. Team Lotus used Dunlop in Formula One, but Dunlop wasn't an Indy specialist and after Clark's big scare in 1964 on the F1 tyres, he simply ruled out even trying them.

Clark had the clout to command equal opportunity from the other two tyre makers. He even had racing overalls made up bearing both their logos. Clark went back and forth between the two makes, making minute adjustments, feeling out not only their grip and longevity but also their driver feedback. Ultimately he went with the Firestones. Jim Smith knew why: 'Jimmy saw a chunk come off one Goodyear, just one chunk. But it was enough.'

'I won't drive on them,' Clark said. Safety for Clark was paramount—so sad that three years later his fatal crash at Hockenheim in Germany was caused, almost certainly, by a puncture.

'Jim was just three years older than me and he'd done a lot more in his life,' Moffat recalled. 'He wasn't exactly a hero. I've never really had those. He was more a benchmark really, an aspiration.' Just like Clark, 'repetitive testing is part of my DNA', Moffat added. 'You can only improve if you've got the miles under your wheels.'

Allan Moffat did more work than Jim Smith during the race. Team Lotus and Ford had both identified the Achilles heel of past efforts—pit stop speed and efficiency would not let them down this time. They brought in the Wood Brothers, a Ford stock-car team begun back in 1950 by brothers Glen and Leonard in the Blue Ridge Mountains of south-west Virginia. Their family were timber cutters and haulers.

The Wood Brothers invented the current practice of pit stops. In the good old days, a pit stop was a casual affair. Sometimes the driver would even have time to get out of the car and have a quick smoke. The Woods worked out that a race could be won in the pits. They developed a routine that was almost balletic. When other teams cottoned on to it, they simply refined and improved their act in order to remain the best in the business.

They came to Indianapolis for the first time in 1965 to work exclusively on Team Lotus. They were employed by the Ford Motor Company, not Lotus, and it was money well spent.

'I was already concerned about the coupling between the fuel filler hose and the car,' Jim Smith said. 'Unless you got it totally square, it just wouldn't connect. I'd started to file a little bit off here and there. But then the Wood Brothers arrived. They took the coupling off the car and fitted it to a packing case in the pits and just started practising over and over again, modifying the coupling until they could literally throw it at the car and it would fit.'

In the race Clark stopped twice, on laps 66 and 137. His first stop lasted just 19.8 seconds. (A.J. Foyt's crew took more than 40.) The second stop was a little longer—24 seconds—but they had time on their hands.

The Wood Brothers Racing team stood out. While the Lotus mechanics were in green, the Woods were in tight white stove-pipe jeans and short-sleeved shirts—their names emblazoned in red and gold across their backs above the racing number of their NASCAR. No fireproofs, no overt safety precautions. There was no pretence that they were part of Team Lotus either—they were gum-chewing specialists, there to do a job. They helped bring Bobby Johns home seventh, too, the best result he'd ever enjoy at Indy.

Moffat learned from that. Even when he held out the dixie cup on its long pole to give Clark a drink, it had to be part of the Wood Brothers' choreography. 'I built my own race team inside its own ecosystem,' he said many years later. 'I couldn't have been all that easy to work with, but I guess those who stuck with me did so because they shared the same intense commitment that has always driven me.'

Jim Smith, on the other hand, found the race an anti-climax: the Wood Brothers had usurped him. 'I had nothing to do for the whole race,' Smith said. 'I was there only if something went wrong with my car—no way that was going to happen, thank you.'

Jim Clark and Team Lotus set multiple records that day—the first rear-engine car to win Indy; the first winning average above 150 mph (150.63 mph/242.36 km/h); the first non-US resident driver to win since Dario Resta in 1916; and Clark's Lotus was the first winner to be painted green since 1920.

Moffat and Smith have different recollections of post-race celebrations.

Smith remembers an Italian restaurant, falling asleep in his pasta and being prodded awake by Clark: 'It was Memorial Day and it was alcohol free, so we were drinking from teacups— red tea.'

Moffat remembers being in Colin Chapman's room at the Holiday Inn, serving drinks: 'Jim Clark was just so pleasant. That day at Indy lives with me as one of the greatest experiences in my motor-racing life.'

Both men treasure the team photograph taken the next day on the Yard of Bricks—Moffat standing, Smith perched on the wheel, Jim Clark in the cockpit, with Colin Chapman kneeling alongside.

In 1996 Jim Smith, in Sydney, received an unexpected phone call from Allan Moffat, in Melbourne. The four-time Bathurst 500/1000 winner was planning one last shot at Mount Panorama. It would be his very last race, not driving, but as an entrant. Jim, who'd spent 30 years at sea, mainly on tankers and bulk carriers, had dabbled in motorsport over the years, but his life had been in the marine industry.

'Allan asked me to come to Bathurst to work in his crew,' Jim said. 'And you know what, I did.'

Moffat had let the money run out. He was down to a one-car entry, used once a year at Bathurst. The old Falcon was well past its prime.

Moffat brought out German touring-car ace Klaus Niedzwiedz as the lead driver and traded off the second driver's seat to the engine builder Ken Douglas in return for his mechanical services.

Smith turned up to help fettle the car. And against all odds, they brought it home tenth. 'There would have been a time that I'd be so distressed by that result it would be unbearable,' Moffat said. 'But that night I allowed myself a small smile of satisfaction. My team had achieved something amazing and if it had to be, it was not a bad way to draw a line under the career of both the car and its team owner.'

Moffat never raced again. Neither did Jim Smith.

Allan Moffat's former wife Pauline is a prominent resident of Indianapolis, named the city's 2012 Woman of Influence. Pauline runs the IndyFringe, a celebration of arts and culture, which is part of a global movement inaugurated more than 50 years ago in Edinburgh. She was the real deal when she was married to Moffat. Their partnership was very public—she would run his business, run his pit wall (at least the lap-scoring part of it), and join him on the winner's podium. They were in all respects a power couple and complementary: for every person of influence he'd risk offending with his sometimes caustic, single-minded, full-frontal approach, she'd charm two. 'Allan was always 110 per cent,' she said with a smile. That meant there was invariably collateral damage for her to clean up.

Her husband is now motor-race engineering legend Lee Dykstra, in the early 2000s the technical director of CART (Championship Auto Racing Teams), the open-wheeler road-racing series that was spun out of the now-healed split in the Indianapolis 500 ranks. Lee was also one of Allan Moffat's earliest influencers at Ford Kar-Kraft and his trusted fly-in-fly-out international engineer throughout his long race career.

There was nothing untoward in Pauline and Lee getting together. Lee admits an attraction back when he was helping Allan run his Ford Falcon GTs at Bathurst (who wouldn't?— Pauline was the flame to a lot of unrequited moths) but he didn't make his move until well after the Moffats separated. Pauline wonders why he waited so long.

Together Lee and Pauline are now the power source for the IndyFringe. A stucco-clad gable-fronted Pentacostal church, abandoned for many years, provided the bones for a restoration that encompasses new theatre and staging facilities. Lee designed and installed lighting, sound and staging technology. Pauline is IndyFringe's CEO.

The Dykstras have lived in Indianapolis almost twenty years—but both had been coming to the race long before that. 'Allan loved the place. For him, motor racing was all about Indy,' Pauline said. 'We used to organise paying tour groups from Australia to come here each year and Allan would give them a unique insider's perspective.'

Indianapolis is a fast-changing metropolis. Its downtown is just 6 miles (9.6 kilometres) from the speedway, but culturally it's a world away. Seated with the Dykstras in a bright restaurant on a Monday night, you could be in any of the world's major cities. There's a contemporary street buzz. 'You can't believe the change,' Pauline said over a glass of Australian sauvignon blanc. 'Ten years ago, the windows were boarded up, the street was dark, and it was dangerous to be out at night.' Indianapolis, the city once revolving on the hub of its Memorial Day motor race, is discovering a new identity.

'The Indy 500 needs reinventing,' Lee agreed. 'It's no longer truly the Month of May. There used to be people in the grand-stands all month long. Now there's not. They need to find a way to attract a younger audience . . . get kids involved.'

The Indy 500 still holds one of the best street parades in the US. Since 1957 the 500 has made a point of coming to town— bridging the divide between the racetrack and its greatest source of audience participation. Le Mans does the same thing. The City of Bathurst has just reinvented the idea after 30 years, bringing the stars of the show to the city to create a connection with the townsfolk. But Indy does it the best of all. 'There must be 100,000 people at the street parade,' Pauline said. 'Roger Penske [new owner of the Indianapolis 500] is the best thing that could happen for the speedway.' The Dykstras, who'd not been to the race in years, planned to go back.

7

The Bruce, Denny *and* Chris Show

Denis 'Denny' Hulme, New Zealand's first and only F1 world champion, was just getting up to speed at Indianapolis when small droplets began to course across his windscreen—like light rain. He was north of 180 mph (289 km/h), still accelerating, when behind him there was a *whump!* And heat, horrible, intense heat. His McLaren M15, the first car built by his countryman Bruce McLaren to race at Indianapolis, had exploded in flames and Denny was the only one who knew it.

The McLaren was running on methanol fuel, which burns invisibly. A fire in the pits during refuelling, where they usually happen, can result in anyone standing close doing the 'methanol dance'. They'll prance and flail about and no one can see the flames. For years, every Indianapolis pit had been equipped with a 44-gallon drum of water—all the better to put out a fire than a chemical extinguisher. Just jump in the drum or reach for a bucket.

But Denny was on track, away from instant assistance, and he was being burnt alive. At the insistence of racing officials, the McLaren's snap-down fuel filler cap had been fitted with an extra spring to help it flip open at fuel stops. It was a measure intended to prevent an accidental gush of fuel, which could cause a fire. Now it had exactly the opposite effect. Under high-speed vibration the cap unclipped, which it would not have done without the spring assistance, and small droplets of fuel had begun to leak—over the windscreen, over the driver, and onto the red-hot engine and exhaust behind.

Hulme went for the brakes and that started a flood out of the fuel cap. He was wearing a fireproof race suit, but the concept of total protection was in its infancy. He had on thin kangaroo-leather driving gloves and, in an instant, they had begun to melt into his hands.

Under completely controlled conditions, the best open-wheeled race cars can brake from 300 km/h to zero in about four seconds. Hulme took much longer. He steered to the infield, punched the onboard extinguisher without noticeable effect, and at something like 70 mph (112 km/h) undid his safety belts, stood in the cockpit, and bailed out. He jumped backwards so he wouldn't be run over by his own car. He just cleared the rear right-hand wheel.

He was tumbling down the infield grass, doing the methanol dance, when the safety crews arrived. They took him to the Methodist Hospital across town, the Indy 500's level-one trauma centre of choice. He spent two weeks there, his hands, forearms and feet covered in white antibacterial ointment.

The incident occurred on 12 May 1970. The race was on 30 May. By then Denny was back home in the United Kingdom. Every moving moment had been agony. He couldn't open doors, reach for papers, use a knife and fork, dress himself or attend to matters of personal hygiene.

Worse still, he'd left Bruce McLaren—the dominant partner in what the motor-racing world had come to call the 'Bruce and Denny Show'—without a driver.

Bruce McLaren was a motor-racing phenomenon. He'd burst onto the motor-racing scene while still a teenager, sharing a cut-down Austin 7 Ulster with his father Leslie, 'Pop', out of the family garage in Remuera, Auckland. It was good therapy for young Bruce. He'd had a hell of a childhood, struck down at age nine by Perthes disease, which required up to three years in and out of the Wilson Home for Crippled Children. They broke and rebroke his legs, leaving him immobile for months, in traction. Bruce was gifted a left leg 4 centimetres shorter than the right.

By the time Bruce was twenty he was racing a bob-tail F2 Cooper Climax, one of the ones Jack Brabham left behind for sale. Jack used to service his cars at Remuera Road and stayed with Les and Ruth McLaren in their lovely old home just around the corner.

'Jack called them his New Zealand Mum and Dad,' Bruce's sister Jan told me. 'He was like a big brother, eleven years older than Bruce. He'd turn up with black plastic spiders to scare the girls and he'd put bungers up the exhaust pipes of cars.'

Jack brought out two Coopers for the 1958 New Zealand Grand Prix, one for Bruce. With Jack's encouragement, Bruce won New Zealand's first Driver to Europe award and a works F2 drive with Cooper. It was a scheme inaugurated by New Zealand motor-racing authorities to encourage young local talent to take on the world. Bruce took his own orthopaedic clutch and brake pedals to Europe.

The following year he was Jack Brabham's Number Two driver in the Cooper F1 team—simple as that—and at year's end at Sebring he became the youngest winner of a Formula One grand prix. When Brabham left to start his own team, Bruce stayed on to become Number One for Cooper. He won the Monaco Grand Prix and was third in the world title behind Graham Hill and Jim Clark, but Charles Cooper felt forever betrayed by Brabham's departure and he closed shop on design collaboration with his drivers. Cooper felt he'd taught Brabham too much—set him up with the intellectual tools to build his own cars. He wasn't going to make the same mistake with Bruce. He made a bigger mistake by excluding him.

In 1964 Bruce formed his own team to run modified Coopers in the Australian and New Zealand Tasman Series, held over the Australasian summer in the F1 off-season. He found willing financial partnership from wealthy Pennsylvania brothers Teddy and Tim Mayer. Teddy was the money. Timmy was the driver. It was going well, too, until Timmy was killed on the Longford road circuit in Tasmania; he was only 26 years old, lying third in the series with Denny Hulme when he crashed. There's a memorial for him, still, at the roadside, a testament to the immense talent that was never requited. Teddy went home to the US, took some time off to get over the hurt and ponder the morality of building race cars in which young men killed themselves. Then he went back to Bruce and they started McLaren Automotive.

By 1966 they had a Formula One team and a firm business direction to secure them strong financial relationships with automobile companies, tyre makers and fuel suppliers. Motor racing never ran on enthusiasm alone. They could have concentrated just on F1, but Mayer recognised the huge potential in sports-car racing in Canada and the United States. The pinnacle was the Can-Am (Canadian-American) series. McLaren Auto bought the ex–Roger Penske Zerex Special, removed its ex–Brabham Indianapolis Climax engine and inserted a 5-litre V8 Oldsmobile engine. It was the prototype for a series of McLaren sports cars that became the class of the field. They won five successive titles. At its peak, the McLaren Can-Am program was so dominant that they'd stand down during practice sessions—'go fishing'— because they had nothing to prove.

The Can-Am program was Bruce's road to IndyCar. The M15 in which Denny was burned in 1970 was essentially a single-seater version of the M8 Can-Am car.

Denis Hulme was a year older than Bruce McLaren. In seniority alone he should have been New Zealand's first Driver to Europe, but his formative years followed a different trajectory. Young Bruce was coddled by his family, studied engineering at uni, knew Jack Brabham. Denny went to school barefoot. The family had a farm outside Pongakawa in the Bay of Plenty and Denny worked on it while he was very young, loading feed mills and driving trucks. Going barefoot wasn't a sign of poverty. All the kids did it. This was 'Footrot Flats' in the 1950s—archetypical New Zealand. Denny's dad Clive had come home from World War II a hero. He had been awarded the Victoria Cross—the Commonwealth's greatest military accolade for bravery—as a sniper in Crete. And he was tough. He didn't talk about the war much, like most of the veterans, just knuckled down to get the job done. Not a lot of emotional support there for a nine-year-old who looked up to his dad.

Denny's first paying job was in a local garage where he saved enough money to buy and occasionally race an MGTF. And then Clive surprised him. The old man put out for an MGA—the latest in sports-car technology. It worked for him on the track and with the girls.

'He and his mate would sit outside the milk bar and watch the talent go by,' Greeta, Denny's wife, recalled. 'There were girls who loved his car more than they loved him. But one day he said to me, "G'day, are you going to the dance?"' Greeta was 'blonde with boobs—his type'. But she wasn't as impressed by him: 'I started telling him all that's wrong with his car.' They went to the dance anyway. Denny turned up for their date in blue suede shoes and a duffel coat. He was not without sophistication.

Like Bruce McLaren, Denny used an F2 Cooper to attract the attention of the New Zealand International Grand Prix Association. In the 1960 NZ Grand Prix, Brabham and McLaren came first and second in their works F1 Coopers. Denny was tenth after mechanical problems, while George Lawton, three years his junior and son of the local mayor, failed to finish. The association sent them both to the UK, equal winners of the young driver program, which had already lost its works drive component. They got a one-way airfare and the addresses of a few doors to knock on.

Denny and George formed an unofficial 'New Zealand International Grand Prix Team' but if a paid drive emerged, they'd be at each other's throats to get it. They towed the cars to Roskilde in Denmark for the Danish F2 Grand Prix, held on 10 September 1960. It was a strange little circuit, just three-quarters of a mile around (1.2 kilometres), no straights and a lap record of only 44 seconds. In a full field it was very busy. Lawton crashed and died that day. Denny held him in his arms as he passed away. Brabham won.

Jack Brabham was Denny's rock in the hard place of European motor racing; so was Bruce McLaren. At the height of his career, he was driving for both at once. In 1967 Denny won the F1 world championship for Jack and was second to Bruce in the Can-Am series. He raced 36 weekends that year and in his 'spare time' he debuted in the Indianapolis 500.

Denny enjoyed Indy. He scored two fourths in his first two attempts but in 1969 he retired at the three-quarter distance mark. Bruce was in Canada with the Can-Am car, listening to Indy on the radio. 'Right,' he said to his crew, 'let's build a car for him for next year.'

Chris Amon was never a fully-fledged member of the Bruce and Denny Show. 'Too young,' he told me years later, sitting on the exposed timber grandstand seats of the Manfeild track on New Zealand's North Island. It's now been renamed

Circuit Chris Amon in his honour. There was only eight or nine years between them, but while Chris was going to parties, Bruce and Denny were tucking their kids into bed.

Amon had had to spend his whole life living down the mantle of being the 'best driver never to win a grand prix'. He'd had no wins in 96 starts over thirteen years—not a lot by today's standards; enough, though, to lead to Mario Andretti quipping, 'If he was an undertaker, people would stop dying.'

On that day at Manfeild Chris was more annoyed by the reputation than the actuality. He was there, weatherbeaten in a dairy-farmer-up-before-dawn sort of way, chain-smoking, nicotine stains on his fingers, to test a Toyota. Not an F1 car, nor an LMP1 sports car, but a Camry. Toyota New Zealand had been immensely sensible in getting him not only to put his name to their product but to legitimately develop its suspension. In its era, it was the best-handling Toyota in the world. There was time for us to talk. In the hands of a genius like Amon, driving a Camry at speed left a lot of brainpower to spare.

Chris's folks were well off. They had the big farm, a holiday batch down on the water. They sent him as a boarder to the elite Whanganui Collegiate School and he learned to fly a Tiger Moth when he was fifteen, so he'd zoom over and land in one of the paddocks for Sunday lunch with the family.

He'd raced a Maserati 250 F when he was seventeen. Fangio used one to win the world title in 1957.

Chris was racing in England by the time he was twenty. And he was up for a good time. He was a core member of the Ditton Road Flyers, named for the street in which his flat was situated in south-west London, just up the road from the Cooper factory. It was a Formula One frat house, famous in motor-racing circles for its parties. Motorcycle world champion Mike Hailwood, a known party animal, lived there during his transition to four wheels. Peter Revson was a permanent fixture. 'It was never as wild as legend has it,' Chris claimed, but he was grinning broadly when he said it.

Chris raced sports cars for Bruce McLaren, then 'betrayed' him by accepting a Ferrari F1 contract in 1967 just when Bruce was hoping to step up to a two-car F1 team of his own. That caused a rift. But in 1970, Chris was invited to join Bruce and Denny at Indy. It was like they'd put out the welcome-home mat.

All three had been to Indianapolis before they got together in 1970. Amon went in 1967, the same year as Hulme. Amon's Ferrari teammate Lorenzo Bandini had already arranged a start. At the US Grand Prix the year before, Missouri gas station owner Wally Weir had approached the Ferrari team and asked Bandini how much he'd charge to race at Indy. Bandini held up five fingers—$5000. Weir shook his head and raised both hands—$10,000. The deal was done. Weir would prepare a new Gerhardt Ford V8 for their attempt. Amon accepted an opportunity to race for BRP—British Racing Partnership—a company owned by Alfred Moss, Stirling's father, and Ken Gregory, Stirling's manager. The former Indy 500 competitor Alfred was feted at Indianapolis. He loved it there.

Amon and Bandini were to be part of a major contingent of grand prix drivers who'd attempt Indy in 1967. World champions and former Indy winners Jim Clark and Graham Hill would be there for Team Lotus, Jackie Stewart for the Mecom

Lola team, Jochen Rindt would be in Dan Gurney's Eagle Ford; even the Belgian ace (and the following year's Le Mans 24 Hour winner) Lucien Bianchi had found a ride.

Lorenzo and Chris were due to fly to Indy the day after the Monaco Grand Prix, but Lorenzo didn't make it. On lap 82 of 100, he clipped a hay bale at the chicane coming out of the tunnel. His car went upside-down and he was trapped. Flames fuelled by the hay engulfed him. The whole horrible spectacle was made worse by a news helicopter, hovering above, its down-draught creating a vortex into which the fire expanded. The race was not stopped. The field filed past for another nineteen laps. Hulme won, Graham Hill was second, Amon slipped back to third. Bandini lingered in the Princess Grace hospital for three days—then died.

'I flew to Indy by myself and I had a lot of time to think about the what-ifs,' Chris said. He arrived at the pits to be told Lorenzo had succumbed. Then he put on his race suit and went out to have his first-ever practice laps on the Indianapolis Motor Speedway. The records say he spun twice and never found sufficient speed to be able to qualify. He recounted just one spin—a massive, lurid loop when a rear suspension component broke and snapped him around. 'I actually felt fear,' he said.

Mechanics repaired the car, even listened to Amon when he pointed out there was a more deeply rooted problem, but the car—or driver, or both—wouldn't come up to speed and when they found a fracture in the monocoque tub there was no chance to qualify. 'I can't say I was too upset,' Amon recalled.

Denny Hulme was 'The Bear'. It was a persona he'd invented. It started out as an act, an exaggeration, a manifestation of the example that his dad set him. When you become well known, people want a piece of you. Better to draw the shell around yourself, get on with the job. People had started to call him The Bear—approach with caution. At Monaco he had been leading Bandini . . . leading him on. And then lap after lap he'd had to drive past the consequences of the bloke trying too hard to catch him. It must have affected Denny, but The Bear was not Chris Amon and wouldn't show it.

Hulme finished fourth in the Eagle owned and run by 'good ole boy' Smokey Yunick, who ran 'Smokey's Best Damn Garage in Town' in Daytona Beach, Florida. Denny steered the City of Daytona Beach Special through a last-lap melee to claim Rookie of the Year. Then he had to be lifted from the cockpit. His right leg had cramped up so much he couldn't move it except to push the throttle.

In 1968 Bruce McLaren and Denny Hulme narrowly escaped Indianapolis with their reputations—and, they reasoned, their lives—intact. They'd been unwittingly embroiled in a cheating scandal and they'd been subjected to a design and construction program of such incompetence that it put their lives at risk.

Tyre maker Goodyear had signed an exclusive contract with McLaren Automotive for its F1 and Can-Am programs, but they also expected an Indianapolis car. Winning Indy was big on their agenda. Trouble is, they couldn't wait for Bruce to act. They were approached by Carroll Shelby, who'd masterminded their 1966 Ford GT40 Le Mans victory, in which McLaren and Amon won and Hulme came second with the late Ken Miles. Shelby was running a radical all-wheel-drive turbine car, with the motor alongside the driver. Turbine power had briefly become the Indy buzz. The year before, Andy Granatelli, CEO of oil additive STP (Scientifically Treated Petroleum), had invested heavily in a car powered by what was essentially a helicopter jet engine. It developed massive horsepower and it had been carrying Parnelli Jones to an almost-certain victory until a component failed three laps from the end. The designer of that car, Ken Wallis, had moved to Shelby to build an improved version for 1968.

There was massive pressure on McLaren and Hulme to race the new car.

In 2020 Jan McLaren, sister of Bruce, handed me a letter written by Bruce to his family. He had hand-written it, with some frustration, sitting in New York's JFK airport as he flew away from the debacle that had become Shelby's Indy project:

Dear Folks,

I imagine that by the time you get this you will know that I'm not driving at Indy and along with Patty [his wife] and most other people I've talked to you will be pleased about that. I must say I'm not going to miss it. In truth I didn't particularly like any part of it. Indianapolis as a place is pretty miserable and the track and people not that much better, with a few exceptions.

I wish in a way that I hadn't been associated with the whole miserable performance, however . . . my purpose was to learn as much as possible about turbines and four-wheel drive. Well that was a pressure cooker course if ever there was one.

Heaven knows what the NZ papers ended up with, but basically Goodyear hired this guy Ken Wallace [*sic*] to build the turbine cars, Shelby to run them and Denny and I to drive. The fact that both Denny and I were involved meant that the letter of McLaren Racing's contract, which said if McLaren Racing did Indianapolis, $50,000 would be added, was complied with because McLaren Racing agreed to provide Denny and myself as drivers (that paid for the F1 engines, or some of them). Further as bait, if I did Indy a personal contract would be forthcoming, the first I'd had of that type from a tyre company. So, the total benefit to McLaren Racing was in effect $70,000.

Now—Shelby, Goodyear, me and a good many other people, after hearing him talk and acting on the assumption that he designed, single-handedly last year's car, were under the impression that Wallace was the greatest automotive genius of all time. To be fair to myself I did occasionally express doubts, but I was told not to live in the past—this was the dawn of a new era!

Anyway, they went big. I believe that Goodyear came up with one million dollars for the project, handed it to Shelby and he paid Wallace as they went. They went first class. Wallace's office was like something from a movie. A bunch of ex-aircraft people filled the drawing office. Where McLaren Racing buys Mini Vans for transport, they bought El Dorado Cadillacs. Even the toilets at Wallace Engineering had velvet seat covers.

Then they ran $300,000 over budget. By April, the project was running pretty late. By May I had had four transatlantic crossings—first class on Goodyear, and I knew we were in trouble.

At first at Indianapolis the thing was very unstable down the straight and there was very little in the way of brakes, and no way you could go round corners fast. 'Don't worry' was the word from Wallace. 'You will be faster down the straight than any other car in the race.' 'Providing you can keep it between the walls,' was my reply.

Some of the areas on the car I was convinced were ridiculously weak and I got agreement on changing these before the month of May. I tested at Hartford in California; the brakes were bad again and eventually I called 'end of test' when I discovered that most of the bolts holding the brake discs to the Top Hat section had popped their heads off.

Then we had the first week at Indy. I did my Rookies test. This is quite involved, and I won't go into the pros and cons, but it did give me quite a bit of time in the car and I did some laps of about 155 mph [249 km/h]. I think I had to get about four seconds off my lap time to be fast enough to be in the race with a chance—I couldn't imagine it frankly.

Well now it was just a question of trying to make the thing work. 'It feels just plain heavy,' I said.

'But it's right down to weight' was Wallace's reply. Phil Remington is Shelby's chief engineer—and he and I had been good friends for a long time. Embarrassed he told me it was nearly 500 lbs [227 kilograms] over the minimum . . .

The Wallace car was complicated beyond imagination. To make the adjustments and tests that we would run through in half a day with a new car at Goodwood took up to a week at their speed. In time we worked our lap speed up to 160 [257 km/h], but nothing seemed right; from the wheels up, we were in trouble. I refused to drive it one day unless we found something apparent. We found a rear wheel bearing extremely loose. When the upright assembly was taken apart, I was horrified— the rollers were virtually back to back so there was no spread to keep the wheel pointing straight. The detail on the engineering . . . nearly made me faint.

Then Denny had a moment, right in the middle of one of the turns. The rear wheel drive stopped, and it made for the wall. Denny managed to gather it all up and coasted into the pits. From the description Denny gave, he knew, and I could tell, that it had stripped something in the gear department. Not so Mr Wallace—his explanation: just a blocked limiting valve causing an imbalance in torque flow. How could you argue with that? A day later they found it had sheared all the bolts in the rear crown wheel mounting. To make it worse, [they were] nasty old bolts . . .

Well, all this was bad enough but for Goodyear's sake Denny and I were prepared to carry on.

Then—I shouldn't put this on paper but providing you keep it away from the newspapers it doesn't matter: I'd had my suspicions . . . at Hartford the front of the engine was apart but I was not allowed to look at it under any circumstances. I'd poked around in the transporter and found some bits that started me thinking. Finally, when I got back to England, I made some sketches to show Tyler [his engineering partner] and one or two of the boys how it would be possible to cheat within the turbine regulations.

Andy Granatelli with the STP cars told us—'look you guys—I know what happens in the front of that engine once it starts running.'

[Bruce had discovered that the turbine was way outside a new Indy parity regulation that limited the amount of air that could be gulped into the engine, restricting its power so that the Offys and Ford could still be competitive. In 1967 the turbine air intake had been 23.999 inches (60.957 centimetres). In 1968 it was restricted to 15.999 inches (40.637 centimetres).]

Obviously Denny and I had to voice our suspicions to Goodyear. The power on the straight was enormous. There was no doubt about that.

The next thing we knew the cars had been withdrawn 'for reasons of safety'. I don't think the truth will out, but I'm going to have to burn the sketches if I can find them—the scandal could have been fantastic. Goodyear just closed the whole operation down and let Shelby make a statement that was acceptable and allowed him to bow out with some good grace.

I just hope Goodyear don't get too disillusioned over the whole affair—on the bright side maybe they will place more of next year's budget in areas where it has done some good before—i.e., Brabham-McLaren. Anyway, that was the Indy story and now I guess this is my last first-class plane ride this year. It's back to little old McLaren Racing and economy fares—but darn sensible racing cars.

Lots of love,

Bruce

On 7 April 1968, Jim Clark was killed in a Formula Two race at Hockenheim in Germany. He had been telling people at the circuit that he'd just returned from Indianapolis where he'd driven 'the car that would win this year's race'. One month later at Indy, on 7 May, Mike Spence, Clark's teammate, hit

the Turn One wall in the Lotus 56 turbine car. His right front wheel ricocheted back into the cockpit, knocking his helmet off, and he died several hours later in hospital.

Hulme was drafted into Dan Gurney's Eagle Ford team and was immediately at home. Gurney finished second in the race, Hulme fourth—again. The following year, again with Gurney, he was up to second when his clutch failed, and he was classified eighteenth on 145 laps.

At the end of 1969 Chris Amon, inexplicably, fired Ferrari. Amon's omen of doom—that cruelly snatched victory from his grasp time and again—had moved with him to Italy. He was no more successful with the world's most recognisable and revered motor-racing team than he'd been elsewhere. 'It was a damned silly decision,' he told me all those years later and there was still pain in his voice and in his eyes. 'The old man [Ferrari] wanted me to come back, you know.' But he never went. The Italian press had been giving him a hard time, the pressure within the race team was rising, and Amon just decided to move on. The last race he had for Ferrari was in April 1970 in the Monza 1000 and he was fourth.

Amon had signed to drive with the new British team March Engineering. They looked promising but for him turned out to be a total disaster. And then Bruce McLaren called and asked him to drive at Indy in a fully fledged McLaren team. It would be the Bruce, Denny *and* Chris show.

Team McLaren built its first IndyCar, the M15, in just three months. It was based to a large degree on their Can-Am sports car, except it would use a 2.65-litre turbocharged four-cylinder Offenhauser. In late 1969 Denny tested the IndyCar at the Goodwood circuit and spun out. He'd been caught out by turbo lag, the hesitation between the driver's foot going to the floor and the turbocharger spooling up to feed fuel into the engine. It took a very special driving technique to anticipate when power would come on song. Get it wrong and you'd have not enough power, or far too much—either way you were in trouble.

The following weekend while Denny and Bruce contested—and Bruce won—the final Can-Am round in Texas, the M15 was flown to Indianapolis. The Can-Am series had been an immense success—there'd been eleven races and the McLaren team won them all. Bruce was the champion with six wins; Denny second, winning the other five. Bruce wanted to test on the Brickyard before winter set in. Otherwise he'd be arriving in the Month of May with a virtually untried car.

The test was better than promising. Denny was quickly up to a lap average of 168 mph (270 km/h). The team brought in 1968 winner Bobby Unser for a test run and he not only went quicker but also gave Bruce some strong advice on the unique Indy groove—the line of greatest speed around the course. Bruce got up to 162 mph (260 km/h) but it was then that he made the call not to race. Mystery surrounds his decision. Officially he told people that there were many projects that demanded his attention. On opening day of the Month of May, Bruce led Denny and Chris out onto the track in a third car—but it was for ceremony only. He never intended to race.

Amon was delighted to get the phone call. It went a long way, in his mind, to reignite the friendship that had been lost when he had gone to Ferrari. He arrived at Indianapolis in a positive frame of mind.

Bobby Unser was there as coach. The Indy veteran was a good 5 mph (8 km/h) per lap quicker—but, Chris recalled, 'He got out of the car a bit disturbed, hands shaking a bit.' Nonetheless Amon worked at it.

'Get down low on the apexes,' Unser said.

'Any lower and I'd be on the golf course,' Chris replied.

'Develop tunnel vision,' Unser said. 'Make sure you're looking half a mile ahead.'

'But what about the cars inches from me on either side?' Chris replied. 'Shouldn't I be watching them?'

Finally, Amon put in a demon ten laps—nudging an average of 170 mph (273 km/h), right on pole position time. He felt he'd cracked it; he was in charge of the racetrack, not the other way around.

Satisfied, Bruce, Denny and Chris all hopped on a plane for the Monaco Grand Prix. Denny was fourth; Bruce and Chris both retired with suspension failures.

When they got back to Indy, Chris's speed had gone. He couldn't come close to his qualifying pace, let alone pole, and nothing, it seemed, would bring it back. He flogged the thing around the Brickyard but he was just too slow.

In Chris's account, told through the mists of time, Denny's fire was the clincher. He turned to Bruce and the team and said, 'This is not for me', and left the circuit. It would never have been that brutal. The Bear was in trouble and Chris was a sensitive soul. Most likely he waited for the right moment when he was sure Denny was okay. But he did walk out—never to return to Indy. It was a paradox that just one week later, Chris flung his March F1 car without concern through Eau Rouge at Spa, the most frighteningly awesome corner in all of motorsport. 'Perhaps if they painted trees on the Indy walls,' Eoin Young, a journalist close to the New Zealand trio, speculated.

McLaren Automotive—the team with a 'flying kiwi' as its emblem—needed two new drivers. Drivers then trawled Gasoline Alley just as they do now, suits, helmets and, more recently, personally formed seats ready, looking for a drive. If you have a bit of reputation and a team has a need, maybe you'll get the chance to strut your stuff. It seemed an awfully big risk for a team to take—to put someone in their race car on spec. Peter Revson, fifth in Jack Brabham's car the year before, was available and he stepped into the Amon seat.

Carl Williams, a USAC dirt-track specialist but with four Indy starts—although no finishes—under his belt, was named the second McLaren driver. Williams, killed in a motorcycle accident three years later, delivered McLaren a ninth outright. Revson, who would join McLaren on a more permanent basis, retired with electrical breakage. It had started out as a grand assault—it had ended less so.

Bruce flew back to the UK immediately after the race. With Denny incapacitated, he'd take over the test-driving duties at Goodwood the next day. Team McLaren was due to race in the first round of the Can-Am in just two weeks at Mosport in Canada, and the M8D, their new car, had to be sorted out. Even before that, they had the Belgium Grand Prix at Spa. The McLaren team moved at an incredible, breathless pace. No time for rest. Bruce called it 'woosh-bonk'. That was the time it would take to build a car—'woosh', the suspension goes on the tub; 'bonk', on goes the body. So simple.

'Denis wouldn't let me travel to America to see him in hospital,' Greeta told me, sitting at the dining room table of their daughter Adele's home in Rotorua, looking down over the deep-green lawn of their hot spring–irrigated garden (only in New Zealand). Greeta lives within the property, in her separate home, but it's Adele who has an attic full of trophies upstairs, and in the garage is the Ford Zodiac with which Denny and Greeta towed his race cars around Europe in 1961 after George Lawton was killed. It's a happy family home. Adele's husband Michael is a local GP, they have two lively teenage daughters and it's hard to imagine anything further removed from the still-raw events of 2 June 1970.

'Denis arrived off the plane with both arms in splints and we went home where I dressed his burns.' Greeta was a nurse. 'Next day we went into London on the Tube to see the specialist. Denis was quite intent on being ready for Spa the next weekend, but it looked like the healing would take longer than that, at least six weeks.

'We'd left our son Martin [three at the time] with our next-door neighbour Marguerite and I took Denis home, then went to pick up Martin. Marguerite met me at the door and told me she had just heard the news: Bruce had been killed at Goodwood. I went upstairs and told Denis. He was just stunned, silent.'

Chris Amon was driving home through the back lanes of Oxfordshire. He had just been to the March factory to prepare for Spa and his thoughts were on nothing specific when he heard it on the radio.

'It's a moment you'll remember all your life, like where were you when Kennedy was shot. I just stopped the car, got out and stood there. Don't know for how long.'

There were new regulations for the 1970 Can-Am series. Until then the massive aerodynamic wings were able to be mounted to suspension components. In 1970 they had to be body-mounted. It was a substantial change. Bruce was keen to test the new fitments. With Denny not there, the factory made up one car out of two—the body from Denny's car on Bruce's tub.

Goodwood is a marvellous, largely flat 2.4-mile (3.8-kilometre) circuit built within the perimeter of the WWII Westhampnett airfield in West Sussex. Australia's first F1 driver, Flight Commander Tony Gaze DFC, flew Spitfires out of there for 616 squadron in World War II. When the war finished, Tony persuaded the airfield's owner, the Duke of Richmond, Frederick Gordon-Lennox, also known as Lord March, to build a racetrack: 'The chaps have been burning around the perimeter roads all war long.' Today, his Lordship's grandson, Charles, runs the Goodwood Festival of Speed, the greatest celebration of motor-racing heritage on the planet.

On 2 June 1970, it would have been a sparse place, with a prevailing south-west sea breeze for the second day of summer. According to the McLaren log, testing began at 10.45 a.m. Multiple adjustments were made and then at 12.19 p.m. Bruce went out for a high-speed run. He had completed his outlap and was on a flyer when the car left the main Lavant Straight at something above 170 mph (273 km/h) and, with brakes applied, speared right into the infield at Woodcote corner. There was a marshal's barrier—a block of cement—and the McLaren collided with it. The rear bodywork had lifted and without downforce it was uncontrollable. Chris Amon had a theory: with the wing now attached to the body, the downforce was pushing backwards, trying to open the engine cover. If that was the case, it succeeded.

'It was a half-hour's drive to Bruce and Patty's place,' Greeta recalled, staring down the garden. 'I drove and we had Martin with us. By the time we got there, the girls from the Dog House Club had already arrived.' (The Dog House Club was a gathering of drivers' wives—set up to raise funds for safety equipment, sorely lacking at tracks, and simply to support each other in times like this.) Graham Hill's wife Bette and Patty McLaren were in the kitchen drinking wine. 'She was strong, holding up well.' There was no sign of Bruce and Patty's daughter, Amanda, just a year older than Martin. She'd been taken by a neighbour to shield her from the grief. 'People just came and went. Bruce's manager Phil Kerr went to his office to secure his briefcase.' The shock was immense but already there was thought to 'what next'.

'It was 12.22 a.m. [in New Zealand] and my mother sat up in bed and said, "Les, something's wrong,"' Jan McLaren, Bruce's sister, told me. 'Quarter of an hour later there was a call from Phil Kerr with the news. Dad came around to my house and to my sister Pat's, but he didn't have to say anything. Just being there, knocking on the door, we knew.'

Speed King Rupert Jeffkins (at the wheel), a works driver for Velie in the inaugural Indianapolis 500 in 1911, failed to qualify his own car but was relief driver for seventeenth-placed Howard Hall. (IMS)

In 1912, riding mechanic Jeffkins (at the rear of the car) and driver Ralph De Palma came within a lap of winning, but the engine in their Mercedes blew. Their gallant struggle to the finish line remains an Indy legend. (IMS)

Rupert Jeffkins was Australia's first professional international racing driver—a pity his achievements are clouded by his own boastful claims. (IMS)

Carl Fisher, the visionary genius who conceived and built the Indianapolis Motor Speedway and the city around it. (IMS)

The first Indianapolis 500 started five cars abreast. Case teammates Will Jones (no. 9) and Joe Jagersberger (8) contested the first corner from the second row with Louis Disbrow (Pope-Hartford, 5). The Howard Hall/Rupert Jeffkins Velie was well behind, clouded in dust. (IMS)

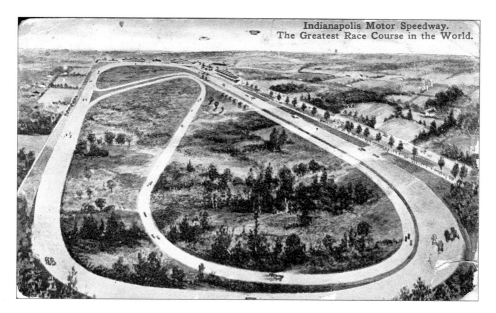

Carl Fisher conceived his Indianapolis Motor Speedway as a multi-track facility with a road circuit on the infield. It took more than three-quarters of a century for his dream to be fully realised. (IMS)

In 1961 Jack Brabham changed the course of Indianapolis racing when his rear-engine Cooper Climax Kimberly Special finished ninth. (IMS)

Rodger Ward (left) and Jack Brabham (right) were both dirt-track speedway champions and kindred spirits. Ward was instrumental in bringing the Australian to Indianapolis. (IMS)

Ron Tauranac AO, Jack Brabham's partner and one of the most successful car designers and engineers of his time, at age 95 in his retirement home in Buderim, Queensland. He died in July 2020. (John Smailes)

The contrast between traditional Indy roadsters and the smaller Formula One–based cars of the European invasion was evident. In 1963 the Lotus 29 of second-placed Jim Clark harries Eddie Sachs's Watson-Offy. (IMS)

In 1964, Clark was on pole position and the 'European cars' had locked out the front row. Clark retired and A.J. Foyt won in his Watson-Offy—the last time a roadster would claim Indy victory. (IMS)

Jim Clark won in 1965. Clark sits in his Lotus 38, with Lotus owner Colin Chapman, in brown jacket, alongside. On the rear right wheel is Australian mechanic Jim Smith; standing next to him is four-time Australian Touring Car Champion Allan Moffat. (IMS)

The beginning of McLaren's horror month. In 1970, Chris Amon practised in the McLaren M15 Offenhauser, but withdrew when he could not find speed in qualifying. (Bruce McLaren Trust)

1967 World Formula One Champion Denny Hulme was badly burned in a methanol fire during practice in 1970. (IMS)

Chris Amon first went to Indianapolis in 1967, hired by BRP Ford. He crashed twice in practice and failed to make an attempt to qualify. Check out the upholstery. (IMS)

Of the New Zealand trio—McLaren, Amon and Hulme—it was Hulme who had best come to terms with the Brickyard. (IMS)

Bruce McLaren briefly drove the M15 at Indianapolis; here with Denny Hulme alongside him and business partner Teddy Mayer to the rear. But he never intended to race. (Bruce McLaren Trust)

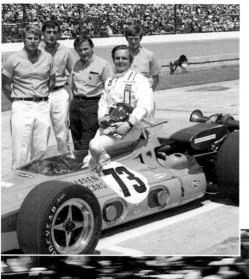

When Denny Hulme was injured in 1970, McLaren secured Peter Revson. This is one of the last pictures of Bruce (third from left), who was killed the following week at Goodwood. (IMS)

Twice Australian Gold Star Champion Kevin Bartlett was in the frame to take over Hulme's Indy drive in 1970, but it went to Revson. Bartlett momentarily qualified this George Morris–built car, but was bumped from the field. (Kevin Bartlett Collection)

1970 could have been Kevin Bartlett's break into the global big time. Car owner Marvin Webster (right) couldn't provide a car fast enough, and Bartlett's second car was tardy in coming up to speed. (Kevin Bartlett Collection)

In 1973 Andy Granatelli (in the red jacket) hired three-time Australian Grand Prix winner Graham McRae (white race suit) to be a third driver in the STP team. McRae's teammate David 'Swede' Savage died. The other, Gordon Johncock, won. (IMS)

Le Mans 24 Hour winner Vern Schuppan attempted six Indianapolis 500s and qualified three times. (IMS)

Schuppan was sensationally third in 1981 in a team he initially funded himself. He is one of only three Australians and New Zealanders to claim an Indy 500 podium. (IMS)

Vern Schuppan has collected classic race cars. This Lago Talbot, with author John Smailes at the wheel and Schuppan alongside, was owned by Australian Grand Prix champion Doug Whiteford, the inspiration for Schuppan's motor-racing career.
(Jennifer Smailes)

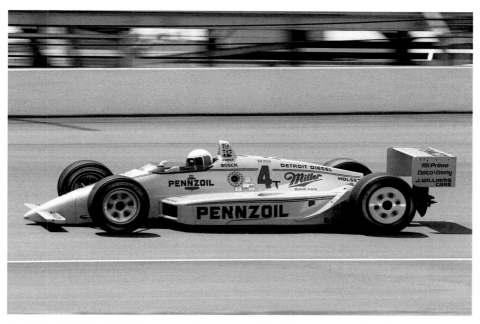

In 1989, Geoffrey Brabham was a last-minute hire by Team Penske after their driver Danny Sullivan broke a wrist in a practice crash. Brabham completed several laps in the team's no. 4T (training) car, but Sullivan returned for the race. (IMS)

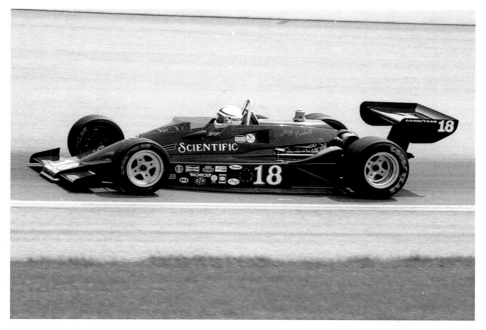

Australian by birth Dennis Firestone was such a talent that Roger Penske arranged for him to race this Penske PC6 as a condition of supplying the car to entrepreneur Jack Rhoades in 1980. (IMS)

The man who rejected Roger Penske. Dennis Firestone was asked if he'd give up his trucking company to race full-time for the Penske organisation. He declined. (IMS)

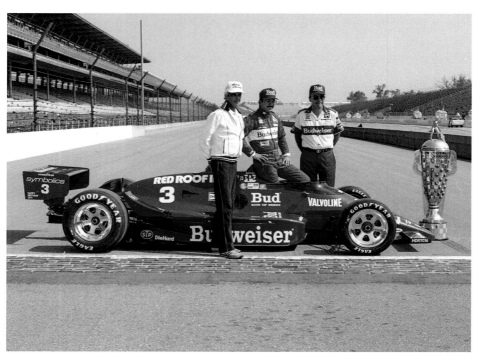

Auckland engineer Steve Horne (right) masterminded Bobby Rahal's 1986 victory. Car owner Jim Trueman (left) succumbed to cancer just ten days after the race—proud that his Truesports team had claimed the Borg-Warner Trophy. (IMS)

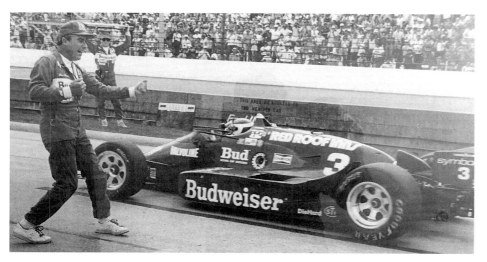

Steve Horne greets winner Bobby Rahal on pit road. Horne and wife Christine would run Truesports as shareholders then start their own Tasman Motorsports team, fostering young talent. (Steve Horne Collection)

Western Australian brothers Barry and Kim Green won the 1995 Indianapolis 500 with Jacques Villeneuve driving for Team Green. (Steve Horne Collection)

John 'Ando' Anderson pioneered Australian engineering success at Indianapolis. He died of a heart attack in 2010, aged 65. (IMS)

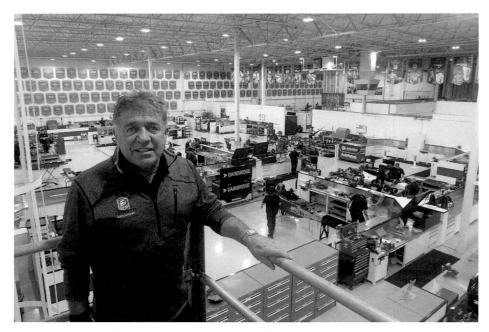

Auckland's Paul 'Ziggy' Harcus runs the IndyCar program for Andretti Autosport out of a giant Indianapolis workshop originally commissioned by Barry Green. (John Smailes)

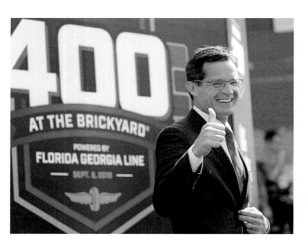

J. Douglas (Doug) Boles, president of the Indianapolis Motor Speedway, is one of the few in motorsport to wear a suit to work and to have an Indianapolis Chevrolet Corvette ZR1 pace car as his company vehicle. (IMS)

The rear-view mirror was invented for Ray Harroun's 1911 winning Marmon Wasp, on display in the Motor Speedway's museum. (John Smailes)

Sydney's Ryan Briscoe (no. 39) was an international karting champion as a teenager, competing alongside Jenson Button (59), later to be world F1 champion. (Geoff Briscoe Collection)

Briscoe in his early teens at Tamworth, New South Wales, with his rally-driving father Geoff as mechanic. (Geoff Briscoe Collection)

This fiery crash at Chicagoland in 2005 came close to ending Briscoe's IndyCar career. He lost his drive with Chip Ganassi, but not his ambition. (Thomas Link, PaddockTalk.com)

Ryan Briscoe claimed pole position in 2012. He and wife Nicole frame the iconic timing tower with his race number and 226-mph (363-km/h) average speed displayed. (IMS)

Almost as good as winning: Briscoe holds the pole position trophy and cheque on the front straight, in a Penske car. (IMS)

'Every driver wants to be you,' Briscoe said of his five seasons with the iconic Team Penske. But without an Indy 500 or IndyCar series win, his contract was not renewed in 2013. (IMS)

Briscoe's basement: a collection of race suits, helmets and trophies testify to a stellar career across Indy and sports cars. (John Smailes)

Jan and I were sitting in the upstairs trophy room of the Bruce McLaren Foundation, a tiny, well-formed museum in an industrial unit at the thoroughly modern Hampton Downs Motorsport Park, 60 kilometres south of Auckland. Downstairs there are several of Bruce's cars, an M8 Can-Am, a Formula 5000, an M23 Formula One car formerly owned by Denny Hulme, and the original 1929 Austin 7 Ulster that started it all. Display cabinets contain Bruce's memorabilia, including the Samsonite briefcase that contained the key to his business dealings.

Unravelling and resolving the McLaren legacy had been a hard and long road. Almost 30 years after Bruce's death, Patty McLaren sued Phil Kerr unsuccessfully for funds she alleged were misappropriated from a Swiss account. Both had since passed away, but the unpleasantness lingered. 'I walked the middle line—there were so many issues on both sides,' Jan said. 'The widow was well looked after.'

Bruce's daughter Amanda was now an ambassador for the modern McLaren car brand in the UK.

The Remuera Road service station had only recently been sold. Jan was keen that it be preserved as a national monument, but that was not to be. It was to become a shop-top, a modern housing development. 'The developer has given me bricks from the demolition. I've got 50 of them,' Jan said. Bruce is interred in Waikumete Cemetery in Auckland, next to Pop and Ruth. 'The cortege from St Mary's Cathedral stretched for two miles.'

And, finally, Jan offered the reason why Bruce did not race at the 1970 Indianapolis 500. It's something really only the family knew: 'It was his leg, from the Perthes disease. He was constantly favouring it and it was hurting him. The g-forces at

Indy were just too much. He'd been to a Harley Street special-ist. Jack Brabham had recommended the surgeon. They were planning a hip replacement which then was a very complex procedure. If it had been done, he would have certainly had to give up racing.'

And The Bear? 'Denny was distraught,' Greeta said. 'Bruce was testing for him that day. He determined that no matter what, he'd drive for Bruce, for the team.' On the night of Bruce's death the team met at McLaren's workshop and vowed to continue. It was Denny's leadership that strengthened their resolve. The pits at Spa were a sombre place without the McLaren team. But a week later there were two orange McLaren M8Ds at Mosport in Canada for the first round of the Can-Am series. Dan Gurney had agreed to drive one in honour of Bruce, and he won. Denny, his hands bandaged and in great pain, came third. He went on to dominate the 1970 Can-Am Championship, with double the points of the second placegetter.

'Once Bruce was gone, there was always a commitment Denny would have a car,' Australian McLaren engineer Steve Roby told me. Denny anchored the team in its post-Bruce transition, first with Peter Revson as his teammate, and then the team's new management replaced Revson with Brazilian Emerson Fittipaldi. Revson went to the new Shadows Team and three months later was killed in testing at South Africa's Kyalami Circuit. Denny had been close to Revvy. He raced on that year and finished seventh in the championship to his teammate Fittipaldi's first. Then he walked away from McLaren.

The Bear kept racing, of course, everything from off-road motorcycles to V8 Supercars. And he would have kept doing it forevermore except his heart was broken: 'It was Christmas day 1988 and we were at our lake house—you could only get to it by boat,' Greeta said. 'Denis had taken our son Martin to the Australian Grand Prix in Adelaide just weeks before. People were so pleased to see him: six feet tall, twenty-one years old. They'd not seen him since we were in the UK. At the lake, there was a rule: no diving between the boats and jetties, but Martin did it anyway. No one noticed for a while, and then it was too late to save him. I looked up to the house and Denis was just standing there. Not moving.'

Four years later Denny Hulme, 56, died at the wheel of a race car. He was racing a BMW M3 in the Bathurst 1000 motor race. They asked him if he was okay to do a double stint and he said yes, so at the pit stop he stayed in the car. A little while later he called in, reporting blurred vision. It was raining at the top of the mountain, so the natural assumption was the windscreen had smeared. But as the yellow BMW—McLaren colours—came onto Conrod Straight, it pulled to the left onto the grass verge. Then it drifted back across the track to the right-hand grass where it rolled to a stop. Denny had suffered a massive heart attack. His last act had been to pull the car safely off the track

Greeta wasn't at Mount Panorama. The rest of the family was. There had been an estrangement and divorce had been discussed but never actioned. 'We'd spoken on the phone that morning, talking about normal things like getting new wheel bearings for the lawn mower,' Greeta said.

'I felt he was coming back to me. He had so much unresolved grief.'

Chris Amon retired from professional motor racing in 1977, the year he married Tish Wotherspoon. He was only 34. They settled in New Zealand and had three children, Georgina and twin sons Alex and James. For the second half of his life he was a largely contented farmer and there would be people with whom he dealt who knew him only as a farmer. He told me at Manfeild about an excerpt from Enzo Ferrari's biography, written when the 'old man' was still peeved with Chris for leaving: 'After his time at Ferrari he drifted from team to team in a vain attempt to overcome the adversities that he was constantly encountering,' Ferrari wrote. 'In the end he went back to his native New Zealand and devoted himself to his family. I wonder if his children believed him when he told them how very near he had been to becoming a motor-racing legend.'

Chris died in 2016, from cancer. He was 73.

8

Big Rev Kev and Cassius

Kevin Bartlett

Twice Australian Drivers' Champion—holder of the nation's coveted Gold Star—Kevin Bartlett swears that Denny Hulme offered him the McLaren seat in the 1970 Indianapolis 500. 'I went to see Denny in Methodist Hospital the night of his fire,' the man they called Big Rev Kev said. 'He was pretty chirpy (no doubt the morphine) and he knew he wouldn't be driving. He said, "I'll have a word to Tyler to get you my car—that'd be good."'

Tyler Alexander was part of the senior Team McLaren management at Indianapolis. 'Allan McCall was at the hospital at the same time,' Bartlett recalled. McCall—'Maori' in the quirky way McLaren had of giving each of its team members a nickname—was one of the leading mechanics on the team. 'He said, "I'd reckon you'd fit in the car real well."'

Bartlett, struggling to find a car fast enough for this, his one and only attempt at the Indianapolis 500, was more than pleased. He'd gone to the hospital simply to visit Hulme and he'd come away with a works drive. But it didn't happen. 'It was down to tyre politics,' Bartlett said. 'I'd been running on Firestones and McLaren was a Goodyear team. "We want a Goodyear contracted driver," they said. "We're going to put Peter Revson in the car."'

There was likely more to it than that. Peter Revson was already a star—a personality who could add to the glamour of America's greatest motor race. When they took his team photograph, coiffured and glamorously perched on the cockpit of the McLaren, he looked like he owned it. Pure Hollywood. Kevin Bartlett was a rookie, and a risk.

The McLaren seat was the launch pad of Revson's career. It could have been Bartlett's. His tilt at the 1970 Indianapolis 500 was equal parts opportunity and frustration. What happened to Bartlett, one of the icons of Australian motorsport, is an annual occurrence in the Month of May, a backstory to the main game as drivers of calibre work the Brickyard's garages and corporate suites in search of a seat. Only a very few succeed. Bartlett's dream would fall short by 2/100ths of a second.

Indianapolis was never big on Kevin Bartlett's radar. He was a street fighter—a road-racing expert who'd back himself against anybody, but always humbly recognised that he was 'a fair size fish in a little pond'. He never put huge tickets on himself, always regarded the international drivers as being one step above him. They had greater opportunity and more experience. 'The one race I recall was in a Tasman Series round in Queensland when I went wheel to wheel with [three-time] world champion Jackie Stewart and we swapped position time and time again. That gave me a benchmark.'

Bartlett was the protégé of 1960 Australian Grand Prix winner Alec Mildren, a person you'd never pick as a race driver. Alec had poor eyesight, so he raced with his spectacles protected behind goggles. He looked like Mr Magoo. But he could race— he held off Lex Davison by just half a second to win the national Grand Prix at Queensland's rural Lowood circuit—a GP track on a country airstrip. When Mildren retired he became a patron. He picked Bartlett out of the obscurity of sedan and sports-car racing and elevated him to his Number One resident driver. 'I'd never been paid to race until then, just gave it away to get the drive,' Kevin said.

Bartlett won the Australian Drivers' Championship title in 1968 and 1969, won the Macau Grand Prix against a top inter-national field, and bravely set the first 100 mph (160 km/h) lap record of the fearsome Mount Panorama racetrack. He was stuck with the name 'Big Rev Kev' because some commentator thought it sounded vaguely onomatopoeic. He hated it: 'It was all wrong—it misrepresented me. I had mechanical sympathy and I think I was smooth and precise.' He was correct on all counts, but he couldn't shake the tag. Most people just called him 'KB'.

He was at the top of his game when Alec quietly gave him the heads-up that he was winding down the team to spend more time on his fishing boat. No urgency—sometime in the next couple of years.

The grapevine knew. Bartlett fielded a call from Frank Matich—the Australian engineer/driver voted as one of the top 50 drivers in the world never to be elevated to F1 status. Matich designed and built his own cars—in that respect probably even more a purist than Brabham, who had Tauranac perpetually alongside him. Team Matich worked out of a small service station at Castle Cove in Sydney but their eyes were firmly on the United States. They planned a big assault for 1971.

'Frank asked me if I'd like to drive for a friend of his in the States,' Kevin recalled, calling his two dogs to heel as they did frenetic laps around us at his property in the rainforest of Maleny behind Queensland's Sunshine Coast. 'He was too busy to go, but he'd be happy to recommend me. I said, "Sure".'

The friend was Marvin Webster, a tall, thin, old-fashioned professorial type of American who'd caught the racing bug years before and run dirt-track quarter midgets for himself and his son. He'd bought one of the original Dan Gurney Eagle Weslakes and thought he'd like to take it racing in the IndyCar series. 'Marvin owned a gear-manufacturing business in Mill Valley, California,' Kevin said. It made Webster well off, but he was still one of the smaller teams—struggling.

'They flew me over to race at Sonoma, California: no money but they covered all my expenses.' There couldn't have been a better track for Kevin to showcase his skills. The hilly twelve-corner 2.5-mile (4-kilometre) course was made for a street fighter. Kevin had been racing in Australia with aerodynamic wings to hold the car down. The USAC racers didn't have wings, but it didn't matter to him. He flung and slid the Eagle around the track to qualify fifth against the stars. He was with them in the race, too, until the old Eagle broke down.

'You know, I'd like to do the Show,' Webster told him. The 'Show' was Indianapolis.

'I came home, did some races for Alec and then flew back,' Bartlett said. 'Indianapolis was pretty old-fashioned; friendly. I got to meet the grounds people, the people on the gates. I made a point of meeting the other drivers. I was surprised. To me Indianapolis was just another race. To them it was the holy grail.'

He met Jerry Eisert, the master mechanic who helped Dan Gurney build the Eagles. Eisert took an interest in the young man from Australia who'd driven so hard at Sonoma. 'You're a real racer,' he told Kevin.

'Marvin's car came to Indianapolis still set up in its road track trim. It even had the frail five-speed gearbox used on the road course. And it was underpowered,' Kevin recalled. This was the year of turbochargers and turbine cars, and Kevin had a naturally aspirated 3.3-litre Ford, a severe disadvantage. Jerry watched as Kevin completed his Rookie Test, the officials flagging him down because he was going too fast: 'All I could see was an open track and I wanted to put the hammer down.'

Jerry came up to Kevin. 'That car is never going to qualify,' he said. 'We need to get you another one.'

You could do that—swap from one car to another, even change teams. The deals done in Gasoline Alley were more complex and most times immensely more entertaining than the racing.

Peter Revson shirt-fronted Bartlett: 'Denny said he wants you in the McLaren. Well, *I'm* going to take it.' But there was an upside. Revson was already entered in another car, the Morris Marauder, a turbocharged Ford V8—loosely copied from the Lotus 56 wedge car—built by mechanic George Morris for George Walther, a wealthy entrant whose family owned the

Dayton Steel Foundry. (Three years later Walther's son David—'Salt'—would crash heavily on the first lap and spend the rest of his life struggling with addiction to the painkillers he took as a result of his injuries. David died, aged 65, of a drug overdose.)

Jerry Eisert brokered the Bartlett–Walther deal and suddenly Kevin was in a far stronger place: 'We'll pay you what we were going to pay Revson,' Walther said. '$5000 plus expenses.'

'The car was putting out 920 horsepower [686 kilowatts] on low boost and it was twitchy—I just wasn't comfortable. I spoke to Mario Andretti and he helped; all the experienced drivers did. I guess they figured if they didn't help the rookies, they could become part of their accident.'

'Use more road,' Andretti said.

'I was having trouble getting close to the walls. But Mario set me right—"If you get close to the walls you won't hit them. The aerodynamics create their own cushion of air and you can actually feel the car pushing away from the concrete." Judging the turbocharger boost was tricky. You needed to keep it spooled up [to avoid turbo lag] so you'd modulate the brakes to set yourself up for the four corners. There was a big boost gauge in the middle of the cockpit, and it was the only thing you looked at. The rate the boost came up would determine what the chassis would do in the corner.

'The acceleration rate was fantastic. Out of Turn Two onto the back straight you'd plant it and it would just go *BANG*—force you back into the seat even with your belts tight. It would go from 150 mph [241 km/h] to 240 mph [386 km/h] in half the straight.'

Qualifying is unique to Indianapolis. Drivers get three attempts, of four laps each. It's best to qualify in the first session because that result cannot be taken away. But the time sticks, and subsequent sessions can move another driver into the field and those on the cusp can be bumped out. 'Your crew has to give you the green flag to start your four-lap qualifying run,' Bartlett explained. 'I got the flag and I was into it—and I couldn't believe the car. It had more power than I'd experienced before. The chassis didn't like it. The whole thing felt so lively. I'd been told by the experts, "Stop if you feel uncomfortable", but I felt obligated. I stayed on it but not at the speed that would qualify far enough up the field to be safe from being bumped, so they waved me off.

'In the pits I asked what had happened. "Oh," they said, "we turned up your boost to give you 1200 horsepower [895 kilowatts]." They hadn't told me. I'd been doing all my training at 920 horsepower. Next day I went out to qualify and I went only marginally better—still not quick enough. Waved off again. "Yeah," they said, "we turned the boost down." They didn't tell me that either.'

The third session was Bartlett's last chance. He recorded a four-lap average of 165.25 mph (265.88 km/h), only 5 mph (8 km/h) slower than Al Unser's pole. It was good enough for 33rd position—last on the grid.

But the following day was Bump Day, a cruelly unique, highly entertaining Indy specialty. It's a sudden-death shootout, the opportunity for anyone not in the field to go faster than those who are. The cars go out one at a time. Bartlett sat there in the line-up, watching the timing tower to determine his fate. One by one they failed; Sam Posey crashed, and then Arnie Knepper, a bit of a goose, snuck past Bartlett by 0.021 seconds. (Knepper had staked his claim to Indy ignominy the year before when he crashed and, instead of staying strapped in or running for safety, stood up in his cockpit and waved his arms at cars approaching him at 180 mph.) Arnie's glory was short-lived. Jim McElreath, third for Brabham in 1966, bumped them both. Then rain stopped play.

George Walther packed up and went home—didn't wait for the race, even though his team may have been called up as a reserve. Bartlett went home, too. He'd gone back to his hotel and called his wife Rana in Australia to vent. Instead, his sister answered the phone and told him they'd been trying to contact him for days: 'You have a son—six weeks premature.'

'When I got to the front door Rana greeted me with tears in her eyes. "Steven is in hospital in a humidicrib." I made up my mind then—no more extended trips away.'

Kevin went back twice that year for a short time to fulfil his commitment to Marvin Webster. Hampered by equipment failure, he was sixteenth at the Continental Divide Raceway in Colorado and failed to finish at the Ontario Motor Speedway in California. 'But I'd had enough of ovals—just didn't enjoy them. I knew then I was never going to be an IndyCar champion, nor a world champion.' It was a strangely unexpected statement from a driver who, in all the conversations we'd had over the years, never indicated self-doubt or limitation. He was KB . . . bulletproof.

Bartlett's Australian career remained stellar. He deployed his considerable skill in a multitude of categories, won the Bathurst 1000, was pack leader in the emerging Formula 5000 open-wheeler series, and survived a horrendous crash at Pukekohe in New Zealand that left him with permanent leg pain. It's tantalising to contemplate what might have happened, what massive change in career path might have occurred, had he not been bumped from his only Indy.

Graham McRae

'I didn't do it, you know. I didn't shoot them; just threatened them.'

Graham McRae, so much older, greyer, in soiled tracksuit pants and white T-shirt, barefooted, greeted me at the door of his world for the last two years: a 5-square-metre room in a nursing facility in suburban Auckland. I had come to talk about his sensational racing career. He wanted to talk about the incident that put him in his current circumstance. It was top of his mind, and whatever was on Graham's mind was what you spoke about. That hadn't changed. He'd always had a singleness of purpose that defied convention.

In 2003 McRae had been involved in an incident involving the police. He'd rented part of a warehouse complex in the inner Auckland suburb of Grey Lynn and he'd taken exception to a rock band that was using another unit there to practise. Graham had used a crossbow as a means of getting their attention. He used the same persuader on his landlord as well. Then he locked himself in his unit, sparking something of a siege. It took several hours and the use of tear gas to get him out.

Graham's good friends, people who knew and respected him for his amazing motor-racing exploits, gathered around him and remain loyal today. They found him the home in which he now lives and ensure that he continues to take his daily meds (a mild antipsychotic concoction). They take him out occasionally but in the main he's content to stay home, his mind lively in a way that not all of us would understand.

'He's looking forward to you coming,' said Brian Lawrence, brother of Tasman motor-racing champion Graeme Lawrence, for years a fierce competitor of McRae. Brian had pushed hard to get McRae admitted to the home: 'Don't you know who he is?' he said to the authorities. 'He's pretty much a national treasure.' The admission fee was waived, and the room made available.

For a time, in the early 1970s, Graham McRae was the class of the field in Formula 5000 motor racing, the stock block 5-litre open-wheeler category that spanned the UK, Europe, Australasia and the US, at a price that was not in the F1 stratosphere. McRae was a marvellous combination—an engineer and designer who could also drive like the devil. He was not shy about talking himself up and that led to people calling him 'Cassius' for Cassius Clay (boxer Mohammad Ali—'I am the greatest'). McRae quite liked his nickname: 'It's better than them calling you "Shithead",' he said, perched on his hospital bed.

Cassius spent his motor-racing life poised on the edge of greatness. He raced at Indianapolis (once) and in Formula One (once), and he seemed to have a special talent for persuading people not to take the next step with him. He could be abrasive, obstinate, obstreperous—and brilliant.

He built and raced his first car while at Wellington University, getting an engineering degree, just like his dad had. It was a beautiful sports car—unusual for a home design—which he called the Maserrari (for Maserati and Ferrari), although it's known today as the McRae 220 S. In typical McRae style, he built a full-size plaster-of-Paris mould to get the body dimensions right. Then he kitted it out with an Austin A70 engine and a four-speed Jaguar transmission. 'I spent every moment working on that car and spent every dollar I made.'

McRae raced it for the first time at the 1.1-mile (1.8-kilometre) clockwise Levin circuit above Wellington: 'I ran against [Kiwi legend] Kenny Smith in a Holden-engine car and I was quicker, but I couldn't get through. I still ended up first in the 1.5-litre class.' That was 1961. By the end of the decade, he'd built his own open-wheeler racing car and had won the New Zealand Driver to Europe award.

Cassius was a true believer. His dedication to motor racing was absolute, to the exclusion of everything else, including a social life and social niceties. He defined his own quality of life by the quality of his race cars.

He won the F5000 Tasman Series in three consecutive years from 1971, and won the Australian Grand Prix three times—twice in a car carrying his own name. He fell briefly into a partnership with UK designer Len Terry, who had started the Leda car company, then bought him out, changed the company's name to his own and set out to take on the world. He won the America F5000 Championship in 1972 against all-comers, defeating Surtees, Lola, Chevron, March and McLaren.

That commanded the attention of promotions wizard Andy Granatelli, chief executive of oil additive company STP. Granatelli, a big-talking Texan, was using motor racing to take STP to global markets. In 1969, Mario Andretti had won his one and only Indianapolis 500 in an STP Hawk. At the end of the race Andy got to Mario on the victory podium before the race queen and planted a huge kiss on his cheek. It was a magic moment. The Granatelli brothers, Andy, Vince and Joe, had been trying to win Indy since 1946. In 1948 Andy even drove his own car and was almost killed in a horrific crash.

In Australia and New Zealand STP had sponsored Chris Amon and David Oxton in the 1971 Tasman Series: 'They were thrashed by me and Frank Matich,' McRae smiled, the old Cassius shining through. 'Next year Andy decided he'd sponsor the two of us.'

It's easy to see why they got along. Granatelli had entitled his autobiography *They Call Me Mister 500*. No shortage of self-esteem. He was simply outrageous. One year he dressed his whole team in overalls patched with STP logos all over, and he wore a similar suit himself. Only Colonel Sanders would have stood out more in Gasoline Alley.

In 1973, Graham's STP McRae cleaned up the Tasman Series—it won three out of eight and was on the podium five times. 'Andy sent his son Vince out to run me,' McRae recalled. 'Vince asked me if I'd like to have a go at the ovals; he'd arranged a test drive at Ontario Motor Speedway.'

Ontario was a bold Californian experiment—a multi-disciplined motor-racing facility that existed only between 1970 and 1980 before it was carved up by real estate developers. The Big O was built as a replica of Indy, 2.5 miles (4 kilometres) around with nine-degree banking, and it was always a bit quicker than Indy.

'They put me in a Lola Offy—it was the first time I'd driven a turbo car,' McRae said. 'It felt heavy, but I worked it up to 184 mph [296 km/h] and they said, "That's enough; when we screw the boost up you'll go faster." And then they offered me Indy.'

In 1973 Granatelli's STP became the principal partner of an outfit run by Kentucky oil magnate Ueal 'Pat' Patrick. Pat sank nineteen wells before he hit Texas Tea. It made him enough money to easily buy a race team. His Indy attempt was going to be his biggest yet.

Patrick had secured the services of one of the most successful chief mechanics of all time, George Bignotti (he'd be responsible for seven Indy 500 victories). He'd made young David 'Swede' Savage, a protégé of Dan Gurney, the star of the show and it was no coincidence they were using the very latest Gurney Eagle chassis, fitted with a turbocharged Offenhauser engine. His other driver was 37-year-old Gordon Johncock, who'd recently fronted bankruptcy court after winding up his own team at the end of a long winless streak. Johncock was an ace, just down a little on his luck. He balanced Savage, who, at 26, was a firebrand.

Andy and Vince inserted McRae into that mix—in a third car, their Lola-Ford. While Patrick and Bignotti would run the other two cars, Vince would look after McRae.

'The first time I saw Indianapolis was when I turned up to race,' McRae said. Being in a team was a totally different experience for the one-man-band driver: 'I just decided I'd do as I was told.'

He passed the Rookie Test, but his frustration was growing. Australian Frank Gardner (British touring-car and European F5000 champion) consulted to Lola and he'd set up the car on Ontario and given it the all-clear. But for McRae it was 'a big heavy slug. It pointed in okay, but it just wasn't nimble.' No matter how hard he tried, he couldn't get it up to qualifying speed. Granatelli put the muscle on Patrick, who offered McRae the team's spare Eagle.

There'd been considerable speculation that 1973 would be the year the 200 mph (321 km/h) lap average barrier would be broken. Just talking about it poured the pressure on. Early in practice, the mercurial young Savage came close—197.8 mph (318.2 km/h).

But Art Pollard, 46 years old and already a grandfather, died trying. He completed a lap at 192 mph (309 km/h) then looped it and was killed. Just hours later, on that same afternoon, Johnny Rutherford did 198.41 mph (319.24 km/h). It was the quickest speed anyone would achieve in the Month of May and JR dedicated his run to Pollard, who'd been his good friend.

McRae qualified thirteenth fastest. Johncock was eleventh. Savage would be off the second row of the grid in fourth. 'I figured I could win it,' McRae told me in Auckland. There wasn't a doubt in his mind, not even now.

The 1973 race was one of Indy's horrors. It took three days to complete.

From the start, Salt Walther assaulted the fence. His McLaren Offy just kept climbing and climbing, looking for a way over the steel safety cables and into the crowd. At its zenith it plunged back to the track, but it sprayed burning fuel into the public area and several spectators needed medical attention. Walther's life, they said, was saved because he was not wearing a six-point harness. He slipped down into the tub of the car while its roll cage collapsed above him. Eight cars ploughed into or around him. British driver David Hobbs was heard to say: 'You'd think the best drivers in the world could come down the straightaway without hitting each other.' They put out the red flag. And then rain started to fall, and the race was postponed for a day.

Next day the 32 remaining competitors were on their pace lap when it rained once more. It wasn't until day three, three hours after the scheduled 11 a.m. start, that the green flag waved. In all that time Graham McRae and his crew never realised that the fuel transfer valve on his Eagle had jammed.

'They say that I got as high as third place,' he recalled. 'I was passing quite a few cars, up around 190 mph [305 km/h]. In those days you had two fuel tanks—40 gallons [151 litres] each on the left and on the right. There was a fuel transfer lever you had to pull. You burnt off the fuel in the right-hand side first, so the car didn't want to tip in the corners. And then you'd pull the lever to activate the left tank. I did that and it jammed. It was a big lever on the right-hand side. I had to pull it back towards me—and it just wouldn't come. There was so much going on, you don't keep trying once you know something is hopeless, you just get on with it.'

Teammates Johncock and Savage were duelling for the lead. Wherever McRae was in the race, it didn't matter compared to this. First it was Johncock, then Savage, then Al Unser in the Parnelli who took the lead. Savage headed for the pits, took on a full load of fuel and charged impetuously back onto the race-track. A car with a heavy fuel load—up around 200 additional kilograms—handles differently to one that's near empty. Savage didn't hesitate. He was challenging Unser when his car slewed inwards on Turn Four, heading for the safety fence that defined the infield before the pit entrance. There was no stopping it. It simply disintegrated.

The crash happened in full view of the grandstands, and the pit signallers. Armando Teran, 23, from Santa Monica, California, was the volunteer pit signaller for Graham McRae. He looked up to see a red STP car plummeting across the track and then exploding. It wasn't clear which of the team cars it was. Didn't matter—Armando started to run, not away from the wreck but towards it. At the same time a fire truck was signalled to head for the scene—up pit lane in the opposite direction of race traffic, allowed under race regulations. The fire truck hit Armando and he was flung into the air, suffering a broken skull. He was pronounced dead that afternoon.

Andy Granatelli saw it all. As horrifying as Savage's crash was, he was focused on Armando. 'I thought it was my son who was killed,' he told the *Chicago Tribune*. 'He was the same size and wearing the same uniform. It was a crazy, freak accident and it flat turned me off racing. I didn't want to do this anymore.' There was a depth to Granatelli's interview, a recognition of the motivations that drive the sport: 'Swede recognised the dangers and his rewards would have been much more than crew members'. They both had the same penalty to pay but the rewards weren't even close.'

When they resumed the race an hour later, the STP team was still in it. There must have been teams even then who had an issue with that judgement call; Savage was in a critical condition, a crewman was dead. But Johncock was second, chasing Unser. In the melee McRae's crew had not been able to release the fuel valve so instead they'd changed strategy and leaned out the fuel mix to get more mileage from the fuel they could access. 'But we went too lean and it burnt out the valves. It just kept getting slower until it stopped, and I was out,' McRae said. Unser broke and Johncock took the lead. On lap 133, the rain came again, and officials simply held out the red flag, not the chequer, and declared the event was over. The 332.5 miles (535 kilometres) that winner Johncock covered made it then the shortest Indy on record.

McRae, 91 laps covered, was named Rookie of the Year. In other circumstances that might have been the perfect result. But the STP crew went to the Methodist Hospital to visit Savage, then had a subdued dinner at a local fast-food restaurant. One month later Savage was dead, without having left the hospital. Dr Stephen Olvey, the Indianapolis Racing League's doctor, said contaminated plasma from a blood transfusion may have caused liver failure.

Graham McRae was keen to return to Indianapolis. He'd learnt a lot about oval racing. For a while he stayed close to Vince Granatelli: 'They helped me with a few of my races.' But then the cracks that inevitably appeared in Cassius's relationships started to show: 'The Granatellis were great PR people,' he said, 'but they were not great engineers. The trouble is you didn't work with them, you did what they wanted. They had some good ideas—they took jet cars to Indy and that could have been successful. But they didn't understand how a mechanical engineer puts a car together and for what reason. After a few more races they told me we'd finished. They never consulted me on anything.'

McRae's attempt to build a Can-Am car, like Bruce McLaren had done, was underfunded and fell away. In 1978 he won the three-race Australian Drivers' Championship in the McRae GM3 Chevrolet. Kevin Bartlett was third. He then claimed his third Australian Grand Prix, a remarkable result.

Later he developed a beautiful little Porsche 356 Speedster Replica—a lookalike for the car in which actor James Dean was killed in 1955. He built 38 of them and they are collector's items, but he is seeing none of the reward. The company he set up to build them was deregistered fifteen years ago.

Graham's small room had become very cramped. I looked him in the eye, not wanting to cross any boundaries, and asked: 'Would you have done anything differently?'

There was a long pause and he gave me the Cassius look of defiant determination we all used to love: 'Probably not.'

9

Third . . . Could
Have Been First

South Australian Vern Schuppan was third in 1981 in the most controversial Indianapolis 500 ever held. If he'd been an American, he might have won it. Post-race, two of the giants of American motor racing, Bobby Unser and Mario Andretti, were locked in an unseemly battle over infringement of the rules. There'd been a blend line infraction, a simple failure to merge properly after a pit stop, and instead of being clear cut, it threw the result open to interpretation. Both drivers were sheepish. Unser didn't drink the ceremonial winner's milk. Andretti, when told next day that the pendulum of victory had swung his way, said: 'For the rest of my life, I'm going to have to apologise for winning this race.' It was farcical. Protests and appeals went on for five months. The two drivers turned petulant: 'Bobby went through all the hoopla and got to experience victory lane and then it was taken from him and given to me and I will never get to experience that myself,' Mario sniffed when they named him winner.

'It's already ruined for me,' Unser bleated when it seemed an appeal might turn back in his favour. 'I'm very bitter. I'm not waiting for a decision either. The damage has already been done and I will paint racing out of my future.'

Outspoken journalist Robin Miller, whose insight and influence were far greater than that of a mere reporter, thundered: 'If Schuppan had been an American they would have declared him the winner.' It would have been a sensible, face-saving way out. But you don't fling two homegrown heroes out of the race in favour of a driver whose major claim to fame at that moment was that he was 'the nicest man ever to drive an IndyCar'.

It took until October for Unser to be declared winner of his third Indy 500. At the same time, officials fined him $40,000 for breaking the rules. How was that possible? 'Unclear' race regulations were the real culprit. TV vision clearly showed the drivers doing the crime. But a smart lawyer got them off.

Two years later Schuppan won the Le Mans 24 Hour race, part of the Triple Crown, and his stocks were on the rise. But by then he'd pretty much drawn a line under his Indy racing career and moved on to management. It was his misfortune that he came into Indy racing at a time of official incompetence and growing unrest. It was all too much for a simple lad from Whyalla who just wanted to race.

Whyalla is a town of red dust. For many years the dust settled on roofs and windows, and infiltrated the cavities of homes that had been built in the 1950s to accommodate a flood of workers attracted by the town's steelworks and ship-building facility. BHP built 64 ships at Whyalla from steel made right there on site. In those boom times the population doubled. The price people paid to live in the town was the dust from the manufacturing process that perpetually caked them. It got in their hair, in their eyes and up their nostrils, and later an environmental protection agency claimed the people of Whyalla presented with levels of lung cancer that were well above average.

Vern Schuppan's family moved to Whyalla from the tiny rural township of Booleroo Centre, population 391. Both towns claim him as a prominent former citizen. There was something to be said for growing up on the shoreline of the Spencer Gulf, the 300-kilometre long inlet up the centre of South Australia. Vern would perch on his dad's knee as they drove out to the Point Lowly Lighthouse to go fishing and while Norm worked the throttle, Vern would throw the family car into opposite lock slides on the wide, deserted dirt road. He was all of five. 'Will you look at that,' Norm used to exclaim.

When Vern was twelve, Norm took him to Port Wakefield, on the other side of the gulf, to watch the 1955 Australian Grand Prix. Motor racing had been banned on public roads in South Australia—it was a danger to stock and rural livelihood—and Port Wakefield was the first purpose-built circuit to host the grand prix. Jack Brabham won it in his Cooper Bristol but the car that caught Vern's eye at his first-ever motor race was the glorious French-racing-blue Lago Talbot, formerly raced by Louis Chiron. In the hands of Doug Whiteford, it finished third after a battle with Brabham and Reg Hunt's Maserati 250 F.

Vern didn't know how to spell epiphany. But that's what he had. 'You know, as a kid you watch cowboy movies and you want to be a cowboy. Well that day I wanted to be a racing driver.'

Norm bought him a go-kart. Vern won the South Australian championship and started to look further afield. This wasn't in Norm's plans. He'd mapped out his son's future . . . taken him out of school at fourteen and made him an apprentice in the family panelbeating business.

The 1968 London–Sydney Marathon, a rally from the UK to the east coast of Australia (it covered 17,000 kilometres in ten moving days), was a tipping point. The opening portion of the Australian leg across the 1200-kilometre Nullarbor Plain, full of wombat burrows, held great fears for some of the European amateur crews. One hired a local expert, illegally, to take the wheel. 'I had to duck down under a blanket when we got to the control point at Ceduna because all the officials knew me,' Vern laughed.

A year later Vern was off to Great Britain to seek his motor-racing fortune: 'If you go, don't come back,' his father threatened.

The townsfolk backed his dad: 'You don't know what you're doing to your father,' the barber entreated.

'Stay here, settle down with a nice girl,' Norm pleaded.

Vern married the nice girl and took her with him.

Vern and Jennifer had a plan. They had a budget of £2000 and a deadline of two years to win a major championship. Vern built up a Ford 10 van, fitted it out for camping and towing, and arranged passage on the *Angelina Lauro*, a 24,000-tonne passenger vessel that offered far less costly travel than an airline. Two and a half years after setting sail, Vern was in Formula One.

There were other Australians and New Zealanders in the UK, all tilting at the big time. Tim Schenken from Melbourne, who went on to drive for Ferrari, and Howden Ganley from Hamilton, New Zealand, who'd drive in more than 40 Formula One grands prix and later form a race car manufacturing company with Schenken, greeted Vern warmly and pointed him in the wrong direction.

'Tim told me to go production sports racing,' Vern recalled. 'It was a ticket to nowhere.' These days Vern and Schenken, who is the long-serving race director of Australia's Supercars Championship, are the best of friends. They go camping together up in the Flinders Ranges north of Adelaide.

'I spent £900 of my budget to buy an Alexis Formula Ford,' Vern said. At his first race meeting at Oulton Park, the four-year-old chassis came twelfth in a gun field of 32, a promising start. While Vern networked, an acquired skill for a boy from the bush, Jennifer went to work in a bakery 'which meant she could bring home free bread'.

There are stepping stones in motor racing; the skill is knowing when to step. Some would have stayed in Formula Ford to attempt to win the series. Schuppan stepped up to the more meaningful Formula Atlantic and won in that instead. His car was down on power compared to the opposition, but his growing understanding of car set-up made the difference. Big Louis Stanley, the boss of BRM F1, offered a test drive, which led to a 1973 race contract, secured purely on talent. Then a young Austrian, Niki Lauda, arrived with talent *and* money, and Schuppan was out.

Schuppan turned to the burgeoning Southeast Asian motor-racing scene, won the Singapore Grand Prix and the Macau Grand Prix—both times for enthusiastic, mega-wealthy Macau casino owner Teddy Yip. 'It was the first time I'd met many Australian and New Zealand drivers,' Vern recalled. 'I'd never raced in Australia so here I was in Singapore, Malaysia, Japan and Macau racing against guys I'd otherwise have known at home. And they were all on deals.'

The pits at the Southeast Asian circuits were like a big bazaar. You could enter them with a car that was clean of advertising and before long, as you racked up practice results and bargained a bit, you'd amass enough sponsorship and decals to pay for the weekend and make a profit. It was all foreign to Vern.

'If you want to do something special in the region, just go and talk to him,' offered Max Stewart, Australian Gold Star Champion and another boy from the bush (he hailed from Orange in the Central West of New South Wales), indicating Yip.

Teddy—a Portuguese-Chinese version of Errol Flynn complete with a pencil-thin moustache—became the best patron a driver could have. He persuaded Vern into F1 drives—he would drive for Ensign, Hill and Surtees. He arranged Formula 5000 opportunities. Vern drove for Theodore Racing (Teddy's team) when he won the 1976 Rothmans International Series in Australia, all the time building a strong reputation. He earned touring-car drives with Peter Brock and Allan Moffat, and especially sports-car drives—almost a parallel career—in big events such as Le Mans. By the end of his active racing days, he'd amassed a first, two seconds and a third at Le Mans and had become one of the feted *Pilotes Anciens*, a select group of Porsche heroes who travel the world representing the brand.

Living inside the Yip cocoon came with risk as well as reward. The risk was to your constitution. Teddy never seemed to sleep, and those who travelled with him dared not drop off, either. A welcome party, in whichever country he may have been, could involve 100 or more people and a fully booked restaurant. It could get punishing.

Schuppan wasn't the only Yip-supported driver. Australian F1 world champion Alan Jones was another; and Ron Tauranac designed and built a car for Theodore Racing. In Macau, Ayrton Senna drove for Yip and won the grand prix. In the US, Yip offered his support to Dan Gurney.

'I'd raced in the last two rounds of the American F5000 championship for Teddy against Gurney's Eagles, one driven by Bobby Unser, the other by James Hunt,' Vern said. 'In the last race at Riverside in California, Hunt spun in front of me and I T-boned him. That's when I met Dan.'

Gurney phoned Schuppan at home in East Horsley in the UK two months later: 'Do you want to drive for me? Bobby's going to concentrate on the ovals.' That's code for 'he's not quick enough on the street circuits'. As a clincher Gurney added, 'I'll give you a percentage of the prize money.' Teddy Yip also gave Dan $10,000 to put Theodore Racing branding on the car.

Vern and Jennifer moved to the United States, got themselves an apartment in Santa Ana, near Gurney's All American Racers (AAR) headquarters, and began to understand US motor racing: 'For some people, America is like second prize, but as a kid I'd always bought the US motor magazines; I watched the Indy 500, loved NASCAR. I loved the big close-ups of guys in their cockpits, Al Unser in his blue-and-yellow Johnny Lightning car.'

Vern scrambled to eighth in the F5000 championship, the chronically understeering Eagle no match for the UK-built Lolas. 'Dan could be intimidating to work for,' Vern said. 'He was my boyhood hero and I pinched myself that I was driving for Dan Gurney. But he was a notorious tinkerer and he'd be working on the car right up to the time the flag fell.' Dan also thought he could go faster, a notion supported by history but debunked by age and driving currency.

'In 1976, Dan knew I wanted to drive Indy,' Vern said.

'If we get Pancho Carter qualified, we'll give you a go,' Gurney told him.

The 60th Indianapolis 500 was run in 1976 and it was memorable for many reasons. Rain made it the shortest 500 race ever held, just 102 laps, 255 miles (410 kilometres). Johnny Rutherford's win would be the last ever for the Offenhauser engine (the Offy won 27 Indy races—almost half of all those held up to that point), while Janet Guthrie became the first woman to enter the 500. And on the night of the race Elmer George, son-in-law of Indianapolis Motor Speedway owner Tony Hulman, was shot dead in a confrontation with his wife's alleged lover.

Pancho Carter qualified sixth in the first week. Carter had replaced the previous year's winner, Bobby Unser, who'd moved on from AAR. People thought Pancho was Mexican but the name came from 'paunch'; that's what his racer dad called him while he was still a baby bump. He was born while his parents were driving to the Milwaukee Mile race.

'It was common practice for rookies to walk down to the Turn One infield to watch the cars come through,' Vern said. 'We'd already been for several familiarisation laps with race veteran Wally Dallenbach so we knew what to expect. But one of the drivers, Ed Miller, was very nervous. We were standing close to the track, in kind of an open passage behind the low steel barrier with a chain-wire fence behind us. He lost it, hit the wall, and then headed for the infield, just past us, and somersaulted over two more fences. Holy shit. It's not the sort of thing you want to see before you go out yourself.' Miller compressed two vertebrae in his neck and never attempted Indianapolis again.

'The Rookie Test was a piece of cake, really,' Vern mused. Though he sought as much help as he could get.

Gordon Johncock, whom he'd raced in F5000, advised: 'Ram your left foot into the firewall. Otherwise you'll always be tempted to ride the brake.'

Some drivers, Vern knew, planted one foot on top of the other to stop their throttle from lifting. 'I just couldn't go flat into Turn One. The challenge was to lift as little as you could and not touch the brake at all.'

Recalling the experience at his home in Adelaide, Vern compared the IndyCar feeling to that of the powerful Porsche prototypes he drove later in world sports-car racing. 'The 962 Porsche on the banking at Daytona wasn't a problem. It would push well down on its suspension and you could feel it through the seat of your pants. The IndyCar, past its limit, could fly off the road . . . no time to feel it . . . just fly off.' It was important to know your limit.

The same applied in the pits: 'Gasoline Alley was small but not as small as some pits I'd been in.' More, it was a closed shop.

'A.J. Foyt worked behind closed doors,' Vern said. Garrie Cooper, the Australian owner of Elfin racing cars, for whom Vern occasionally drove, snuck in when the door was open and was taking pictures of Foyt's Coyote. 'Foyt yelled at him to get out and then started pushing him, violently, to make his point.' Fair enough, too. Industrial espionage has always been rife in motor racing, but Cooper, surely, should have known better than to pick a fight with Foyt, of all people.

There were two sides to A.J.: there was the take-no-prisoners, suffer-no-fools racer, who was always on public display. And then there was the sheer enthusiast who appreciated it when someone was having a big go. That year, he loaned Janet Guthrie his spare car when hers did not qualify. He wanted to give her the opportunity to prove she had speed and to help her save face. Janet lapped at better than 180 mph (289 km/h) and would be back to race the following year.

'The biggest trouble I had was getting used to the centrifugal force,' Vern said. He sat very still in his car in Gasoline Alley as mechanics cut foam rubber to size and packed it all around him. 'There was no such thing as a moulded seat in those days. The mechanics just packed in the foam until I could not move and then custom-fitted it with race tape.'

Schuppan qualified his Eagle seventeenth, and was the fastest of the rookies. In the race he had the unusual experience of having Dan Gurney in his ear. 'I wasn't used to driving and talking to the pits. Even when I first drove for Porsche, it was one-way to them.'

A contemporary race driver is part of a team—a brains trust of driver, engineer and, in the case of Indianapolis, spotters placed around the track. All have input into ever-changing race tactics.

It's hard to think of a team being competitive without the almost constant communication between them. The Schuppan car lost comms early in the race and it could have cost them dearly.

'I was getting understeer [pushing]. The car just wasn't handling right. I thought it was the right rear going off.' (The right rear is the most critical tyre on the car at Indianapolis because it takes a disproportionate share of the load.) Vern felt he had no choice. He charged to the pits without warning under green flag conditions—pretty much the last thing any driver wants to do. 'They couldn't find anything, so they sent me back out.'

Then Roger McCluskey hit the wall, bringing out a yellow caution. With the field slowed and compressed, Vern was back in. 'This time they found a blister on the tyre—it was losing pressure.' They changed it and he resumed, in last place.

His drive from that point on was exemplary. By the time the rain came and stopped the race, he was already up to eighteenth and he'd well earned the Rookie of the Year award. He'd spent the last few laps in a wheel-to-wheel dice with A.J. Foyt, who was admittedly several laps ahead.

On 19 March 1977, Max Stewart and Vern Schuppan were practising for a rich but ultimately insignificant F5000 race at Calder Park outside Melbourne. Calder was yet to morph into Australia's only Thunderdome, a banked tri-oval built by its owner, tyre magnate Bob Jane, to American specification. It would field left-hand drive NASCARs turning left and right-hand drive local vehicles, AUSCARS, turning right. But back

in Vern's day, the Calder road circuit was a 'two straights and a squiggle' track.

Schuppan was in Garrie Cooper's Elfin MR8, Stewart in his Lola T400. Coming out of the stop corner at the end of the main straight, Schuppan suddenly lost power. A car behind him moved over to avoid him, but Stewart, travelling right behind, possibly thought it was moving out of his way. He accelerated hard and ran straight up the back of Schuppan's Elfin. Stewart took the impact of the Elfin's engine and exhausts in his full-face helmet.

Vern didn't know that, not immediately. All he felt was an impact that left him dazed. He was taken back to the pits by medics and soon after, because he was complaining of a sore neck, his father drove him to hospital. 'I walked up to the reception desk to ask how Max was and they said, "I'm sorry, the prognosis is he won't last the night." It was the first I knew. I was winded, it felt like someone had dropped me off a twelve-foot wall. It was the worst day of my life.'

Vern Schuppan is the only Australian to win Indianapolis's Jigger Award. Leon 'Jigger' Sirois, son of a successful Indy 500 mechanic, was the unluckiest Indy driver ever. He tried for six straight years to qualify and never succeeded. But it's the big one that got away that immortalised him in the annals of Indy. It was pole day in 1969 and Jigger, from the small town of Shelby in northern Indiana, pulled three pretty average qualifying laps and his crew waved him off before he completed his sequence of four. Then it rained and no one else qualified at all. The media room noted that if Jigger had competed his run-of-four, he would not only have been in the field, but would have been on pole position.

Try as he might, Jigger could not replicate the attempt and he failed to qualify for the race. The American Auto Writers and Broadcasters Association mounted a small gold-coloured whiskey jigger on a plinth and handed it to him as something of a consolation prize. The Jigger Award was born, and it's been awarded every year since. The Jigger has become a badge of honour. Pancho Carter, Johnny Rutherford, Janet Guthrie, even Roger Penske have their names engraved on it.

In 1977 so did Vern Schuppan. The Brickyard had been totally resurfaced, the first time it had a complete makeover since 1910 when they first laid the bricks. With an accompanying increase in allowable turbo boost, lap averages soared. Suddenly Schuppan was doing in excess of 190 mph (305 km/h) but Tom Sneva grabbed pole above 200 mph (321 km/h), the first time the double tonne had been cracked. To recognise the achievement, the speedway filled Sneva's helmet with 200 silver dollars.

Schuppan's attempt was comedic. With the end of the qualifying session fast approaching, it was now or never. Twice his crew chief failed to wave the green flag to signify his four qualifying laps had begun—nothing more than brain fade. When the flag waved, the session had ended but anyone still on the track was allowed to complete. Schuppan's first lap was 190.43 mph (306.4 km/h), his second 191.61 mph (308.3 km/h), his third 189.63 mph (305.11 km/h). One more lap and he was in the field. Instead his car ran out of gas. The laps he'd wasted, waiting for the green flag to wave, had run the car dry. Hello Jigger.

It was the start of a downward trajectory. It can happen to any elite sportsperson. Sometimes they can arrest it; other times they're along, unwillingly, for the ride.

The next year, Vern was at the track, helmet in hand, ready to qualify Pancho Carter's Lightning. Carter had been badly injured in a test crash the previous autumn and Vern had been driving his car in USAC championship races at the beginning of the season. But not at Indy. 'Pancho arrived with his left leg in plaster,' Vern said. 'No way he wanted me in that car a moment longer, especially at Indy.' Officials gave Carter a special test—to see how quickly he could get in and out of the car. He qualified it 21st but then retired mid race. Carter would carry the disability for the rest of his career.

Vern next drove for a start-up team. They could afford him, and he wanted the drive. With a bit of help, a first-time team owner can pull together an effort and chance their arm. Herb and Rose Wysard had been very successful in business. They thought, 'Let's do Indy.' They bought the Wildcat that Gordon Johncock had driven to third the year before and from the pool of available talent they chose Schuppan. It was a tight-run ship. In order to afford him, they couldn't allocate money for a spare engine as well. 'There were about six or eight cracks in the chassis,' Vern recalled. He nursed it until just after halfway when the transmission failed. He and the Wysards accepted $20,537 for 21st place.

Herb and Rose continued in the sport, hiring and helping a cornucopia of drivers including Australian Geoff Brabham, Englishman Derek Daly, South African Desiré Wilson, and American Hurley Haywood who won the Le Mans 24 Hour with Schuppan for Porsche in 1983. The Wysards would never be a top team but they conducted themselves with dignity and epitomised the spirit of a second-tier entrant. When Herb celebrated his birthday, his son Jeff commissioned a model of Schuppan's Wildcat.

In 1980 Vern knew the downward spiral had to stop. It was becoming embarrassing. While his career in sports cars was going through the roof in Europe, here he was in the US, once more, just treading water in the talent pool. He signed on as a one-off to drive the Sugaripe Prune Special. When his teammate and Number One driver Tom Sneva crashed in practice, Vern had to hand over his own car. He never got to qualify.

'I said if I come back to Indy again, I'll do it with my own car': a simple statement with big intent. It was to be Schuppan's major shot at the main prize. In truth, the big works drives were most likely out of his grasp and the drives he could get would not bring the result. It was time to put together his own dream team—all he could afford of one, anyway. The year was 1981.

'I'd made some money from racing,' he said. He spoke to Roger Bailey at McLaren and used it to buy the M24 that had been Johnny Rutherford's back-up car in 1977. He secured the services of Professor of Mechanical Engineering John Sullivan with whom he'd collaborated on the Wysards' Wildcat: 'He was a clever bloke especially around turbochargers.' Vern had also worked with one of the most proficient team managers in world motorsport, John Horsman—'The Horse'—who ran John Wyer's Mirage team at Le Mans and before that was on the Ford GT40s. The Horse offered to run Vern's show. The team all came out of friendship. The only paid employee was the truck driver.

'The car cost me about US$120,000, ready to race, engine and all. I bought another new engine as well,' Vern said. Still, he needed sponsors to run it.

Young Jimmy Immke, the tearaway son of one of the founders of the Wendy's Hamburgers chain, was keen to get his dad involved as a sponsor. It led to a huge falling out between father and son. Father Len didn't see motorsport as part of his future. Jimmy invested a bit of family funds anyway and turned up for a good weekend. The big sponsorship came from Red Roof Inns, a motel chain owned by Jim Trueman, who would soon figure prominently in the sport. Trueman was already sponsoring a car in a feeder category driven by Bobby Rahal, later to be an Indy winner. 'There was no inside running—I simply put up a deal and it was accepted,' Schuppan said.

And it was time to get back in touch with Teddy Yip. 'We'd never had a falling out—it was my choice to distance myself. His parties were just too intense. You couldn't be flat out at practice and then go to Las Vegas all night. I was there to race.' Teddy was delighted to reunite. He gave Vern US$25,000— enough for the new engine—and Theodore Racing was prominent on the engine box of the M24.

'To put it in perspective, we were there with about US$90,000 of costs plus the car. Roger Penske had a car, too, and a budget of about $1 million,' Vern said with justifiable pride.

Third place was a massive result for the Schuppan team. It didn't come easily. The car developed a fuel leak even as they pushed it onto the grid, and they had to put a blanket underneath it to soak up the alcohol.

'We'd had handling problems and just couldn't find a solution,' Vern said. 'On the night before the race The Horse took 30 millimetres off the top of the rear wing—just on a hunch. I didn't get to drive it like that until the race. He came on the radio and asked, "Any better?" I was able to report yes.'

Vern finished just one lap behind the duelling Unser and Andretti. The crew were elated. 'It was only when we looked down as the celebration began that we noticed that both right tyres had deflated. We were within a lap of not finishing, and we hadn't known it.'

It was five months after the race that Bobby Unser's Penske was eventually proclaimed the victor. Mario Andretti, who had been told he was first, was relegated to second.

'USAC was so incompetent,' Robin Miller told me from his semi-permanent seat in the Workingman's Friend diner in suburban Indianapolis ('the best double cheeseburgers in the world'). Robin didn't hold back: 'Obviously Unser and Andretti had cheated the blend rules so if big bad USAC was going to enforce the rule book, they'd both have been penalised and Vern would have won the race. A fine on Unser was probably the right call—ditto for Mario—but in typical USAC fashion they did the wrong thing and it dragged out for months while a panel decided it.'

Schuppan maintained a respectful silence on the whole distasteful blend-line controversy. His third-place purse—$87,974—went a long way towards justifying his decision to go it alone. But it wasn't the $270,401 that Bobby got for winning.

'The upside for me was that Jimmy Immke's father said, "Well if he can get third with an old car, what can he do with a new one?"' In a complete about-face, Len Immke bought Vern a new March, totally built up as an IndyCar, a huge reboot to his US career.

'It arrived at Riverside in California as we were qualifying for a race. I took it out of the crate, and it was immediately faster than the McLaren so I decided to race it.' But something broke in the suspension and the car thumped and pirouetted itself to near destruction. Vern stepped out unscathed.

'The March people said they weren't going to pay for the repair—even though they should have, it was a new car. Len Immke got so scared of the downside of motor racing that he ran away and never came back.'

In his 21-year career Vern raced Le Mans sixteen times, did eight F1 races, entered six Indianapolis 500s and competed in three. He contested 254 races, won 21 of them and was on the podium 65 times—a podium percentage of better than 25 per cent. People count these things. After his last race in 1989 he moved into management and fostered the careers of young hopefuls, including New Zealand's Scott Dixon. He acted as an intermediary between the South Australian government and F1 boss Bernie Ecclestone and was influential, perhaps instrumental, in bringing the F1 World Championship Grand Prix to Adelaide in 1985.

He has become an avid classic car collector and trader. He secured the ex-Steve McQueen Ferrari 275 GTB/4 in poor condition, had the Classiche division of Ferrari fully restore it and sold it at auction for A$14.1 million. He owns a McLaren M24 IndyCar—not the one he raced—and he has restored it to show order.

Vern and Jennifer split their time between their homes: one in Adelaide, a glorious two-storey penthouse overlooking the Supercars street course, and the other in the Algarve in Portugal. Their children, Paige, a novelist, and Kerrin, a fashion designer and online retailer, are both successful.

And Vern is still a boy at heart.

At the end of my visit, he opened the security doors of an air-conditioned warehouse in Adelaide where he and a friend kept their toys. The walls were lined with classic motorcycles. On the floor there was something delicious sheathed in a proper car cover, not just a tarpaulin. He pulled it back, not theatrically, but with great care. And there was the French-racing-blue Lago Talbot driven by Doug Whiteford in the 1955 Australian Grand Prix. Vern was grinning hugely. It was as if he was twelve again. Except now he could drive this automotive masterpiece wherever and whenever he chose, in historic races across the country and perhaps even across the world. 'It feels like a big go-kart,' the 76-year-old told me. He was completely at ease with his seven-figure purchase, and, it seemed, with his life.

10

Son of the Father

Geoffrey Brabham, first son of three-time world champion Sir Jack Brabham, drove in his first Indianapolis 500 in 1981, the year Vern Schuppan drove his last. He was nine years younger than Schuppan, the next generation, and despite his surname there were no free rides. Brabham's teammate, Mexican teenager Josele Garza, was far younger, *Vogue*-cover handsome, unbelievably wealthy and, despite failing to finish while Geoff came fifth, was named Rookie of the Year. Who knew it was a personality contest? Josele kind of set the tone for Geoff's career. There would always be flashier show ponies and perhaps even drivers with more pace, but if you wanted the job done with fearless and resolute determination, you called on Geoff. He was steadfast.

The pinnacle of Brabham's career was not Indianapolis but the IMSA GTP Championship, a US series for prototype sports cars. Nissan built a succession of red-hot racers that had the ability to completely dominate. They could have hired a superstar to steer them but the concern, always, is that the driver might consider himself better than the car. They plugged Brabham into their program and he brought the cars home first four years in a row, from 1988 to 1991—a record that still stands.

There could be no better recognition of his professionalism than at the Le Mans 24 Hour race in 1993, ten years after Schuppan won for Porsche. Brabham was driving a French car—a Peugeot Talbot—for a French team in a French race with two French co-drivers. Yet when it came time to decide which driver would have the honour of guiding the winning car over the finish line, the French team manager Jean Todt, later the autocratic president of the French-based Fédération Internationale de l'Automobile (FIA), the world controlling body of motorsport, nominated the Australian.

'My father used to turn up at my races when he thought I had a fair chance of winning,' Geoff, now long retired and the father of a racer himself, young Matthew, said over coffee and croissant overlooking his dock on a Surfers Paradise canal. It was his way of bringing balance to the long-held belief that Sir Jack gave his sons nothing except tough love, and that being a Brabham in motorsport was most times a handicap. Sir Jack was nobody's fool. He knew that he'd got lucky, that he'd enjoyed massive success in a less-regulated era where there was room for the maverick to succeed; where to take risks, cut corners and win out of sheer nerve, especially off the track, was revered. It was an era when, Geoff said, 'people were getting killed left, right and centre'.

The way of life back then was best summed up by the means Jack used to get to races—flying in his own aircraft, as many of the racers did. It wasn't a corporate jet with a couple of pilots but a self-fly Cessna: 'Mum didn't like it much; there were too many near misses; no restrictions.' Geoff recalled Jack running out of runway and spinning the plane on full throttle to avoid an upcoming lake; and losing all power mid-air and gliding a long way because there'd been no discipline about switching the fuel taps. They all did it. When Indianapolis 500–winner Graham Hill perished in foggy conditions along with key members of his F1 team in 1975, he was flying what was technically an unregistered plane without an appropriate night-flying licence.

Jack knew that his sons Geoffrey, Gary and David would have to make it in an atmosphere defined by far more stringent boundaries, and he wasn't sure that he wanted that for them. He liked it the way it was. 'The only driving advice my father gave me was, "There's the throttle, brake and steering wheel—if you crash it, don't come back,"' Geoff half-joked.

It would have been somewhat close to that. Jack once told a prominent TV interviewer when quizzed on the secret of his success: 'You're either fast, or you're not.' He wasn't being supercilious. Jack's communication skills were limited. Even though he and designer Ron Tauranac had a great rapport, neither was loquacious even about technical matters. A debrief was . . . brief.

'I think there were times he would have liked to teach me more, but he just didn't know how to put his knowledge into words,' Geoff said.

Geoff absolutely discounts the notion that you're born a racing driver, that it's in the genes. Despite the evidence of the multiple generations of Unsers, Andrettis and Brabhams, he believes strongly that ability comes from constant exposure: 'It's not genetic—it's a disease.'

In his case he was privileged, more than his brothers, to see his father's lifestyle up close and learn by osmosis. Gary was nine years younger, David, thirteen. They didn't travel much, not like Geoff did. He was at Mexico City in 1970 for Jack's last Formula One race when the crowd invaded the track for the duration of the event, making it incredibly dangerous, and Jack's engine blew while lying third: 'Well, what the hell do we do now?' Jack asked his eighteen-year-old son. It was a question about life in general. Geoff made a point of souveniring Jack's steering wheel before somebody else did. It's proudly in his trophy cabinet at home, an annex devoted more to his father than himself.

In Sydney, Ford funded Jack into a major dealership in the city's south-western suburbs. It was the time of a power struggle between Ford and Holden where a win on Sunday meant a sale on Monday and either company would have paid dearly to have Brabham's name on their masthead. Ford won—although six years later when Jack made his celebrated comeback along-side Stirling Moss at the Bathurst 1000, they did it in a Holden. The dealership ran a couple of racing cars, not for Jack—he'd had a gutful, or at least that's what Betty told him. One was a Formula Ford open-wheeler driven by local ace Bob Beasley. Geoff took the car to the nearby Oran Park circuit and when he improved a couple of seconds in the session, his old man said, 'You may as well do a race.' But after him. Jack snuck the car down to Melbourne to the 1971 Formula Ford Race of Champions involving the biggest names in domestic motor racing—Allan Moffat, Bob Jane, Bib Stillwell, Frank Matich—and he won. At least Geoff knew the capabilities of the car.

Geoff was third in the next year's Formula Ford Championship and won the Australian Formula Two title, which earned him the right to leave home and head for the UK Formula Three championship, the F1 nursery.

The stories of Jack being of no help to his boys are so wrong. Geoff had worked out of a corner of Jack's garage (he had Vauxhall in Great Britain) with a bit of sponsorship from ESSO, which used to look after Jack, and his parents gave him $10,000 seed money. Roseina, his girlfriend, went with him and they shared an apartment in Wimbledon with an Aussie assortment that included, variously, Larry and Raelene Perkins, Paul Bernasconi and his girlfriend (both of the blokes were racers), and Greg and Jill Siddle.

'Pee Wee' Siddle had management skills and he'd latched on to a Brazilian with money—Nelson Piquet—who would become three-time world champion. Piquet rented a transporter from Jack, and when Geoff's funds ran down to zero, Piquet let him throw his car into the truck to get to races. 'I was at a race meeting—a total one-man band. The battery lead came off and I had to undo my belt, get out, remove the seat, fix it and repeat the procedure, and it was then I realised I was pissing in the wind,' Geoff said.

Geoff was fourth in the F3 series, a spectacular result against the money teams, but he retreated to Australia to race with Jack in the 1977 Bathurst 1000 in which Allan Moffat and Colin Bond staged a 1–2 finish in their Ford Falcons. The Brabhams were eighteenth, 22 laps behind, but the weekend had an upside. Geoff and Roseina were married at Orange just up the road.

Motor racing breeds characters. David Psachie was one of them. David was short and stout, of Polish parentage with a thick Brooklyn accent, who sold Learjets in Orange County, California. Jack had Jack Brabham Aviation at Bankstown Airport, Sydney. Naturally they'd talk. David loved motor racing and he was in awe of Jack.

When Geoff turned up in California, David had cobbled together a deal to go racing in a Formula Super Vee, a feeder series to IndyCar, and he'd arranged for his girlfriend to let Geoff and Roseina stay in one of her houses. First time out Geoff threw the car into a fence: 'I thought, that's it, my US career is over.' But they battled on to the next round where 'the guy who owned the car found he'd tuned the engine all wrong. He fixed it and I put it on pole.'

Then came the Milwaukee Mile, America's oldest surviving banked oval. It was the first time Geoff had done a banked track and Milwaukee is just a constant, punishing left-hand turn: 'Halfway around my neck was gone. I don't mean it was just painful; I had lost control of holding my head up. My neck just went to jelly. I thought, "Holy crap", and I just prayed for a yellow flag to slow the field down.' But Geoff was hooked.

He sped back to the UK, sold his Formula Three car and built up a new Ralt chassis—Ralt had been owned by Jack's partner Ron Tauranac—and fitted it with the series' control VW Golf engine. 'David didn't have the money to do the whole series, but he scraped up enough,' Geoff recalled. The team lived off a rotating sequence of credit cards. Geoff won the Super Vee Championship and attracted the attention of the larger formulae.

By 1981 he was driving for Belgian Count Rudi van der Straten's Team VDS and he'd won the Can-Am Championship— the powerful V8 sports-car series made immortal by the Bruce (McLaren) and Denny (Hulme) Show a decade before. 'It was the first time I'd ever been paid to go motor racing,' Geoff said. The count's family owned the Stella Artois brewery. It was a win–win.

They were different times, almost as unstructured as Jack's era. 'Roseina and I decided to buy a house in Los Angeles,' Geoff recalled with a smile. They had little money, no credit rating, weren't even citizens.

David Psachie fixed it: 'They have $100,000 in gold bullion,' he swore on a stack of legally binding affidavits.

The junior Brabhams got the house and David introduced them to his new Formula Super Vee charge—the eighteen-year-old Mexican Josele Garza. America's *Sports Illustrated* magazine described Josele as 'a young man so handsome that girls walk into walls when he passes and so rich that his boyhood pet lion had its own room in the family's 54,000-square-foot house in Mexico City'. In contrast, the magazine described Geoffrey as 'an intense young Australian'.

Psachie claimed that Brabham had been tutoring the young Garza, but Geoff poured water on the suggestion. 'I answered his questions when he asked,' he said. Geoff had a pragmatic Brabham-esque view on driver coaching: 'Everyone has a ceiling and I guess coaching can get you there faster. But if coaching could take you beyond your natural limit then we'd all have tennis lessons and win Wimbledon.'

Josele's elegant mother, Nadina, widowed for the past eleven years after her banker husband had allegedly been assassinated, was keen to indulge her son who wanted to drive in the Indianapolis 500. She was prepared to invest whatever it took. How much? A million dollars should do it, was the speculation.

Brabham, with some experience on ovals, went along as well, part of a two-rookie team—one a 29-year-old dual series winner, the other a youngster who forged his entry form to get around the age limitation. Josele was nineteen years, two months and nine days when he drove the 1981 Indy 500. The rules said he had to be 21. His entry form claimed him to be 22. Josele and David Psachie both claimed they had no idea how the error occurred.

The Psachie-Garza team, because that's what it was called, bought the two Penske PC9 full ground effects cars from the Penske Team's works 1980 assault. Ground effects (GFX) was recently new in IndyCar. The PC9 was Penske's first full GFX and it upped the ante for a pair of rookies. It gave them speed and had the ability to encourage them to exceed their level of skill.

'It was amazing,' Geoff recalled of his first drive on the Indianapolis oval. 'I was trying to get the car slowed for Turn One and Gordon Johncock drove around the outside of me still on the throttle. I thought, "What am I doing?"' A different technique was required. 'On a road course it's still slow-in-fast-out. Here you drove deep into the corners. Conversely it's no wonder the Indy old-timers found it hard on the road courses.'

David Psachie had successfully lobbied USAC officials to

adopt a Rookie Orientation Program in the month of April to enable first-timers to become comfortable with the speedway. It was a great idea. 'But we'd done no pre-race testing with the GFX before the final phase of the Rookie Test and you're not allowed on the racing line; so here I was in the inside lane, rough as hell, with cars going *wow . . . wow . . . wow* past me. I felt a bit like a Christian going out to fight lions.'

The feeling grew when it came to getting up to speed: 'You can't see around Turn One. Your brain tells your foot to stay flat and your foot says, "F—k off, you're not the one who's going to hit the wall first."' It was all a mind game. 'The engineers would bullshit you—you never knew what downforce you were carrying.' Geoff explained that without telemetry, now the defining factor in car set-up but not available back then, 'it was up to the driver to work it out'. He said he went flat on the second lap of his qualifying attempt and then stayed flat for the rest of the four laps: 'The car was so good.'

His average, 187.99 mph (302.47 km/h) in the first session, was well above the bump zone. Of course, he could have trimmed it out, taken off the downforce, made the car more skittish, not stick to the ground so well, maybe gone quicker still, but what he did was solid. It turned out he'd been conservative. Young Garza did 195.1 mph (313.9 km/h). Brabham would start fifteenth, Garza, sixth.

For Brabham, Indy was an eye opener. 'On the last day of qualifying people were desperate. I sat on pit lane and watched them running up and down the line of cars waiting for their last run. They were carrying suitcases full of cash, ready to buy a drive in a good car. "Take your guy out and stuff me in the car," they were saying. You just had to look in their eyes, they didn't care if they died. They just wanted to get in the race.' Apart from anything else, 'In those days if you made the race you might make enough money to live on all year.'

At lap 64 in his first Indy 500 Brabham was in close company with the Hawaiian Danny Ongais. They called Ongais 'On the Gas'. The flyin' Hawaiian had topped 200 mph (321 km/h) in practice. Suddenly he had a major crash. Heading into Turn Three the car known as The Batmobile swapped ends and headed for the wall. 'It was like watching an aeroplane crash,' Geoff recalled. 'There were bits of crap all over the road. His legs were hanging out the end of the car like pieces of spaghetti. It was the first big accident I'd seen and I thought he was dead. I had to shut it out of my head and keep racing.' Ongais would recover to compete in the next year's race.

Garza was driving out of his skin, joining a four-way battle for the lead—the veterans Bobby Unser, Andretti and Johncock, and the teenager. Garza hit the lead twice and then he hit the wall. It was just the gentlest of kisses out of Turn Three, but his suspension was broken and he was forced into retirement. The kid's brave effort earned an ovation from the crowd. Show pony. But he'd never replicate it, never win a race.

Brabham finished fifth. His engine had been losing power for some time: it blew up as he crossed the finish line, right over the Yard of Bricks. 'Without that I think I would have been a good shot for third,' he said.

Geoff Brabham entered an even dozen Indy 500s. He placed in ten of them and failed to qualify only in the very last race he attempted. He endured the full gamut of emotion the Brickyard had to offer—except the elation of drinking the winner's milk. His best result was a fourth.

In 1982 he had 'the worst season ever'. He'd agreed to drive a March for George Bignotti, the chief mechanic turned team owner who discovered A.J. Foyt, and who was regarded as the man who engineered Indy wins. In Geoff's view the reputation was overrated: 'I never knew when the car was going to break. At Pocono Raceway the steering came off its rack and gave me my biggest ever moment. At Michigan the suspension broke at 200 mph [321 km/h] and I'd spun three times before my brain caught up with the fact that I was spinning.'

At Indianapolis, though, George delivered Geoff what seemed to be the fastest, strongest car he'd ever driven. 'It was King Kong.' This was the car to deliver pole position 'except George forgot to put the green flag up'. For a driver to begin his four-lap qualifying run, the team must raise a green flag to signify to officials that the attempt has begun. George neglected his duty.

Before Geoff could try again, Gordon Smiley was dead. The 36-year-old Nebraskan was a road-race specialist; he'd even raced F1. That year officials reduced the number of warm-up laps before the qualifying run from three to two, just enough to get warmth in the tyres. Smiley was completing his second warm-up and getting on the gas for the run to the start line when the car stepped out on Turn Three. He instinctively counter-steered, a road racer's reaction, and the March bolted for the wall.

'That was the biggest accident I've ever seen,' Geoff said, and even after all the years he was still shaken by the recollection.

'The car broke up and he was like a rag doll spiralling through the air.' TV caught the lot and they replayed it over and over again. 'You couldn't get away from it. People told me to look away, to make a point of not watching, but it was right in front of you.'

The manner of Smiley's death was horrendous, and his head injuries were graphic. Sir Jack was there that year. He counselled his son as best he could: 'Every living racing driver is proof it always happens to someone else.'

Sitting in Surfers Paradise, Geoff's whole manner, his body language, toughened up. 'I think they've gone too far with counselling these days. They're just covering their ass. The legal system has a lot to answer for.'

The next morning *The Indianapolis Star* had a front-page picture of the millisecond of impact. Smiley's helmet was head-on, facing the wall, just a fraction away from it, and there was nothing in front.

Brabham qualified 21st and he drove his incredibly powerful car into the top ten by the tenth lap. The engine blew up on the eleventh.

The next year he turned up with his helmet under his arm looking for a drive. He got it when John Paul Jnr broke his foot. Paul was a name motor racing tried to sweep under the carpet. John Snr and John Jnr both did time later in the 1980s for drug-related activities—anything to feed a motor-racing habit. John had followed his dad into the family distribution business at age fifteen. John Snr absconded to neutral Switzerland for a while and they finally got him on a variety of charges. John Jnr was done for trafficking and got four years, out in two and a half. The state offered him a deal but that would have meant fingering his father, and love and honour prevented that. Instead of being forgotten, the Pauls became celebrities—of the notorious kind.

Brabham took over John Jnr's Team VDS Penske PC10, qualified it 26th, and with great resolve worked it up to the front of the field. In that no-man's land of unresolved pit stop sequences, he was at one stage classified second. But on his last stop he stalled exiting the pits. 'It was the methanol,' he said. 'The fumes are nasty stuff.' In his pit stops Geoff tried to shut his eyes and hold his breath but this time he took one deep gulp. It pretty much knocked him out. By the time he got moving, he was fourth and that's where he stayed to the end.

Brabham drove four different makes of car with five different makes of engine for eight different teams in his Indianapolis 500 career. The best he ever qualified was eighth in 1984. That was the year the team had a problem just before the race started, down in the V of the engine. In his haste, one of the mechanics neglected to properly tighten up the fuel line to the injectors. As soon as Geoff hit the throttle at the start, the line fell off and fuel pumped over the motor. 'I looked in my mirrors and I could see the fire, even as the car went on seven cylinders.' He was the first to retire—one lap in—and was classified 33rd overall. The prize purse was still US$55,077.

Geoff drove for three years for Rick Galles, whose family owned car dealerships in New Mexico. The Galles had been stalwart members of the Albuquerque community since great-grandfather Nick rode down the Sante Fe trail and started a stagecoach-building business in the mid-1800s. Galles loved to do it right, no compromise. 'Each year there was a new and better chassis—a March or a Lola,' Geoff said. When Honda wanted to put a toe in the IndyCar water, but not do it in a way that brought attention to its effort, they approached their long-time partner Sir Jack who suggested they use the Galles team as their means of entry, and his trusted engine maker John Judd to put it together. As a subterfuge they named the engine a Brabham-Judd. Disappointingly, it was down on power. Geoff managed 71 laps in the 1987 race before it retired.

Honda Performance Division would enter IndyCar almost a decade later and for six years it became the sole engine supplier to IndyCar and the Indy 500. In 2020 it continued to be one of two competing engine brands at Indianapolis. It had won twelve Indy 500s—including the years when it was a control engine.

'I still won't drink Budweiser and neither will my father.' J. Douglas Boles, president of Indianapolis Motor Speedway, was sitting at the wheel of his Chevrolet Corvette C7 Grand Sport, the official pace car for the Indianapolis 500, and we had just completed several sighting laps of the Brickyard, Doug at the wheel, booting it hard up the back straight, grinning broadly. 'I haven't forgiven them for the disgraceful way they treated Geoff Brabham in 1989.' It doesn't pay to piss off a fan, especially when he may become president of the Brickyard.

In 1989 Jim Trueman's Truesports team, run by New Zealander Steve Horne, had secured Budweiser as its naming rights sponsor. Steve was keen to have Geoff as his driver. 'I'd agreed to do it, all we had to do was sign the papers,' Geoff said. 'But when my name came up, the whole deal came close to being scrapped. Bud wouldn't employ an Australian.' Steve had to secure Scott Pruett instead. The homegrown Californian, 29, won Rookie of the Year. Somewhat ironically Pruett, now in his semi-retirement, has become one of California's better boutique winemakers, not a beer man at all.

The Brabhams and the Boles are good friends. It gets a bit complicated. Doug's wife Beth was formerly married to UK racer Derek Daly and the Dalys were the next-door neighbours of the Brabhams when they lived in Florida. Beth and Roseina rode jet skis together. Not cream-puff rides up the canals: they were doing JetGP—about as serious as outright competition could be. Both had become champions in their categories—Beth standing up, Roseina sitting down. When Beth became Mrs Boles, the friendship continued. 'They come to us for Thanksgiving,' Doug said.

Geoff Brabham rounded out his Indy 500 career driving for the richest man in Wisconsin. John Menard Jnr, a billionaire philanthropist and owner of the Menard chain of home improvement stores, was also in the top 200 of the world's, and top 100 of the United States', wealthiest. But he was on pole in Wisconsin. John had caught the racing bug and had the money—lots of it—to back up his ambition.

'I wasn't really trying to get back into Indy racing. My long-term deal with Nissan in IMSA GTP was working very well,' said Geoff. And there was a parallel series called International Race of Champions (IROC) pitting drivers of all disciplines against each other in identical stock cars. Geoff did well in that, too—he took four wins each on the streets, on the Indy ovals and on the NASCAR bowls.

But he accepted the Menard offer and drove the Lola respectably up through the field until the engine gave out with just 26 laps to go. 'They asked me back the next year at the very last moment, but the car was pushing [understeering] and I couldn't get it up to speed.' His last crack at the Brickyard was also the first in which he did not qualify.

In 1992 Geoff's NPT-21 Nissan sports car flew off the track at Road Atlanta with tyre failure. His teammate Chip Robinson suffered the same fate. It was a turning point for what had until then been a dominant team. Dan Gurney's Toyotas had been pushing them for a season and cracks were showing.

Geoff had a great relationship with Gurney, one-time F1 teammate and employee of his father. The tall American shared some of his adult stories with Geoff, the things that as a kid he'd not seen: 'The middle of the night kerfuffle at the old Nürburgring where the Brabham team thought they'd caught a thief entering their room, until it turned out to be Dan sneaking home just before the dawn of race day; Jack's aircraft overloaded with race car components just struggling airborne; the Fiat Bambino that ended up on the roof of a police van.' It went on.

Gurney was a true innovator. While other IndyCar teams were building ground effects tunnels under their cars, Dan exploited the hurricane of air from the exhausts, which otherwise would be wasted. With typical Gurney humour, he called it BLAT—boundary layer adhesion technology. Geoff drove the BLAT car twice, before it was banned for being too fast. It was

30 years before Dan's idea found its way into Formula One. They banned it there, too.

Geoff had won four IMSA GTP sports-car championships for Nissan; then Gurney countered with a contract with Toyota and brought Geoff's winning streak to an end. Nissan took the opportunity to withdraw while it was still close to the top of the mountain, but Gurney was a victim of his own success. With nothing left to prove and no Nissan to beat, Toyota, too, withdrew its support.

Four years later Geoff joined his younger brother David to win on another mountain—Mount Panorama—where the Brabham boys made their parents proud by bringing their BMW 320i home first in the 2-litre version of the Bathurst 1000.

11

The Man Who Rebuffed
Roger Penske

They were 'overpaid, oversexed and over here'. They were the one million serving members of the United States military who used Australia as their base in World War II. The population of Australia at the time was only seven million so they hardly assimilated. They stood out in word and deed.

The girls loved them; in fact, they were encouraged to do so. In many cases entry to a cinema or a night club was prohibited unless accompanied by a member of the military. Morale was a priority.

At the end of the war, 10,000 Australian war brides, many with infants, shipped out of east coast ports to join their new husbands in the US. It was the largest exodus of women and children in the history of the country. Dennis Firestone, five-time Indianapolis 500 competitor and eight-time aspirant, was among them. He was two years old at the time.

Dennis's mother Paulette had been born in Sydney but moved to Brisbane before the war. She was a seamstress, busily producing uniforms for the Australian war effort. The Americans would not join the war officially until 7 December 1941 when the Japanese raided Pearl Harbor but there was already a plan in place. Australia would be strategically important for the war in the Pacific. Just three weeks after Emperor Hirohito hit the Go button, 45,000 Americans had turned up in Brisbane.

The Americans had chosen Townsville, 1400 kilometres to the north of Brisbane, as the logical staging place for their defensive, hopefully offensive, operations. Townsville, a seaside sugarcane city, nestled under the 280-metre-tall Castle Hill from which you can look out to Magnetic Island and the Great Barrier Reef, had a population of 30,000. That would more than double as 50,000 troops, the majority American, moved in. Townsville was Australia's equivalent of a wild west town.

'My mum became a dancer with the Australian army,' Dennis Firestone said down the phone from his very successful transport company in California. 'My dad was ground support in the air force.' Dennis was born in July 1944. By then hostilities had moved further north, but if you count back some, Paulette Harbulow and Earl Shaughnessy got together right in the thick of it.

The Americans were treating Townsville like an aircraft carrier. They were flying B-17 bombers into the Battle of the Coral Sea, and Curtiss P-40 Warhawk fighters patrolled the seven airfields that made up the Far North Queensland complex. The Japanese bombed Townsville with long-range flying boats based in Rabaul.

Things occasionally went wrong—the US Air Force's 435th squadron mistakenly attacked an Allied naval force including the Australian cruisers *HMAS Australia* and *HMAS Hobart*; fortunately, they missed. The most serious incident, the Townsville Mutiny, an uprising of African-American troops in response to being locked out of Townsville's nightlife by their own comrades, was suppressed under a D-notice and only came to light in 2012. People died that night when Americans turned machine guns on fellow Americans. Future US president Lyndon Baines Johnson, a young congressman at the time, was sent to Townsville to deal with the flak.

When Dennis was born, his dad had moved on, up into Rabaul and beyond, driving the Japanese out of the Pacific. Paulette took the youngster down south, ready to sail to the US to join his dad at war's end. It took a while: 'I was walking before I boarded the ship,' Dennis said. Sydney had a big send-off for its war brides. There was a perception of impropriety; whispers of 'good-time girls' and one-night stands swirled. The Australian government moved to make the war brides heroic. At a ceremony on the lawns of NSW Government House, overlooking Sydney Harbour, in front of assembled newsreel cameras, the young wives and mothers were told they were establishing 'a new bond of kinship'.

They were filmed placing wreaths on the graves of unknown US soldiers at Rookwood cemetery, and there were streamers at the dockside. When they arrived in San Francisco, there were scenes of passionate and happy reunion. But Earl was not there for Paulette and Dennis. 'We caught a bus or a train to San Bernardino, I don't recall which,' Dennis said. 'My parents lived together for some time, but he had someone else in his life and they separated.' No way Paulette was going home—the expectation of coming to the States to start a new life, and the shame of going home, were both too great.

It was a few months later when she met John Firestone and they started dating. John had been a wireless technician on board a US warship and had turned that skill into a thriving business. 'He was quite the businessman,' Dennis said. 'Buying and selling properties.' Dennis took his stepdad's surname.

In his whole life Dennis has been back to Australia just three times. And yet for his entire motor-racing career, he identified as an Australian. Dennis felt it 'added a bit more flavour' to his image. 'I enjoy the fact that I'm not another one of the Andretti boys,' he laughed. 'It's not that I brag about it. It's my heritage. I have an affinity with Australia.'

Dennis became an early achiever. He bought his first truck at eighteen, 'so I could pay the rent', but soon after he bought a specialised furniture-trucking company from an old guy who liked his style. It cost him US$51,000, but the seller only wanted US$8000 for the deposit, and over time Dennis was able to pay off the rest. That business today is worth more than US$75 million and Dennis only recently sold it to his long-time employees.

His motor-racing career spanned just one decade. The father of one of the mechanics in his trucking business built engines for the Indianapolis 500 and that got him interested. 'I'd been desert dirt-bike racing for a while, but I was too aggressive and hurt myself way too often,' Dennis said. So, he went car racing instead.

He won the Sports Car Club of America's Formula Ford runoffs in 1976 against young tearaways including Mike Hull, now president of Chip Ganassi Racing. 'It was the heyday of Formula Ford—120 cars turned up for 36 starting positions.' He dominated the USAC Mini-Indy series, the Formula Super Vees that were the path to Indianapolis. He raced the series for two years, placing second in his first attempt and then winning the following year. In that second year he beat Geoff Brabham. Geoff was third. Mike Chandler, heir to the Buffums Department Store chain and member of a prominent Californian family, was second. All three went on to race Indianapolis.

'We were running the Super Vees as support category to IndyCar and Roger Penske approached me,' Dennis said. 'His son Greg was racing at the time. Roger asked me to take him under my wing, talk to him, give him a bit of advice.' The younger Penske was a competent and enthusiastic driver. In one season alone he would enter 47 races and claim seven podiums. At the last race meeting in the 1979 season, Roger said to Dennis: 'I'd like to talk to you further. Let's see what all this may mean.'

Firestone travelled to Penske's office. 'There was a man called Jack Rhoades with him. I'd never met Jack before,' Dennis recalled. 'Roger said to Jack, "You want to buy one of my Penske PC6 race cars. They're not for sale, but I'll give you the car for a year as long as you use Dennis as your driver. I think he's got talent."'

Rhoades was a true son of Indianapolis—he'd lived there all his life and built multiple businesses, largely in aviation. He'd already rescued several P-51 Mustang fighter planes from the scrap heap and begun their restoration. (Today's starting price for a P-51 is around US$2 million.) He'd entered the Indianapolis 500 with an old McLaren M16 and failed to qualify, but as a big thinker he found his way to Penske.

'He was a redneck,' Firestone said. 'He wanted a speedway driver. But I came with the car.' The deal went ahead. The odd couple 'didn't have a clue' but with a bit of help from Penske they stayed in the top half of the field in the 1980 race until the car expired with transmission failure on the back stretch on lap 137. They were classified sixteenth.

Firestone drove seven championship races for Rhoades that year and earned Rookie of the Year. He was 36, not young, but he was doing well. And he was on Penske's radar.

'Roger sent out a representative to meet me in my truck business office in California,' Dennis said. 'I could tell by his questions that he'd been directed by Roger to discover if I could be a player in his team. He asked me directly: "Are you a racer or a trucker? Would you walk away from trucking and race full-time?" I couldn't turn my back on my business, on everything I'd built, and I answered truthfully, "I'm a trucker." That nixed my future with Roger.'

According to Dennis, an offer was discussed: $70,000 to start and a share of the purse. 'But I wasn't in it for the money. I drove for the fun and the thrill. When you're racing IndyCar you're walking on water. You're next to God. It's something special.'

From that moment on it was tough for Dennis to get decent drives: 'I had this belief in my heart that the day I pulled out a chequebook to pay my own way I would no longer be able to distinguish if I had value as a driver . . . if I was good enough not to have to pay for it. I got good offers but from second-rate teams with two- to three-year-old cars, I scared myself to death.' His best result at Indy was a top ten, his worst a 27th.

In 1986 Dennis had qualified but on Carburetion Day, the final chance to practise on the track for Indy entrants, he hit the inside fence hard. 'It wasn't my fault.' Out of Turn Four onto the main straight, a brake rotor exploded and he skated down the inside wall until the car speared the pit entrance fence. Two mechanics and a spectator were hit, but escaped injury.

The following year would be his last. He would drive for the Raynor Garage Doors Team (later to have as a partner disgraced comedian Bill Cosby) in a Lola T8700—'the car to have that year'.

It was the fifth day of practice and the team had been gathering speed. 'We were in the top three and we were pushing the car away for the day when Mario Andretti, in the same-specification Lola, went faster. The team stopped pushing.' There is a golden rule at Indianapolis. The quick laps are achieved in the main sessions, not in Happy Hour—the twilight session where the track is cooling and the shadows are lengthening. 'We'd promised ourselves we'd never go for it in Happy Hour,' Dennis said. 'But we'd left some speed out there.' The temptation was too great: 'Okay. Let's go for one more round.'

The team worked for two hours, one corner of the car at a time, to get the suspension right. It was 5.10 p.m. and Nigel Bennett, the designer of the Lola IndyCar, sensed what was going to happen. 'He straddled the car as I was being strapped in and said, "You don't have to do this." I said, "It's absolutely perfect; watch me." He backed away.'

Dennis did three flying laps—it was only practice, not qualifying, but each lap he was 200 rpm up on his earlier runs and then on the back straight he was 400 rpm up. Increased engine revolutions equate to more speed. 'Holy shit,' he thought. 'This will be an outstanding, incredible lap.' He came through Turn Three flat but on the short straight up to Turn Four the car was caught in a small crosswind. 'I took myself down low to compensate so I could take Turn Four flat. I was under the white line.' The team has already written 220 mph (354 km/h) on their pit board in anticipation—that would be 2 mph (3.2 km/h) faster than Andretti, the fastest lap of the day. But he never saw the board. The car switched ends through Turn Four and went backwards into the wall. It would have been doing 200 mph (321 km/h) on impact. He broke bones in his left foot and fractured his left leg.

In Methodist Hospital, Dennis asked his team, 'What do we do now?'

The speedway's doctor Terry Trammell volunteered an option: he could put the leg in a cast but, 'If I pin him, I could probably have him in a car in a week.'

Raynor's management said, 'Buy another car.'

Exactly ten days after the crash Firestone was back at the speedway on crutches, his leg pinned.

'I had no business going back, but I did. I started out slowly and carefully, just 208 mph [334 km/h] on the first day. Pole was at 215 mph [345 km/h] and the slowest car in the field was 202 mph [325 km/h] so even with a broken leg I was in the middle of the pack.'

But the team 'had a little surprise' for Dennis: 'They'd used last year's wheels and machined a little off them to make them as good as the wheels I'd been on.' Into Turn Four a wheel broke and 'BANG—I backed into the wall, just like before. The lights went out.'

A race driver is strapped in so tightly he becomes one with the car. There is no torso movement at all; it's safest that way. Dennis wasn't strapped in to that degree: 'I'd left my belts just a little bit loose, because of my leg, so I could reach the clutch.'

Firestone suffered spinal damage: 'Dr Trammell said, "Don't ever think of getting in a race car again, there's far too much risk." I was 43 years old,' Dennis said. 'If I'd been 21 maybe I would have made a different call. But who was I kidding? I made my decision right there in the hospital bed. I had other priorities.'

Dennis has three daughters and six grandchildren. When he plays golf, he doesn't have the mobility he'd like and it's difficult for him to turn his head. Recently he bought a vintage racing car, a Formula Ford like the one that started his career: 'But I don't race it. I just do fast laps.'

He has remained good friends with Geoff Brabham. Dennis's daughter Shannda is part of the jet-ski racing fraternity and she races against Roseina Brabham and Beth Boles. 'It's been a good life,' Dennis said. The business, his other career, has been good to him. 'You become an old racing car driver—what are you then?' he asked philosophically.

12

The Civil War

Tony George, son of Tony Hulman, and third-generation owner of the Indianapolis Motor Speedway and the Indianapolis 500, knew in his heart he had to do it—unleash the boldest move he'd ever make to protect his family's speedway from vested interests that wanted to manipulate it for their own gain. It was akin to the American Civil War. What beliefs did you stand for? What vision did you believe in?

George, a mild-mannered man, uncomfortable in the company of strangers, according to his friends largely misunderstood, declared that his family was asserting its control. The Indy 500 was the jewel in the crown of US open-wheeler racing: it had a value, historically, commercially and emotionally, that made it the lynchpin of any ambition that a team held to go racing Stateside. And he owned it.

On 23 January 1995, at Walt Disney World in Florida—ironically in the Magic Kingdom portion of the park—George's newly formed Indy Racing League (IRL) announced its rules of engagement. From 1996 onwards, the Indianapolis 500 would be open to all-comers, but 25 places on its 33-car grid would be reserved for members of the IRL. Anyone who chose to remain outside the new tent George had erected could fight for the rest. It became known as the 25/8 Rule.

It was a stand worthy of Carl G. Fisher, and especially of his successor Eddie Rickenbacker who in 1933 stared down a drivers' strike one hour before race start. That stand-off was sparked by the Brickyard's refusal to let a driver compete on medical grounds, but it was exacerbated by a multitude of factors—reduced prize money in the Great Depression and changes to qualification rules. Rickenbacker wouldn't relent. If the majority of drivers didn't get in their cars and race, he'd simply lock the gates and walk away. They raced. You either loved the Brickyard or you didn't.

George's pronouncement sparked outrage. And it created opportunity for the stock-car racing NASCAR community to seize an ascendancy that IndyCar has not clawed back even a quarter of a century on. The first IRL championship to be held in 1996, George announced, would occur over just five oval-track race meetings (two would be postponed to the 1997 title)—but its grand finale would be the Indy 500. And no promoter of any other series could match that.

The motorsport civil war raged for more than a decade and created confusion that damaged the franchise.

Someone, somewhere in a war room, had an idea of what was going on, but the fans didn't. All they could see was mayhem.

'The problem is that George had no one to lean on; no one to tell him the truth.' Robin Miller was keen to tell it as he saw it. Miller, a journalist and commentator, was ultimately one of the casualties of the civil war. He lost his job on *The Indianapolis Star* after 33 years of covering the 500 because, he claims, he was seen as staunchly anti-IRL.

'One of the biggest influencers in Tony making the decision was Bill France Junior—the boss of NASCAR,' Miller said. 'Bill played Tony.' History shows that NASCAR benefited hugely when the open-wheeler series lost direction. Their fan base migrated and to a degree so did the commercial support. 'Bernie Ecclestone played him too.' In his quest to make the Brickyard more globally relevant, George came to terms with Ecclestone to run Formula One racing at the speedway (eight times from 2000).

'George spent $70 million on a new road course, new facilities,' Miller alleged. 'And then Ecclestone raised his sanction fee so high it made continuation impossible.' The pits built by the speedway for Formula One are not used by today's Indy 500 racers. They still push their cars out of Gasoline Alley and work from temporary pit pods in front of the F1 structure.

In 1902, the American Automobile Association became the peak body representing the customers of the burgeoning US motor industry. The AAA was the motorist's friend, providing roadside assistance, maps, even teaching driving etiquette.

In 1904 it became the sanctioning body for motorsport including, from its inception, the Indianapolis 500. The AAA provided the rules of competition and enforced them through inevitable howls of protest.

Half a century later the AAA cried enough. The 1955 Le Mans 24 Hour catastrophe in which more than 80 perished, and the deaths of Bill Vukovich at Indianapolis and Alberto Ascari at Monza within four days of each other had exposed its vulnerability. The AAA wanted nothing to do with a lethal sport that was, at best, a sidebar to its core business of caring for 60 million American motorists.

In response, Tony Hulman, owner of Indianapolis Motor Speedway, set up the United States Auto Club (USAC), starting in 1956. It neatly headed off suggestions that either the Sports Car Club of America (SCCA) or the National Association for Stock Car Auto Racing (NASCAR) should become the pre-eminent administrator. Hulman's USAC provided an umbrella for smaller promoters. It created the USAC National Championship Trail, a title scored across dirt and paved ovals, one occasional hill climb (Pikes Peak), and later road circuits. A national champion was crowned each year. The USAC promoter's cooperative was making a heap of money for the tracks, but not for those who competed on them. Dan Gurney became the competitors' voice.

On 27 October 1977 Tony Hulman died of a heart attack. He was 76 and he'd been honoured that year when four-time Indy 500 winner A.J. Foyt had insisted he join him on his victory lap. No one had done that for the promoter before. Then, on 23 April 1978, a plane crash killed seven USAC officials on their way home to Indianapolis and served to weaken the organisation. It would be distasteful and disrespectful to suggest either was a major factor in what happened next.

In 1978 Dan Gurney wrote what has become enshrined as the Gurney White Paper. It was a call to arms to team owners and their commercial partners to seek equitable treatment from USAC: 'We the car owners are the ones who have put forth by far the most effort, by far the most commercial stake, with little or no chance for return. We have let the track owners, or the promoters and the sanctioning body lead us around by the nose while they reap the benefits.'

The concept was not unique to the USA: Bernie Ecclestone broke the track owners' stranglehold in F1, and in Australia the fighting, spitting rock music impresario Tony Cochrane did the same for what became V8 Supercars.

Gurney's white paper had struck a chord.

On 30 November 1978, Championship Auto Racing Teams (CART) was formed by the team owners to work with USAC to mutual benefit, but USAC rejected the offer of collaboration. CART determined to go it alone. If Tony George's declaration almost twenty years later was the Civil War, this was the War of Independence. CART would run races in opposition to the USAC promoters but of course it still wanted to race at Indianapolis. There was no racing without Indy. It took a court order to make that happen.

CART rebranded its race series as IndyCar. It was a smart idea, adopting the name that the cars had been known by pretty much since Carl Fisher turned the first sod at the Brickyard. 'Indy' was at the heart of all that they did. They started the IndyCar World Series. It was hardly global—but they did eventually race in Canada, Brazil and Japan as well as Australia.

In 1991 they ran an international race at Surfers Paradise, won by John Andretti. The popular Gold Coast Indy 300 was also won by world champions Nigel Mansell and Emerson Fittipaldi: a bit confusing for the Australian fans—'I thought they were F1'—but not so much for the US cognoscenti who'd become used to Lotus, McLaren and Brabham invading Indianapolis. But they were racing in the right place; the Gold Coast, with its heady high-rise mix of sun and surf with a little bit of sin thrown in, was the ideal location for a car race.

Australia fell in love with IndyCar racing, and welcomed it back for seventeen years at some cost to the Queensland state government (A\$217 million, according to a report, with an economic benefit of A\$750 million). The last race, a non-championship points-scoring 'demonstration' in 2008, was the first won by an Australian, Ryan Briscoe.

Dan Gurney made a prescient remark in his white paper: 'Many of the car owners and team directors are excellent businessmen in their own lives outside of racing . . . but we are so intent on racing each other that we do not stop to look and analyze our own situation.' He was spot on.

No one was paying attention. They were fighting each other on and off the track. The cohesion necessary to make the great idea work was missing. Costs were escalating, and rules were blurring, creating opportunity for those who wanted to exploit them. There were allegations of CART being elitist, serving the interests of the most powerful teams. And there was the ever-present fear that the one race that really mattered—the Indy 500—could be taken away on the whim of one man.

In 1992 CART strategically decided to welcome Tony George to come to their board meetings as an observer; better to have him with them than against them. It didn't go well. He was, according to the team owners, petulant, and they were puzzled by his behaviour. Perhaps, they speculated, he was out of his depth. Or perhaps he was being guarded.

Tony George left the board of CART in 1994. He thought about all he'd seen, then acted with his Disney World pronouncement.

'He f—d up America's greatest race. He bought a bunch of donkeys and mules to the Kentucky Derby.' Robin Miller, with some passion even after all these years and speaking like it was yesterday, was referring to the 1996 Indianapolis 500.

CART elected to stay away (although as businessmen they were quite comfortable to sell their redundant equipment to struggling teams that did turn up). The 25/8 Rule, they said, was a lockout. Instead, on the very same day as the Indy 500, they ran the US 500 at Michigan International Speedway—a 2-mile (3.2-kilometre) oval shaped like the letter 'D'. A lot of mud was slung. Indy had year-old cars, seventeen rookie drivers—the greatest number of first-timers since 1919—and even Danny Ongais had been brought back after ten years to fill out the field. Buddy Lazier, who'd failed to qualify four years out of six attempts, was the winner. Up the road in Michigan, eventual winner Jimmy Vasser and Adrian Fernandez made contact on the warm-up lap and precipitated an eight-car crash, bringing out the red flag and causing a one-hour start delay. 'Who needs milk?' Vasser said when he stepped from his winning car.

On both sides there was a lot of PR spin needed to convince the fans, and the sponsors, that they knew what they were doing. Obviously, CART could not continue to use the IndyCar moniker so it rebranded again—this time as Champ Car. On the technical, rule-making side, the IRL fired USAC: 'A lot of Tony George's guys [USAC] were completely incompetent,' Lee Dykstra, who was CART's technical chief for four years from 2003, told me during our interview in Indianapolis.

Champ Car (CART), owned by the teams, went to the public for additional funds. A stock market issue of 35 per cent of its shares raised US$100 million. The IRL, steeped in tradition and old money, didn't need to do that. Robin Miller estimated that the Hulman-George family tipped in $700 million during the civil war. But then he quickly added that Tony's sisters refuted the claim: 'We didn't see Robin Miller at any of our board meetings,' he claims they said to him.

No civil war can sustain itself forever. Brother against brother will always crumble under reassessment of true beliefs. From the outset, Tony George had offered CART teams the option of competing in IRL races and they began to do so. TV coverage was the catalyst. While the IRL could make money from its TV contracts, CART had to pay the TV companies to turn up. In 2002 Chip Ganassi crossed over to IRL and brought his department store backer, Target, with him. Roger Penske followed. The sport's most prominent influencer, who would become the most successful IndyCar team owner of all time, committed to IRL and brought his hugely important tobacco company sponsor with him. The sponsors wanted the coverage TV could provide. In 2003 CART declared itself bankrupt. The civil war—so intense and so introspective—had ignored the harm it was creating in the motorsport community. It was its own biggest loser.

But it had drawn a line under one era of the Indianapolis 500 and opened another. The Brickyard was ready to build a new breed of champions. Drivers from Australia and New Zealand would stake their claim for the greatest prize of all. Two, Scott Dixon and Will Power, separated by a full decade, would be the biggest winners.

13

The Groomsman

Young Ryan Briscoe, with tightly curled blond hair and boy-band looks, was the very model of a 'groomed' racing driver. He was plucked from an Italian kart track by a talent scout for the world's best-funded Formula One team and placed in a development program on a trajectory to the world championship. They taught him to act, think and speak like a racing driver. They taught him Italian and French and the etiquette of media engagement. They took over development of his still-maturing physique so that his muscle progression would be in tune with the demands of a high-powered Formula car. They entered him in nursery championships—still blindingly fast—and coached him on how to win. He repaid them by becoming champion of the first two series he entered.

They made him their F1 development driver and they plastered an immense vinyl picture of him—ten metres tall—across the windows of their European headquarters. They brought him right to the peak of his potential. And then they let him go.

Ryan was a boy from Beecroft in Sydney's Hills District, and he travelled each day to Trinity Grammar School, close to the city's edge, because it was an International Baccalaureate affiliate and Ryan had a bit of a brain. In Sydney it mattered where you went to school. In that city's social scene, it's part of the ritual of introduction.

But Ryan wasn't there long. His dad Geoff was a motor dealer and a handy rally driver—consistently in the top half-dozen in the state championship. Like Saturday afternoon sailing on Sydney Harbour or weekend golf, rallying fails the family-friendly test. Geoff sold the rally car and took Ryan karting instead.

'He was eleven and we had no idea what we were doing,' Geoff said. 'We bought a senior kart and it was far too large and heavy for him and no matter how much he tried he seemed to be locked into coming fifth.' Then they bought a smaller Ryan-sized kart, a lightweight Dino, and at his first race meeting at far-flung Lithgow over the Blue Mountains 'he passed the four cars in front of him down the hill and romped away with the race'.

Karting is a huge talent pool. The Italian team Tony Kart discovered Ryan at an international race in Sydney: 'This huge crate arrived at our office, and it was full of free karts,' Geoff said. But it was rival CRG that asked him to race, full-time in Italy. Ryan was fifteen.

Ryan's parents established the ground rules—their son would

live in the home of one of the team's principals, Giancarlo Tinini, and he'd treat Ryan like family. But when others in the team were provided with better tyres and after two years they didn't pay him (Tinini countered that Ryan was being rewarded in experience), he moved to Tony Kart. It was a step up: 'We did debrief sheets like we do now in IndyCar,' Ryan said. And it was Tony Kart's principal Roberto Robazzi who told his friend Ange Pasquali about this kid who had the right stuff.

Pasquali had recently joined Toyota in its Formula One start-up. In the first decade of the new millennium, Toyota would become the top-spending outfit in the world championship; a shame it didn't reap commensurate results.

'I got a phone call one night from Ryan, saying, "Dad, there's this guy who wants to test me in a car,"' Geoff said. It was very secretive. Ryan and several other hopefuls had to sign a non-disclosure agreement. They went to Autodrome dell'Umbria, a tight 2.4-km track outside Perugia in Central Italy. From there fewer aspirants, survivors of the weeding process, moved to the A1-Ring, now the F1 Red Bull Ring, in Austria. And after the test was over, they asked Ryan to stay back.

'They came to me with a seven-year contract with each stage of my progression mapped out. There was a four-year path to F1 and there were millions of dollars to be earned,' Ryan said. He was nineteen. The offer left the teenager with a moral dilemma. There were people who'd helped his career and, right up to Robazzi, they made it clear they deserved some of the windfall. Pasquali headed it off. He introduced Ryan to his friend Max Angelelli, a driver manager and a handy steerer himself. Australian IndyCar commentator Leigh Diffey later nicknamed Max 'The Axe'. And Max lived up to his name.

Toyota's F1 headquarters in Cologne, Germany, was testament to the wealth of the corporation. At the time there was no better facility in Formula One. Toyota Team Europe had been developed by Swedish rally driver Ove Andersson who'd shown confidence in the Japanese brand when no one else did, and he'd built a rally team on the back of that faith. He'd won the 1993, 1994 and 1999 World Rally Championships for them. When they bought his business, he stayed on as president to lead them into Formula One. Cologne became the biggest bunker in motorsport; massive corridors led to secret places where all the development, fabrication and testing were done in-house. Andersson was well respected in the world of motorsport: they called him 'Påven'—the Pope.

Andersson had a great affinity with Australia and Australians. He'd come within one night and 600 kilometres of winning the 1968 London–Sydney Marathon, sharing the driving with Roger Clark. His Celica GT-4 had won Rally Australia twice with Juha Kankkunen and whenever he visited the country he'd turn off his mobile phone and spend two days driving the winding, picturesque coast road from Melbourne to Sydney to escape from the world.

He took on Ryan as a great personal responsibility. These days most of the big teams are Formula One factories for drivers. Young hopefuls are fortunate to get in and equally fortunate to emerge with their careers and self-esteem intact. It's brutal, survival of the fittest. Teams can afford to churn and burn when there's such a huge catchment of talent.

Andersson and Angelelli placed Ryan with Dr Riccardo

Cicarelli, a specialist sports physician with a clinic at Viareggio, a quaint, canalled seaside village just south of Italy's Cinque Terre. Cicarelli challenged and supported the youngster, providing a balanced environment that was intense but not severe. He went to school, learned languages, developed specific strengths, got his mind around the demands of competition.

Pasquali arranged races. There was no holding back. Toyota contracted Angelo Rosin's Prema Powerteam, one of the best young driver development operations in the world, to give Briscoe the skills. Toyota's investment in Briscoe's racing alone over three years was conservatively estimated at A$2 million. Briscoe won the Italian Formula Renault 2000 Championship—five wins and seven podiums out of ten starts. He won the Formula Three Euro Series—eight wins and ten podiums from twenty starts.

Andersson inserted Briscoe into Formula One early, ahead of the plan. He had counselled Toyota that it was best to enter F1 without making major promises or to hold great immediate hopes, and to build to a fully competitive stance over a period. That meant bringing in safe, reliable drivers to begin with, not stars: Mika Salo who'd driven with Ferrari, Tyrrell and Sauber; and Allan McNish, who'd been part of Toyota's sports-car program. Andersson had determined the team would grow its own stars. Ryan was the chosen one. He did a lot of laps in the test car, the TF101. It was a sensational opportunity to build confidence and speed, working with Salo and McNish.

The Påven preached patience to his masters in Japan, but when on the F1 team's debut in the 2002 Australian Grand Prix, Salo came sixth and earned a single world championship point, the sermon fell on increasingly deaf ears, replaced by an urgent weight of expectation. When the car went no better for the rest of the season, the drivers were replaced; and when the new drivers did only a little better, Andersson was replaced.

A system of consensus was introduced into the team's management. History proves corporations don't run great race teams—but Toyota had not yet discovered that. The vibe in Cologne was different to the Andersson era's. Ange Pasquali lost his job—and later earned a judgement of unfair dismissal in a German court. And Ryan Briscoe, despite his best efforts, was increasingly taking on the look of Tonto without the Lone Ranger to lead the way.

In 2004 Toyota determined that it needed star drivers to guide it to victory. It hired Jarno Trulli and Ralf Schumacher for the 2005 season. It was year four of Briscoe's Toyota plan and he was still third driver, not likely to face the starter except in exceptional circumstances; not what he'd been promised.

There was a chance of moving to Jordan F1, but they needed him to bring money and that was not Briscoe's style. 'Once you bring money to a race team, that's what will be expected of you forever,' Angelelli told him.

Geoff Briscoe recalled: 'I got a call from Ryan and he said he was contemplating going to the States. "Not the ovals," I responded. I was aghast. I'd watched him at high speeds in strange places, but the ovals are dangerous.'

'Well,' his son replied, 'there's nothing for me here.'

It was such a waste, made more so because just three years later Ove Andersson was dead. With his Toyota payout he'd bought a share in a game reserve in South Africa. He loved elephants. He was driving an historic Volvo—Swedish after all—in a fun rally and a bus hit him head-on. The steering column wasn't the collapsible kind and it pierced his chest.

'IndyCar was like a breath of fresh air, so good,' Ryan told me. 'The politics in F1 were overwhelming. You'd walk into an F1 pit and you wouldn't be game to look left or right; not know who to talk to. Indy was just so welcoming—the team, the drivers, even the other teams.' He had lost the golden curls and there were a few laugh lines around the eyes, but his boyish enthusiasm, bordering on innocence, still shone through. We were standing around the big island kitchen bar of his lovely two-storey-plus-cellar home outside Hartford, Connecticut, his two beautiful daughters playing in the family room, and his wife Nicole, a popular sports presenter on ESPN, dialled into the conversation. Outside, a bobcat was ready to dig the hole for the new family swimming pool for the upcoming summer. Connecticut, north of New York, is a long way from IndyCar central but they live there because ESPN's studio is just up the road. Nicole needs to be there daily. Ryan can commute to his racing.

As soon as Ryan landed in the States, he joined top-ranking IndyCar team Chip Ganassi Racing. It was a third-car deal, made sensible because for the first time the IRL was running its series on road courses as well as ovals—and Ryan's road course experience was exemplary. 'I learned later that Kinoshita-san had supported the move,' Ryan said. Yoshiaki Kinoshita was executive vice-president of Toyota Motorsport and Ganassi was using his engines. Ryan had left F1 on good terms, it seemed, with his reputation intact. (Perhaps Toyota was even a little embarrassed.)

Ganassi was a multi-series team. Ryan's first drive for them wasn't in Indy but in sports cars. He came seventh for Ganassi in the Daytona 24 Hour, co-driving with Scott Pruett, in a Lexus-powered Riley chassis. His manager Max Angelelli won the race.

But in IndyCar the Toyota engines were down on power. 'We were doing some crazy things, trimming the cars out to try and get more top-line speed at the cost of grip and handling,' Ryan said. The situation was exacerbated because rival Roger Penske was also running Toyota engines and doing better. 'Penske was having their engines built by Ilmore Engineering [a Penske-owned company]. Ours came straight out of the crate.'

Indianapolis was 'immense'. For the first time Briscoe understood its importance. 'Honestly, I'd not grown up with Indianapolis as a priority. I was about F1. But to see it on race day, it's incredible. I don't get emotional in a race car, but it gave me butterflies. I realised I was grateful to be there.'

Turn One was 'the scariest corner in the world. Wind direction determines how you're going to take it and you just look at the flags flying to see where the wind is coming from.' It's no more sophisticated than that.

'In 2005 qualifying, it was easy to go flat at Indy,' Ryan said. Lack of power determined that. But as the team continued to trim out the aerodynamics in search of more speed, it became 'a bit like a high jump competition in track and field, where you keep raising the bar until you can't get over it anymore'. Briscoe qualified 24th, splitting his two teammates Scott Dixon and Darren Manning. They were within 1.3 mph (2.09 km/h) of each other, and Ryan averaged 224.08 mph (360.54 km/h). Briscoe was the only one of the three to finish, tenth, a lap down on the winner, British driver Dan Wheldon. But he didn't get Rookie of the Year. That went to Danica Patrick, placed fourth in front of him.

'That year, I was fearless, trying to get pole every single race, setting up the car to be loose because that's the fastest way around,' Ryan said. He was crashing 'a lot'. The ovals held no great fear for him, but Ryan's inexperience showed. He'd spent his racing life—from karts onwards—in a bubble. If something went wrong, there was money to fix it. Chip Ganassi was the son of a successful businessman and he was fast following in his dad's footsteps. He ran the race team very personally, counting the dollars. It was new territory for Briscoe. 'Mid-season there was a big meeting and we were told, "There's too much crash damage."' Darren Manning was released from his contract.

Around the kitchen table, Briscoe was caught up in his own introspection, because he knew what he was about to introduce into the conversation: the crash that changed his life.

It was Chicagoland, the fast 1.52-mile (2.44-kilometre) tri-oval built as a joint venture only four years before by Tony George and Bill France Jnr. 'I got pole,' Ryan said. 'But the pole was taken away. The team was attempting every possible innovation to claw back our speed deficit. We'd fitted a device to hold the wing down, but it was deemed illegal. As punishment, I had to start from the back of the field.'

Geoff Briscoe got the call at home in Sydney at around 5 a.m. It was a woman from the Ganassi team. 'Ryan's okay, but he's had a bad wreck,' she said. Local TV crews were knocking on the Briscoes' door soon after. The crash—full of fire and vertical lift, caught on multiple cameras—was one of those that will be replayed forevermore.

'I'm not religious but I was thinking, please God make this stop,' Ryan said. He had been low on the track going for the corner and Alex Barron, an Indy Rookie of the Year, dropped down on his line. Briscoe's car touched the left rear of Barron's and then flew over the top, gaining altitude. It slammed into the 'SAFER' barrier, a uniquely Indy invention to absorb impact energy, and then up into the catch fencing where it separated into three pieces like *Apollo 11* losing its boosters. Its fuel cells exploded, releasing a firestorm that lasted only two seconds but looked like *Saturn V*'s lift-off.

'I blacked out and then found marshals all around me. The first thing I did was wriggle my toes to make sure I wasn't paralysed, but my back was killing me. They put me on a stretcher and as we moved to the ambulance they said, "Wave to the crowd, let them know you're alright."' The video shows Ryan raising his left arm for a moment, difficult since it was broken.

They took him to Methodist Hospital in Indianapolis—200 miles (321 kilometres) away: 'the most painful ride of my life', but it was the IRL's trauma centre of choice. Ryan's mum, Marion, got on a plane and was there in 24 hours.

Ryan didn't race again that year. 'Some people had lots of doubts if I'd return,' he said. Ganassi didn't renew him for 2006. 'It wasn't that they said they weren't going to keep me. They simply employed Dan Wheldon.'

He went to Italy so Dr Cicarelli could put him back together. And as he was walking down a pit lane, on display, gun for hire, pit reporter Nicole Manske exclaimed: 'You're alive.' They married four years later.

Ryan took odd-job rides—sports cars; a doomed one-make global open-wheeler championship called A1GP ('and it took six months to get paid'); even the Holden Racing Team in Australia. The most important gig was with IndyCar race team Dreyer and Reinbold. They got him back on the horse: 'I was terrified. I wasn't sure I could do it.' It took only four laps for him to get up to speed, and he found he had a new maturity. 'I didn't measure how I was going in time—it was all about how comfortable I felt,' Ryan said. He gave the team a podium at the Watkins Glen road circuit—their only one of the year. Then Roger Penske came calling. The meeting was set up by Max Angelelli and his business partner, racer and sports-car team owner Wayne Taylor. 'The Penske organisation wanted to talk to me about driving their sports cars.'

Penske sent a private jet to pick up Briscoe for the Detroit meeting. It's bound to impress. 'We were sitting in the meeting, myself, Roger [some call him that, most say Mister], his president of motor racing Tim Cindric and business advisors,' Ryan recalled. 'They outlined an upcoming Porsche program for the American Le Mans Series. Penske would run the team, I would sign a contract directly with Porsche. Then Roger said, out of the blue, "We should run Ryan in the Indianapolis 500 next year." Tim Cindric's face went white. You could tell he was thinking, "How are we going to do that?"'

There's always a way. Penske does things on a grand scale. Its motor-racing workshop in Mooresville, North Carolina, is impressive on a Toyota Motorsport level. It has more than 40,000 square metres of floorspace laid with off-white Italian tile. A Zamboni ice-hockey resurfacing machine, like they use in match breaks to repair the playing field, is in constant motion keeping the tiles clean. It must have been a back-to-the-future feeling for Ryan. Penske gave him a home just like he'd known.

Except they were now using Honda engines. Toyota had withdrawn, hurt.

Roger's son Jay had set up Dragon Racing within the Penske organisation. Ryan would drive that car. 'It was 100 per cent Penske car, leased from the organisation,' he said. There was a stipulation: Penske was running two works cars for past winner Hélio Castroneves and defending champion Sam Hornish Jnr. 'We were to help them, even get out of their way if they came up to pass.' It worked as if it were well scripted. Rain would stop the race short on lap 166. 'They'd both overtaken me just before the red flag came out,' Ryan said. Castroneves would place third, Hornish fourth and Briscoe fifth separated by just 3.5 seconds. Briscoe's performance and his discipline had been impressive. Next year he was elevated to the works team.

'There was a feeling of "Wow, I've made it",' he said. 'An appreciation of what it means to be a Penske driver. I'd walk down the pit lane in those iconic colours and every driver there wanted to be me.'

Over five seasons Briscoe would claim seven IndyCar wins for Penske and stand on the podium for the team on 22 occasions. But he would not win at Indianapolis, and he would not win an IndyCar Series. Roger Penske, so hands-on, would pay Ryan the honour of being his race strategist—in his ear constantly during the race, driving by remote control. 'Roger hated saving fuel. He always wanted me to be flat out. It was occasionally frustrating. There were races in which I could have done better, but he'd tell me to go rich [use a more volatile fuel mix]. I'd never argue.'

There were incredibly good times. Briscoe won the Milwaukee Mile—his first victory in IndyCar—clocking up

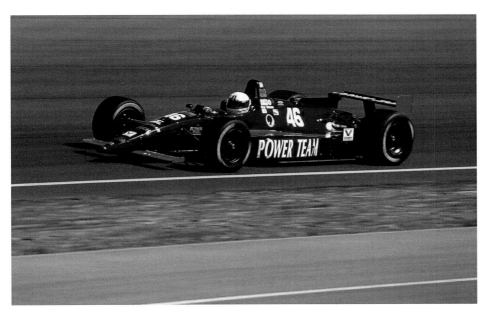

Auckland's Rob Wilson struggled to keep his one and only Indy ride on track in 1996 practice. According to A.J. Foyt, the evil-handling car's failure to qualify 'saved Wilson's life'. (IMS)

'Get after 'em' was Jack Brabham's (left) advice to all aspiring racing drivers, including young Rob Wilson (right).
(New Zealand Classic Driver)

Rob Wilson runs a bespoke race-driver school helping the sport's top talents come to terms with 'transient harmonics'—the art of throttle-weight transfer. (IMS)

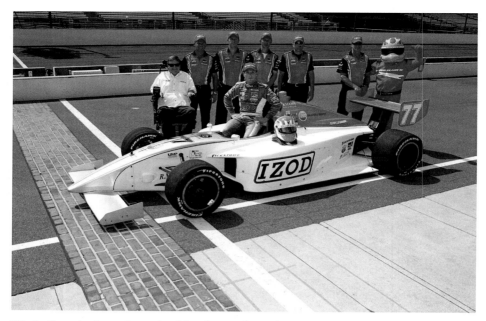

Wade Cunningham from Auckland won the Indy Lights Freedom 100 at the Indianapolis Motor Speedway an unprecedented three times, twice racing for former driver Sam Schmidt (far left). (IMS)

In 2011, Wade Cunningham (in the red car) was part of the fifteen-car pack-racing pile-up at Las Vegas Motor Speedway, which launched twice Indy 500 winner Dan Wheldon (no. 77) into his fatal impact with the catch fencing. (Shutterstock)

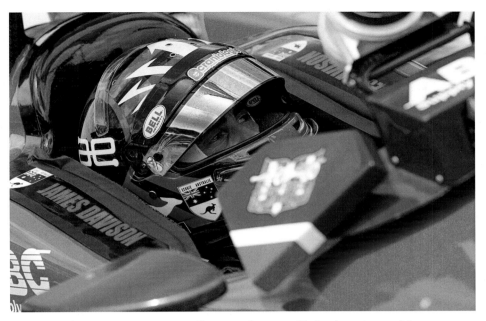

Melbourne's James Davison proudly wears his grandfather's racing emblem Ecurie Australie on his helmet and his cockpit cover. Lex Davison was a four-time Australian Grand Prix winner. (IMS)

James Davison powers out of the Indianapolis pits in 2015 in a Dale Coyne car funded in part by connections of the late Paul Walker, star of the *Fast and the Furious* movie series. Davison started 30th and was classified 27th. (IMS)

Matthew Brabham (left) and his mentors, father Geoffrey (centre) and Brett 'Crusher' Murray (right), who brought a third generation of Australia's most successful racing family to the Indy grid. (BAM Media)

For this epic PR picture, Crusher secured three generations of Brabham cars: Sir Jack's 1961 Cooper Climax Kimberly Special, which finished ninth; Geoffrey's 1985 March Cosworth, which came 19th; and Matthew's Pirtek Dallara DW12. (BAM Media)

Matthew Brabham brought his car home 22nd in the Indianapolis 500 and put his and Crusher's names in the record books. (BAM Media)

Back home in Indiana: Matthew Brabham and his partner Kimberly Bogle in their condo at Clearwater Cove, north of Indianapolis. Sir Jack is ever-present over Matt's shoulder. (John Smailes)

The largest sporting crowd in the world. Indianapolis Motor Speedway has seating capacity of more than a quarter of a million people. Drivers say the full stands change wind flow and alter car handling into Turn One. (IMS)

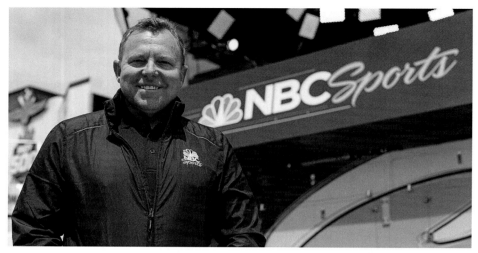

In 2019 Brisbane's Leigh Diffey became the first non-US-born commentator to call play-by-play for the Indianapolis 500. (IMS)

Robin Miller, one of the Indianapolis 500's most ardent supporters and at times most outspoken critics. (IMS)

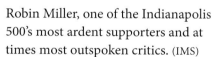

In 2020 motor-racing billionaire Roger Penske (left) bought the Indianapolis Motor Speedway and the Indy Racing League from Tony George (right). (IMS)

Australia's twice world MotoGP champion Casey Stoner won the Indianapolis MotoGP in 2011 and crashed in practice in 2012, finishing fourth in a heroic ride. (IMS)

Tasmanian Marcos Ambrose, the only Australian ever to win NASCAR Sprint Cup rounds, competed seven times at Indianapolis. (IMS)

Mother of Matthew and wife of Geoffrey, Roseina Brabham is a multiple jet ski champion, competing against Beth Boles, wife of Indianapolis Motor Speedway president Doug and mother of Indy 500 competitor Conor Daly. (Geoff Brabham Collection)

In 2008 Scott Dixon (Target Chip Ganassi) and Ryan Briscoe (Team Penske) shared the front row start with Dan Wheldon (Target Chip Ganassi). Dixon took the lead from Wheldon with Briscoe tucked in behind. (IMS)

Winner Scott Dixon drove a perfectly judged race in 2008. Including his pole position, he claimed a total purse of US$2,988,065. (IMS)

Dixon was made a Member of the New Zealand Order of Merit (upgraded to Companion in 2019) and named New Zealand's Sportsman of the Year—an honour he earned again in 2013. (IMS)

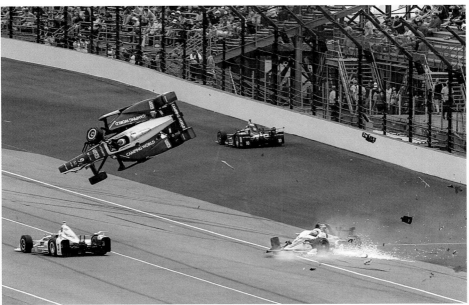

Two forms of Indy flight: Matt Hall in the Red Bull Air Race, held within the infield, and Scott Dixon's massive 2017 aerobatics. (*Top*: Red Bull Content Pool; *Bottom*: Brady Whitesel)

Indy 500 winners drink milk, a tradition since 1956, but in the Indy Racing League championship Scott Dixon (left) and engineer Blair Julian, also a Kiwi, have access to champagne. (Chip Ganassi Racing)

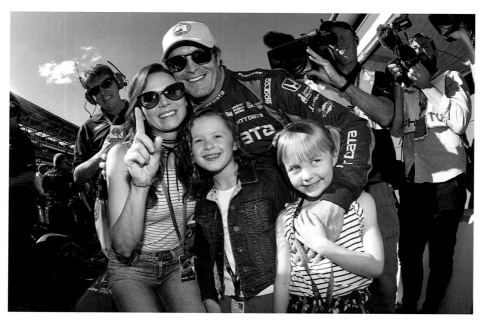

Scott Dixon's tight-knit family: wife Emma and daughters Poppy and Tilly were joined by son Kit in December 2019. The Dixons have become motor-racing royalty in the US. (IMS)

Scott Dixon (left) is one of the original members of Jim Leo's specialist training facility PitFit in Indianapolis.
(John Smailes)

In 2019, Scott Dixon had raced with Chip Ganassi for an unprecedented eighteen years. He had outlasted and, with very few exceptions, outdriven a chain of teammates.
(Chip Ganassi Racing)

The Ganassi–Dixon partnership netted a record five Indy Racing League titles between 2003 and 2018.
(Chip Ganassi Racing)

Scott Dixon and Chip Ganassi: 'I tell Chip that he pays me to do media. I do the driving for free,' says Dixon.
(Chip Ganassi Racing)

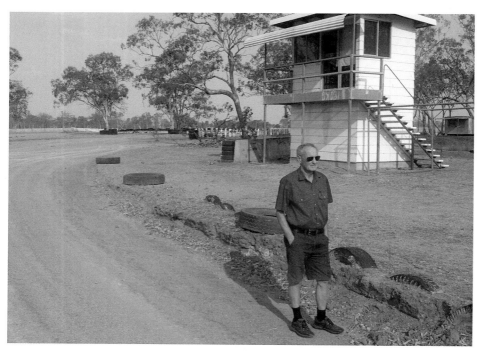

Where it started: Bob Power, father of Will, stands on the main straight of Millmerran Raceway on the Darling Downs, Queensland, where his seventeen-year-old son won his first 'major' race, the Millmerran 100. (John Smailes)

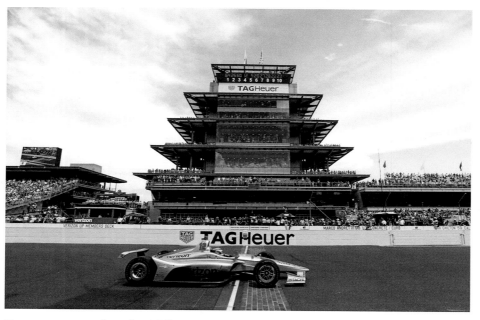

Twenty years on from his Millmerran victory, Will Power crosses the Yard of Bricks in 2018 to become the first Australian to win the Indianapolis 500. (IMS)

Indy 500 winner Will Power, congratulated by Penske Racing president Tim Cindric (left) and Roger Penske. Power delivered Team Penske its seventeenth Indianapolis victory. (IMS)

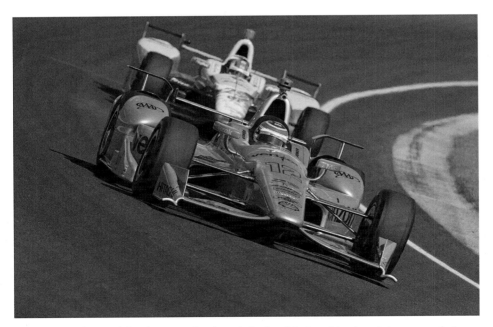

Will Power (no. 12) leads seventh-placed Carlos Muñoz (Andretti Autosport). In 2018 Power took the lead for the last time with just four laps remaining and won by 3.15 seconds from Ed Carpenter, with Scott Dixon third. (IMS)

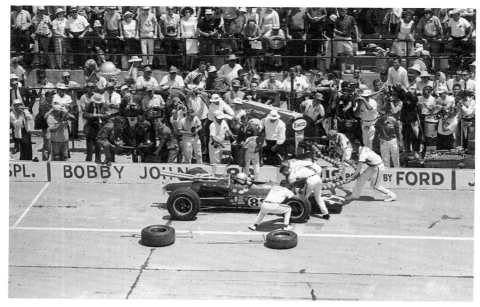

In 1965 the specialist NASCAR team, the Wood Brothers, defined pit stops as a race-winning advantage. They presided over the stops of Jim Clark and his Lotus teammate Bobby Johns. Clark, who won that year, took just 19.8 seconds in his first of two stops—A.J. Foyt took 44 seconds. (IMS)

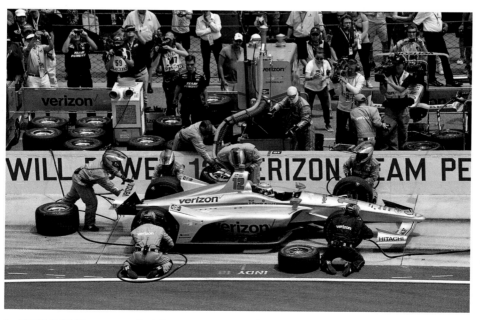

In 2018 Will Power needed four stops to win his Indianapolis 500. Each was half the time of Jim Clark's back in 1965. But Power's two main rivals needed to dash to the pits for fuel four laps from the finish—it was the deciding factor. (IMS)

In the basement of his home Will Power has built a special 'rotisserie' to strengthen his core muscles. It rotates him through 75 degrees, simulating on-track G forces. (John Smailes)

No one celebrates Indy victory like Will Power. 'Show me respect!' he screamed over his radio in 2018. On victory lane he sprayed milk while wife Liz, in her lucky red shirt, shared the moment. (IMS)

In Team Penske race headquarters in February 2020, president Tim Cindric (left) and Will Power greet new recruit Scott McLaughlin, twice Australian Supercar champion. (John Smailes)

In 2008, when Scott Dixon won his Indianapolis 500, Will Power drove the Team Australia car to thirteenth on his debut. The ambitious Australian venture was disbanded the same year, after boosting several careers. (IMS)

The Speed King's gravestone, in Liverpool Cemetery, New South Wales, with no recognition of his achievements. (John Smailes)

Team Penske's 300th overall race success. That was a major milestone. He beat Scott Dixon to do it. He won the Gold Coast Indy 300, the first Australian to claim his home race. He set pole position at the Indianapolis 500, a 226.48 mph (364.4 km/h) four-lap average.

But there were also mishaps and mistakes. At the 2008 Indianapolis 500, Briscoe's car squeezed Danica Patrick in a pit stop release. He was released into her path; the pit road is big enough for two. Patrick moved right, but Briscoe hit her with his right rear wheel. The impact sent Patrick spinning towards the pit exit. Both drivers were out of the race and each fined $100,000 for an aggressive pit road incident.

In 2009 Briscoe had the IndyCar Series in his grasp. He could win the championship at the Twin Ring Motegi circuit in Japan, with a full round to spare. But leaving the pits, leading by a lap with no pressure, his car turned left and hit the wall. The team said he'd disabled the electronic speed limiter too early and the rush of power took him to the wall. It was a massive error. The final shootout for the title in California was a race between three drivers: Dario Franchitti won the championship from Scott Dixon; Briscoe was a frustrated third.

He hit the Indianapolis wall in 2010 and 2011. The next year he claimed pole, a huge statement, but a gearbox full of neutrals dropped him to fifth in the race, his equal best. There was a lot of tension building. At the Sonoma road course in California, he was censured by Tim Cindric. The team was running two Australians, Will Power and Briscoe, and they were 1–2 in the race. Briscoe seized the lead on a pit stop cycle with just ten laps remaining and won the race. 'Tim had been Will's strategist. Roger was mine,' Ryan said. 'Roger told me to keep pushing.

Tim came at me and demanded why hadn't I pulled over to redress the position. I said, "I would have if Roger had told me."'

Briscoe felt the weight of what he perceived as Cindric's displeasure. 'A couple of times he'd pull me aside and tell me he wasn't happy with things I'd said. I heard he'd told people I wasn't a team player,' Ryan revealed. In Formula One that would almost be a compliment. In IndyCar, it's the opposite.

'I really wanted to go to Roger and talk it through. But Tim was the head of Penske Racing. I'm not a forceful personality, and I was conflicted. I never did go to Roger and I regret it.'

Tim Cindric is a tall, well-built, clean-cut guy, a former basketball letterman. He's a Penske man through and through. His dad Carl used to build race motors for Penske at Herb Porter's Speedway Engines business. 'When I was a kid, I used to sit behind the Penske pit, wishing I could meet him,' Tim told me. He got the chance because his wife Megan was the daughter of fellow team-owner Jim Trueman. 'One night we got a call at home. It was Roger Penske who said, "My IndyCar team hasn't won a race in two and a half years. I need someone to run it." I knew everything about him, knew his team. I'd been a Penske historian for years.'

We were speaking in one of the many meeting rooms in Team Penske's Mooresville race team headquarters. Cindric works out of it—his home is nearby on the sixth hole of the Trump National Golf Club, The Point. Billionaire Penske, though, is headquartered in Bloomfield, Michigan. His businesses claim a consolidated revenue of more than US$32 billion and he employs more than 60,000 people. He travels a lot. While motorsport is his passion, and the kernel of his empire, he must place trust in his key people.

'We wanted Ryan to come here and be a champion,' Cindric said, no emotion, just matter of fact. 'But he was the only full-time driver we've had since 2000 who had not won a major title or won the Indianapolis 500.' There is a guiding principle pervading the Penske organisation. Everyone calls it 'the Penske Way'. Even the road leading to race headquarters is called Penske Way. It's a big deal. It's a code of commitment and it's a two-way street. 'Roger and I address it all the time,' Cindric told me. 'Have we fulfilled our obligation to the person? Have we given them sufficient opportunity? Have they reached their level of expectation with us?'

Looking straight at me, neutral, Cindric said: 'We didn't fire Ryan. We didn't renew his contract.'

'You said the most honest thing I've heard for a long time. You said, "I feel lucky".' Robin Miller was interviewing Ryan Briscoe on Racer.com, the race fans' streaming service. Briscoe smiled broadly.

A Penske-alumnus is always in demand. You don't fail at Penske. The judgement is simply by how much you'd succeeded.

Chip Ganassi had rehired Briscoe for the first half of the 2013 season, including the Indianapolis 500: 'I'd just come off five years with Penske. I think they wanted to learn what I knew,' Ryan mused. But Miller didn't know the half of it.

Mike Hull, team principal of Ganassi Racing, had given Ryan the heads-up that there would soon be a works Ford sports-car program working out of their Indianapolis headquarters. Ryan would be one of the drivers. 'We made a list of all the drivers we would place in that team and Ryan was one of them,' Hull told me in Indianapolis.

The deal included a year in IndyCar. Ganassi ambitiously fielded four cars: 'But there was an A-team and a B-team. I was in the B,' Ryan said. He came twelfth at Indy in 2013 and scraped an eighteenth in 2014 and thought it would be his last. Ganassi still wanted him for its sports cars, but not for its IndyCar program.

He was a driver at large in 2015 when Canadian James Hinchcliffe had a huge crash in Indy practice. A suspension component speared into the cockpit and impaled his leg. He lost a lot of blood and first-intervention crews on the spot saved his life. Briscoe was called up by the Sam Schmidt team to take Hinchcliffe's place. He started from last and worked his way up through the field. It wasn't easy. He spun early to avoid someone else's crash. A full course caution thirteen laps from the end compressed the field and anyone in the pack could have won it. Briscoe claimed twelfth, just 5.6 seconds behind the winner, Juan Pablo Montoya. Montoya had moved to Penske after Briscoe was not renewed.

For four years, from 2016, Ryan anchored Chip Ganassi's Ford GT works entry in the GT Le Mans (GTLM) category of sports-car racing. The Ford GTs, built to evoke the emotive spirit of the GT40s in which Bruce McLaren and Chris Amon won Le Mans in 1966, won nineteen major events and Ryan was at the wheel for eight of those victories. The works program came to a halt in 2019. In the first month of 2020, Ryan Briscoe won the Daytona 24 Hour race outright. His co-drivers in a prototype car co-owned by Max Angelelli and Wayne Taylor were Scott Dixon, Renger van der Zande and Kamui Kobayashi. Kamui had been a test and development driver at Toyota F1, post-Ryan, and he'd advanced to do just two races for them before the Toyota team disbanded.

'I don't miss the days of him getting into an open-wheeler,' Nicole Briscoe said. She was speaking as a wife and a mother. As a sports reporter, she had a keen appreciation of the man–machine continuum, working at the edge of their ability. But now with daughters, there were times she'd take the kids from the room when there was racing on, turn their backs to the screen. 'What he does now is significantly safer.'

14

The Driver Whisperer

In early May 1996, 44-year-old Rob Wilson was sitting in the office of his good friend Gary Bahre who, with his dad Bob, owned the one-mile Loudon Speedway in New Hampshire north of New York. They were enjoying a cigarette, which was their constant habit, when the telephone rang. It was Tony George, owner of a significantly larger speedway, who was wondering if Gary would do him the favour of *not* hosting a CART race if he was asked, but instead come on board with the Indy Racing League. 'The Bahres were good friends with the Hulman-Georges,' Rob told me with the rasping voice of a pack-a-day Marlboro Red man. 'It was a really easy response. They were making their money out of NASCAR. They'd happily take IRL over CART—they didn't care.'

George went on to tell Bahre of the difficulty he was having raising a field for his first IRL Indy 500. Gary looked across the desk to Wilson and said, 'What about Rob?'

'Send him over,' was the reply.

Just like that Rob Wilson, Auckland born, who'd seen his first race as a twelve-year-old and had been living as a motor-racing gypsy ever since, was an entrant in the Indianapolis 500.

Today Rob Wilson, large, imposing, with a presence that commands respect, is unique in the world of motorsport. He is a 'driver whisperer'. You won't find him online or in the telephone book, but at a small privately owned airport 18 kilometres to the south of Central Leicester in the United Kingdom, he conducts a bespoke clinic for elite racing drivers that sharpens their technique of dynamic weight transfer. He sits beside his clients—not students: they are not there to learn in the accepted sense but to be enlightened—and almost by osmosis he assists them to come to terms with the concept of transient harmonics, the anticipation of balance required to enter and traverse a corner. It's not done at particularly high speed. He uses a Vauxhall Astra (goes through a set of tyres a day and a set of brake pads a week) and it's helmets off because he doesn't like the separation caused by a radio communications system. It has to be personal—just the two of them, like a communion.

While he may be obtuse, he is not discrete. His clients include F1 drivers Kimi Räikkönen and Valtteri Bottas. 'Lance Stroll, F1-driving son of a billionaire, flies in once a week by helicopter.' He claims that nineteen of the 33 drivers on the previous year's Indianapolis 500 grid had visited him at some stage, that 2018 winner Will Power had discovered a miniscule advantage in holding on to a cornering line for a half-breath longer, thus altering the geometric arc he applied as he moved out to the walls of the Indianapolis Motor Speedway. Seven-time world MotoGP champion Valentino Rossi had been with Wilson, as had Juan Pablo Montoya, David Coulthard and Marco Andretti. Throw in a couple of princes from the British royal family. They all had his telephone number. He didn't gouge them. His fee was not fixed but by negotiation; an elite driver would spend about £2000 for a session, an aspiring one from a junior category a bit less.

Wilson had been a motor-racing enthusiast very early. In January 1965 the pre-teen stood at Auckland International Airport's terminal, little more than a shed, and got the autograph of stars as they arrived for the New Zealand Grand Prix. A week later Rob watched the grand prix, won by Graham Hill in David McKay's Scuderia Veloce Brabham. 'But it was Jim Clark who caught my eye—there was something different about the way Clark drove. I thought, "That's what I want to do."'

The young Wilson rationalised that if you came first in New Zealand you might only be mid-field in Europe: 'Those guys were harder edged.' He saved his money, went to the UK when he was twenty, attended a race-driving school at Goodwood, and kept himself alive by playing bass guitar in a rock band.

New Zealand industrialist, race driver, yachtsman and

philanthropist Sir Tom Clark was his salvation. Clark, who died in 2005, was one of New Zealand's great characters. He inherited a struggling ceramics company, turned it into a corporation, and became a sports participant and patron. He cheated death when he barrel-rolled his Formula One Ferrari 555 Super Squalo at the Bathurst 100 in 1957. He won the 1970 Sydney to Hobart Yacht Race in his 73-feet plywood *Buccaneer*. He mentored people he thought were special. Two-time America's Cup winner Sir Peter Blake, who died at the hands of pirates at the mouth of the Amazon River in 2001, was one of them. Race drivers Graham McRae and Rob Wilson were others. McRae founded his career on the back of Clark's Crown Lynn potteries sponsorship. Wilson accepted support from associated brand Royal Grafton China.

Wilson raced a Formula Ford for TIGA owned by F1 racers Tim Schenken (Australia) and Howden Ganley (New Zealand), and for the British Reynard operation. He built both cars in their factories by day and played bass in 'dodgy SOHO clubs at night'. He came sixth in the 1978 British F3 Championship behind Nelson Piquet and Derek Warwick and ahead of Nigel Mansell and Stefan Johansson. All four would race F1, and two would become world champions.

It's the racing driver's lament—money counts: 'Piquet would spend $100,000. We'd spend $12,000.' Wilson was to have driven with Tyrrell F1 in the Belgian Grand Prix at Zolder but Italian Michele Alboreto turned up with a pile of money and bought the seat from under him. It hurt. Alboreto won two grands prix with Tyrrell while Wilson 'semi-stopped for two years'. Then Alboreto was recruited by Ferrari. 'The phone rang,' Rob said, 'and it was Ken Tyrrell.'

Ken said, 'Michele's leaving. I want to hire you.' But instead of being asked to return to racing, Ken went on: 'You play in a band, don't you? I want you for his farewell party.'

Half a lifetime later Wilson is still unimpressed. 'I was being asked to be the court jester.'

In the US, the Barber Saab Pro Series and Rob were made for each other. The one-make open-wheeler formula was an equal playing field. He won more races than any other driver in its seventeen-year tenure and captured the title outright in 1990. Drives in Indy Lights, the feeder series to IndyCar, and in the Busch Series, the feeder to NASCAR, followed. He raced in the Le Mans 24 Hour, the Sebring 12 Hour—wherever a vagabond racing driver might be considered useful.

'The IndyCar drive was a complete mistake.' Wilson said it more in bemusement than in lament.

'Tony George knew me from races we'd done together so I wasn't a complete surprise to him,' Wilson said. George spent a full season racing Indy Lights. 'He booked me a room at the Speedway Motel [opposite the racetrack] and took me to meet my new team. On the way across he warned me that it was a bit of a con.'

Project Indy, owned by Andreas Leberle, former chief mechanic for Euromotorsport, which was owned by Antonio Ferrari, grand-nephew of Enzo, had a reputation as a pay-to-play organisation. Wilson wasn't paying. He presumed the money came from Tony George, intended as an investment in strengthening his field. 'I walked into the garage and there was an Unser sitting beside a Reynard tub they were working on. He was pleasant enough, but he made it clear that no one was going to work on my car until they got this one right.'

There are as many Unsers in IndyCar racing as there are Windsors in Buckingham Palace, and in their own space they are just as royal. Eight Unsers over four generations have actively raced. Three have won Indianapolis a total of nine times. Bobby, born 1934, won it three times; his brother Al, born 1939, won it four; and Al's son, Al Jnr, won it another two. Rob Wilson wasn't certain which Unser he was talking to that day but whichever one it was, he was there overseeing the fortune of Johnny Unser. Johnny was having his rookie drive at Indianapolis. Back in 1959 Johnny's dad Jerry, born 1932, the eldest of the three second-generation brothers, had died of blood poisoning as the result of a practice crash at the speedway, one year after his rookie year. The Unsers were deeply invested in not only Johnny's success, but also his safety.

'The car was frightening,' Rob recalled. 'Anything over 200 mph [321 km/h] it vibrated so badly I couldn't see the corners very well. The windscreen was directing air underneath my helmet, so it was twisting sideways on my head. Going past the pits, people thought I was turning left to look at them, but I was trying to look straight ahead.'

True to the unknown-Unser's demand, Project Indy had concentrated on Johnny's car. He qualified it well—226.11 mph (363.81 km/h) to put it on sixteenth grid position. 'I couldn't do much above 214 mph [344 km/h] and then I had to slow for Turn One,' Rob said. The Indy old guard kicked into action.

'Parnelli Jones [winner in 1963] took me for a run around,' Rob recalled. They did six or seven laps. 'Going with Parnelli, one of the Indy gods, was a special occasion. "Don't bother looking for a turn-in point," he said, "because by the time you get there it will be gone." Bill Simpson, the racer who revolutionised safety with his own brand of helmets and fire suits, fitted me properly with a new helmet. And A.J. Foyt gave me a new screen to have fitted to the car.'

A.J. was in the next garage, and as was his wont the four-time winner took a paternal overview of Wilson. 'If he likes you, he likes you,' one of A.J.'s crew said when Rob wondered why a legend was assisting him.

His own team was not as helpful. 'They were well aware of the vibration, but their response was, "If you qualify, then we'll spend the money to fix it."'

Sometimes it's best to go to a quiet place and just think it through. Wilson went back to the Speedway Motel: 'I was sitting there playing the piano, having a sing-song with Tony George [seriously], and I told him about the problems I was having. He said, "If you can qualify at just 200 mph [321 km/h] I'll start 34 cars so you'll be in the field."'

Wilson headed back to the track. Just after noon, the pole sitter Scott Brayton went out to do some set-up work in his back-up car. The right rear tyre suffered a rapid deflation, a result of track debris it had picked up, and Brayton was killed instantly against the Turn Two wall.

'I went out at 5.45. The balloon goes up at 6 p.m.—no further opportunity after that,' Rob said. 'I was doing well, 218, 218, 218, three almost-identical laps. It was a bit like riding a pushbike on a greasy surface. One more and I'd be in the race, but going down the back straight, the engine stopped.' Rob coasted to a halt. 'A.J. Foyt walked up to me and said, "That just saved your life." He could see the vibration from the outside.' The car was unsafe at any speed.

And then Foyt did something exceptional, just as he'd done for Janet Guthrie twenty years before. He loaned Rob Wilson his car. It was too late to qualify, too late to switch teams—he just wanted Wilson to discover what Indianapolis really should have been like, and maybe to restore a bit of the driver's confidence: 'It was so easy. I did fifteen laps and I was lapping at 224 mph [360 km/h].' Wilson was way off pole but well within the qualifying window. 'It was a pleasure, so easy to drive.'

Bob and Gary Bahre had a VIP suite high in the grandstand and Rob watched the Indianapolis 500 from there. He watched as Johnny Unser rolled to a halt on the formation lap, his transmission broken even before he got the green flag. Unser would go back four times more, part of the family tradition, with his best result an eighteenth.

The Bahres sold their Loudon Speedway for US$340 million. Once a year, Rob's country-rock band, Grand Prairie, flies from the UK to New Hampshire for a private party thrown by the family. The headliner can be anyone from Diana Ross to Willie Nelson. 'We warm up and mop up—we're the "other" band,' Rob said. Rob is the vocalist and the Bahres love to hear 'This is What I Get for Loving You'. Rob composed it: 'It's a Midwestern hard-luck story of the results of certain ambition.'

15

The Ones That Got Away

Tony George was about the best dad a girl could want. When James Davison, a promising racing driver from Melbourne, came into his daughter Lauren's life, Tony bought her new suitor a racing car, gave him workshop space and a full-time engineer, and sent him off to contest the Indy Lights championship, the feeder category to the main game. Davison repaid the faith by coming second in 2009, a grand effort.

It was James's moment inside the Court of Camelot. He lived with the George family within their gated estate, and enjoyed private jets and Saturday night cook-outs with Lauren and her circle down in the RV parking lot at the family speedway. Her friends called Lauren 'GOM'—for Goddess of Motorsport. They were just a couple of kids—Lauren, in her late teens, and James, 21, were having the time of their lives.

Lauren was a fixture at the Brickyard. It was the family business and they ran it that way. When she was born, she was taken straight from the hospital to trackside because it was the Month of May and her mum was needed to help A.J. Foyt. When she dinged her scooter in front of a gathering of drivers, the biggest names in motorsport nicknamed her 'Crash'. On her birthday Scott Dixon—like so many others, she called him 'Dixie'—gave her one of his winning helmets. GOM made the rounds of social media, and a picture was posted of her and her 'significant other'. 'I speak better Australian than James,' she told her followers.

'I never asked Tony for help,' James told me. 'My plan had been to put together a program to present to Michael Andretti's team in the hope that I could find budget.'

James and the Georges hit it off right from the start when he and Lauren started dating. He was a nice young man, bushy haired, bright eyed, well spoken and respectful. And he was from the right stock. Like the Georges in Indianapolis, the Davos in Melbourne had been entrenched in the strata of society for generations. 'They invited me to jump on their jet and go with them to the last year of the Gold Coast 300. And then Laura, Lauren's mother, said, "Why not stay at our house?"' It was a vast improvement on the itinerant existence James had been leading. 'In February I got a text from Lauren saying, "Dad has bought you an Indy Lights car. It's in the shop." I never saw that coming,' James said. 'It kept my career going. I was done for if not for that.'

The shop also contained an IndyCar driven by Tony's stepson, Ed Carpenter. Ed, five years James's senior, was Laura's son from her first marriage, but Tony, in a brief telephone conversation we had, said: 'I never thought of him as my stepson. He was always my son.'

Tony brought in engineer Lee Dykstra to run the Indy Lights assault. Dykstra had recently stepped down from running rival CART's technical program. He knew of James and had watched his career. 'When he crashed and rolled a Formula Atlantic car [which was running alongside the CART series], I bought him an upside-down cake,' Lee said.

'Lee had little patience,' James recalled. 'He demanded a high level of performance.'

Bringing Dykstra on board was probably an even better investment in James's future than giving him the car. Davison's career had been erratic. The year with Dykstra went a long way to fixing that. There was a near 50-year age gap between them, Dykstra a crusty old dinosaur, and James learning at the feet of the master. He won only one race in the hard-fought fourteen-round series, but he was on the podium five times, finished every race and slipped outside the top ten only once. He'd learned how to race with consistency. He came second in the series to J.R. Hildebrand; the young New Zealander Wade Cunningham was fourth.

And then, quite suddenly, it stopped. Close observers—and the speedway had a lot of them—said there had been unrest in Camelot for many years, ever since Tony rode off on his crusade under the heraldic flag of the IRL. The Global Financial Crisis of 2008 served to focus the family's fiscal attention. It was reported that Tony's sisters moved to rein in their brother's management style and expenditure. In 2009 Tony resigned from the board of the family company, and the race team he'd set up—ironically called Vision—closed its doors.

The drawbridge had gone up, too, for James. Lauren enrolled in the University of Notre Dame in Indiana and James returned to Australia. 'We spent a lot of time apart that summer,' James said. 'And distance just took care of itself.' The break-up 'didn't get too messy'.

Oddly, in our conversation, James seemed not to acknowledge the link between his relationship with Lauren and the dream drive he'd been gifted: 'Tony said he was determined to get me another drive,' he said, 'but I probably relied too much on him. Ed Carpenter was always going to have priority.' He was right. The father-and-son team went on to successfully set up Ed Carpenter Racing. In 2020 their team was joined by Conor Daly, the talented stepson of Indianapolis Motor Speedway president Doug Boles. Once more the Court of Camelot had demonstrated a preference for keeping it in the family.

James Davison knows all about dynasties. He is the grandson of four-time Australian Grand Prix winner Lex Davison; the step-grandson of Tony Gaze, Australia's first F1 Grand Prix competitor; the cousin of Supercar racers Will and Alex, and of Formula Ford competitor Claire; the nephew of Australian F2 champion Richard, and of Chris, the owner of several Formula Fords who is also keeper of the flame of Ecurie Australie, the family's own motor-racing talisman. His grandmother Diana, matriarch of the clan, and her daughter Catherine raced and rallied historic vehicles with great elan. His brother Charles promotes motor racing in China, and they are the sons of Jon, an enthusiastic figure who wears his family pride on his sleeve. Jon raced a fearsome F5000 in honour of Lex and for eighteen years ran Sandown racetrack in Victoria. His motor-sport passion was never more on display than on the day he threw open the gates of Sandown to hold a memorial service for the late legend Peter Brock. He stood there, side by side with Allan Moffat and Mark Skaife, all three of them crying, and the mourners joined in.

'We all know motor racing is part of our pedigree,' James said.

James's cousins headed overseas to pursue their motor-racing ambitions, but Jon held James back. 'He never wanted me to get into motor racing. It killed his father,' James said. Lex had died at Sandown in 1965 in his Brabham Climax. It was a big crash, his car landing alongside irrigation tubing. The coroner later found that he'd died of a heart attack, aged 42, maybe not the result of a race crash at all.

The impasse was resolved when James's mother, Julie, bought him his first go-kart. When Jon came around, they took over the Formula Ford that had been used by his cousins. James came sixth in the Victorian championship in a car that was approaching its tenth anniversary.

'I grew up with a book on the coffee table—*The Illustrated History of the Indianapolis 500: 1911–1994*—and my father and I saw that it was more realistic to make it in America,' James said. They'd watched Will Power race against the best in Formula Three in Europe: 'He topped them all and it still didn't work out.'

In the early 2000s BMW introduced a Junior Development Series, a one-make wings and slicks car, for maximum traction unlike the Formula Ford, powered by a 1200cc motorcycle engine. Series races were held all over the world and because the cars were identical, they provided a true measure of a young driver's performance. World champions Nico Rosberg and Sebastian Vettel won in them on their way to Formula One. Australia's Daniel Ricciardo was third in the Asian series.

James and Jon went to Valencia to audition for a scholarship but 'despite being first and second quickest in two sessions, we didn't get it. They knew we'd enter anyway.' BMW's rejection was the start of a long, slippery slope of relying on diminishing parental funds and other people's money.

Motorsport Australia, formerly the Confederation of Australian Motor Sport, helped out through its Australian Motor Sports Foundation (AMSF), set up to supplement the aspirations of young drivers like James, and in 2005 he claimed sixth in Formula BMW USA.

Queensland entrepreneur Craig Gore had a plan of his own— to form Team Australia, which would help youngsters and promote his products, principally a winery, to the world. Gore was the son of Michael Gore, the 1980s developer of Sanctuary Cove resort. It was said of Michael that he was Queensland's original 'white shoe', a not-too-complimentary way of referring to freewheeling businessmen from the Sunshine State. Gore picked up where Motorsport Australia left off and James entered America's Formula Atlantic Championship. But it was a struggle.

James's season ended before the championship came to a conclusion: 'James Davison has moved to deny claims made by Team Australia that he still owes monies to the team following his program in the Champ Car Atlantic Series this season,' an online news service reported. 'The team announced that it was seeking a judgement against Davison and his father Jon.'

Jon Davison responded that he had made 'a significant financial commitment and he was disappointed in the team management's performance in not fulfilling undertakings it had given'.

It was not a good look, and unsettling for a young driver, and it had the ability to tarnish a good name. 'I took one step backwards to go two forward,' James said. The Davisons moved to the 2007 Star Mazda Championship Series, a lesser car than an Atlantic, and James came second. With a decent result on his CV, James and his dad approached Sam Schmidt Motorsport to move up a gear again. Schmidt had become a quadriplegic in a race crash in 2000. Inspired by tetraplegic Frank Williams in Formula One, he formed his own race team.

'I tested for Sam at Sebring and he offered us a deal for the year at one-third the price,' James said. 'Dad still had to put in a couple of hundred grand.'

In 2008 Davison claimed a pole position, a win and a second, and came home ninth in the Indy Lights series. 'After that I knew I needed just one more year. Some people develop at a different rate. But one thing is for certain, that was absolutely the last year Dad could help.'

That winter, James met the George family.

Most people in IndyCar racing will tell you that James Davison is one of the most talented drivers never to get the right break. It wasn't for lack of trying.

'Driver training is a good way to meet people of influence,' James said. Like many young drivers he was supplementing his income working as a driver coach, 'mainly for older, wealthier enthusiasts'. He'd sit beside them in their expensive, high-powered cars and guide them around the track. He was always respectful. 'I never asked them for support, just told them about my ambition.' The goal, always, was Indy.

It's a delicate juggling act. Most Indy teams—except for the very top ones—have a seat for sale. It's a matter of negotiating the cost of that drive, and then finding the funds to buy it.

'Team owner Dale Coyne offered me a test and a race seat for a round of the Indy series at Mid-Ohio,' James said. 'It was US$50,000, which was more than I had, but I knew it might be my only chance of ever driving an IndyCar.' James called his contacts. Little by little he worked through his gentleman-racer address book and he got the money, promising to 'take them on the dream'. Tony George gave him US$10,000, Zac Brown, now boss of McLaren and one of James's gentlemen drivers, another US$10,000.

James finished fifteenth in his 2013 IndyCar debut. Mid-Ohio is a 2.2-mile (3.5-kilometre) permanent road course. 'Driving the IndyCar there was massively physical, so painful I wanted to cry,' he said. 'The race went green for more than 90 laps and I wasn't sure I'd hold up, but towards the end I felt fine and I was pushing the car in front.'

Dale Coyne said he had a seat at the next race—Sonoma. 'Dale owns a chain of barbecue equipment shops; he's not mega wealthy, so he sells drives in his race cars because there's no other way,' James explained. 'But occasionally he reaches into his own pocket.' James's Sonoma drive was one of those occasions.

'I was doing really well,' Davison enthused. 'I started at the back of the grid and got up to ninth. But then I was chopped, finished eighteenth, and I thought, "There goes my Indy career."' Except with two races under his wheels, he could now legitimately claim to be an IndyCar driver, not a complete novice, but someone with experience—someone who knows how to race and to pit stop (which is an art in itself), and he hadn't crashed. It led him to think: could he do Indianapolis?

'The 2014 Indy 500 had 32 secured entries and they needed 33,' James said. 'Normally it costs US$750,000 to buy a drive but because that space needed to be filled, as a one-off opportunity I could get to the grid for $200,000. I was maxed out at that.'

Some of the money came from an unexpected source, via connections of the late actor Paul Walker, cult-hero star of the *Fast and the Furious* movie series. Walker had died in a fiery road crash in 2013. His associates had taken over his automotive franchise called Always Evolving and they decided to back Davison in honour of their friend, who had always wanted to get to Indianapolis. Davison sourced a car from Adelaide-born, UK-educated, US tech billionaire Kevin Kalkhoven, who ran KV Racing with former racer Jimmy Vasser.

'I was on a short program. I had only one engine, half the allocation of tyres and I could only practise on Fast Friday,' James said. 'It was like my right foot had a brain of its own. When you're doing 230 mph [370 km/h] facing a 90-degree corner, your brain has to wrap itself around the challenge.' James did a great job. He brought the car home sixteenth and 'came out of the race making more money than I'd ever made in my life'.

Now he could add 'Indianapolis 500 finisher' to his expanding résumé, and he had a growing career in sports-car racing supporting him as well. But Indianapolis remained a hand-to-mouth existence.

'I thought my luck had run out in 2015—until Dale Coyne called me,' James said.

Coyne told him, 'We've picked up your seat from KV Racing and we're fitting it to our car.'

James would be in a team with British driver Pippa Mann and Frenchman Tristan Vautier—'all of us desperately broke'. Halfway through the race, a bizarre incident eliminated all three: Davison was released from his pit box straight into the path of Mann and he spun sideways into Vautier one box ahead. All of Dale Coyne's cars had crashed into each other—two were out and only Mann was able to continue. She finished 22nd.

Davison was recalled to Coyne in 2017 when Sébastien Bourdais suffered multiple pelvic and leg fractures in a Turn Two practice crash. 'I saw the crash on live stream,' he said. 'I started to head back to Indianapolis because I knew they'd be looking for a substitute.' A multiple-car pile-up eliminated James just seventeen laps from the finish.

In 2018 he joined A.J. Foyt. The car was disappointingly slow, and he was high up on Turn Three when previous year's winner Takuma Sato rode up his rear wheel and took them both out. In 2019 he survived a crash with Hélio Castroneves on pit row and delivered Dale Coyne a twelfth place—his best finish to date.

Speaking to James, it's almost like listening to Jon, echoing down the line from a lifetime ago: 'My era has been the toughest in motorsport for the last 50 years. I know why I've made it; it's because I never gave up. People don't understand what my struggle has been.' But, he added, 'I've done five Indy 500s and that's five more than most people who have the dream.'

In 2020, in the midst of the COVID-19 pandemic, James Davison secured a drive in both NASCAR and the Indianapolis 500—a massive achievement.

Wade Cunningham sells Indianapolis real estate. He's person-able, in his mid-thirties, upwardly mobile in a laid-back sort of a way, and he's the go-to person for residential property in the city.

Seven years earlier he'd 'hung on for dear life for 500 miles, putting myself in physical danger' to deliver A.J. Foyt's team fourteenth place in the 2012 IndyCar World Championship on the Fontana oval in California. 'I gave the team their best result of the year and it felt like a win,' Wade said. 'It was the best they'd done on an oval for a year. And there wasn't an ounce of thanks. They didn't care. They were oblivious to it. I wasn't getting a reward—not financially, not emotionally. I thought, "F—k this." I walked away and I've never regretted it.'

Cunningham, the middle of three Auckland kart-racing brothers, was a serious talent. He won on the Brickyard three years out of five in the Indy Lights series after his first attempt in 2005 but when he raced IndyCar, just the once at Indianapolis, he managed only 42 laps before the Foyt-entered car coasted to a halt with electrical problems. It would be all too easy to suggest that a young man, born to privilege, whose father had no concerns about buying him drives in the US—'I told him he could reimburse me when he earned more than me,' Bob Cunningham said—was in it for the fun, and happy to walk away at any time, without the sort of gut-wrenching commitment that drove James Davison. But that would be underselling both his sincere motivation to win Indy and the trauma of his involvement in the most horrendous multiple-car high-speed crash of Indy's modern era.

In October 2011 British driver Dan Wheldon, twice Indiana-polis 500 winner, died instantly in a fifteen-car crash at the super high–speed Las Vegas Motor Speedway. TV commenta-tors, speaking in the moment, said: 'It was the horrible accident everyone hoped would never happen.'

There is a phenomenon called 'pack racing' in which the race cars are so close that they are propelled by their combined momentum. It is like the peloton in the Tour de France, except at 220 mph (354 km/h). The danger involved in the pack race was exacerbated at Las Vegas because 34 cars had been crammed into a 1.5-mile (2.4-kilometre) tri-oval, a far greater track density than they ever run at Indianapolis. Even worse, the unique surface at Las Vegas allowed for multiple racing lines—cars could dart anywhere, unexpectedly.

'You are six inches from the car alongside you and the whole pack is covered by just half a second in lap time,' Wade explained. 'It's crazy. There is little visibility of the others around you. There is a guy in your ear [a spotter] giving you a play by play and you have to implicitly trust what you hear.' Wade's car was one of those that started the chain reaction. 'At the front of the pack, James Hinchcliffe and I bumped wheels. J.R. Hildebrand went over the back of my car,' Wade said.

Dan Wheldon was Cunningham's teammate, brought in to race for a special US$5 million promotional prize offered only to drivers not contesting the IndyCar Series. Promoters had hoped to attract world superstars, from F1 and sports cars, but got only Wheldon. They stuck to their offer anyway. Wheldon had won the Indy 500 that year but not contested the series. Instead he had been helping chassis-maker Dallara build a better, safer car. Wheldon had to win the race to claim the $5 million and he was hot favourite. The in-car TV camera was broadcasting from Wheldon's car when the crash began. Viewers shared his point of view as the gaps in front of him closed, along with his options. His car clipped one in front and went airborne, then impacted the catch fencing and its concrete supports.

Late that afternoon, competitors drove five laps of the speedway, three abreast, in tribute to their fallen comrade as loudspeakers played a bagpipe recording of 'Danny Boy'. And then everybody went home, and the series was over.

The legacy of Wheldon's death remains ever present in IndyCar. It shocked the motor-racing fraternity. He had become the fifth driver to die in the same year as winning the Indianapolis 500. Dallara named the car he developed the DW12, after Wheldon.

Cunningham came back the next year, picked up the two drives with Foyt—the last because another British driver, Mike Conway, told A.J. that he was no longer comfortable driving ovals. And then Cunningham stopped: 'When you leave motor racing you gain a lot of perspective,' he said. 'In motor racing your last race is the most important thing in your life. I didn't want to live with that negativity.'

'I never considered the risks of motor racing,' Bob Cunningham, a successful Auckland builder and developer, told me. When he and wife Lyndsay took their three boys go-karting, they gave no thought to anything but family fun. They didn't mind spending a bit, 'about NZ$50,000 for a full season, double that when we went international'. Wade followed in Ryan Briscoe's path, dropping out of school and heading for Italy with kart maker CRG to win the world championship when he was seventeen. 'His headmaster tried to talk him out of going but he was also the first to send him congratulations when he won,' Bob chuckled.

The Dixons—Ron and Glenys, parents of Scott, the most successful Indy Series winner of all—cleared a path for the Cunninghams in the States. Wade even stayed with Scott for part of his first season until Scott's soon-to-be-bride Emma turned up. 'Ron got us a red-hot deal in Formula Ford 2000— around US$80,000,' Bob said. Wade came fifth in the title and then impatiently went up a grade to Indy Lights, 'for around $200,000', which he won in his rookie year.

Bob has fond recollections of going to the Indianapolis 500 for the first time: 'It was like showing up in Rome at the Colosseum. We've been to half a dozen grands prix around the world and nothing compares. The way you get treated by the yellow shirts [the volunteers], it's absolutely fantastic.' Bob's best memory is when his boy took him for a ride in the Brickyard's two-seater Dallara IndyCar. It's the ultimate Indy fan experience with a pillion seat behind the driver. 'We averaged 185 mph [297 km/h]. The g-forces feel ten times more than they really are.'

Wade regards the US as his home: 'I was never an adult in New Zealand, I left there when I was seventeen.' And he's married to Colorado-born Rebecca, whose dad Dick Dodge used to race Pikes Peak. He is not tempted to return to racing although age is still on his side. 'I've watched my friend James Hinchcliffe come close to dying twice—it's heartbreaking,' Wade said. 'The risk-to-reward ratio is just not there for me.'

16

Matty Brabs and the Crusher

In 2016 Matthew Brabham became the third generation of his family to race in the Indianapolis 500 and he did it only because of the intense ambition of an unrelenting larrikin, Australian journalist turned PR operator Brett Murray. Murray, not known for his subtlety, turned out to have a soul. Who would have thought it? He was known on two continents as 'Crusher'. There wouldn't be many of his acquaintances along pit road who could tell you his real name.

For the Month of May the pair become the Odd Couple of Gasoline Alley: the quietly spoken 22-year-old grandson of Jack Brabham, son of Geoffrey, accompanied by his glamour girlfriend, and the gruff beer keg of a bloke with a vocabulary of expletives and the visage of a survivor of seasons of playing American football in Australia, where he picked up his nickname.

Crusher and Matty Brabs came home 22nd in the Indy 500. And Crusher, with not even a hint of modesty, was able to say: 'In another 100 years' time they will go to the record books and there will be the names Brabham and Murray on the same line.'

Matty Brabs had been trying to crack the big time for four years. No one doubted he had the talent and his dad had the contacts. They had pedigree, and don't let anyone tell you that doesn't count for something, but they didn't have money or salesmanship.

'The circumstances have been very frustrating,' Matty told me in his parents' lakeside condo in Clearwater Cove, just north of Indianapolis. (That's another thing he had going for him— rent-free accommodation. His parents bought the place when he first set out to make a go of the American racing scene.)

'If you want to find the money, you have to try to be a personality,' Matty said. 'That's just not us. My dad is very quiet— reserved. The Andrettis, comparatively, are super smart—they generate money.' He allowed a moment for introspection. 'Our personalities don't even fit into motor racing as well as Jack's did when he was racing.'

Matt's climb up the totem pole of success started out modestly: karting success in Australia, then Formula Ford wins in national and state titles. But then it skyrocketed. He moved to the United States in 2012 at just eighteen and in the space of two years he claimed the US F2000 National Championship and the Pro Mazda Championship series, both essential steps on the staircase to Indy Lights and from there to IndyCar.

The trajectory was set. At twenty, all it would take to go all the way would be a bit of luck, and a budget.

Michael Andretti's team, set up to give youngsters a boost, had been very good for Matt in the junior categories. They could see his true potential and they'd continued their support for a time, even after the funding ran out. There was respect. The Brabhams and the Andrettis go back generations.

Geoff and Roseina, too, had been with their boy all the way. The proud parents had his back at race meetings and also in those awkward moments of negotiation when you want to reach out and shake the prospective sponsor because you know you can do the business if only they'd hand over the cash.

Of late, their day-to-day role as the Matty support module has been taken over by Kimberly Bogle, Matt's girlfriend of six years. They'd met at a race meeting when Kim was a spokes-model for one of Matt's sponsors. She 'got' motor racing. Her first job, while still in college—on a Donald Trump Miss Universe Contest scholarship—had been umbrella girl for MotoGP. She was world champion Nicky Hayden's last umbrella girl at Indianapolis. Kim holds a Bachelor of International Business. The pair complement each other. They formed part of a new breed of Indianapolis's motor-racing fraternity. The Brabham condo had become a perfect place for Sunday afternoon lake parties with Indy's young, fast crowd. Kim was helping Matt come out of his shell. 'It was funny at the beginning,' she said. 'He was under 21 and we had trouble getting him into bars.' Even now he looks like he might not qualify.

Crusher could clear the same bar. The just-turned 50-year-old could pass for a serving member of any law enforcement agency, but he plays on being the exact opposite: the cover of his recently published autobiography entitled *You Can't Make That S#^! Up* carries a mug shot of him taken while incarcerated overnight in an Indianapolis prison for blowing positive while riding a jet ski. His life story reads like a Robert G. Barrett Les Norton novel—an irreverent, irascible Aussie knockabout. Crusher started out as a journo with credits such as covering a rugby league Kangaroo tour—a precarious gig in itself—followed by time spent as a footy player in his own right with one US tour cap, a nightclub bouncer in places of the nefarious kind, a voracious punter and schoolboy SP bookie.

Thirty years ago, he moved to the Gold Coast, his natural habitat, and he discovered motor racing. Crusher doesn't just develop an interest. He stands back, takes a run-up and dives in at the deep end. He started his own PR company and he created his own online news service, so he'd have an outlet for his commercial activities (his speedcafe.com.au has become a valuable communication tool in Australian motorsport).

He took on PR for the Gold Coast 300 IndyCar race and was integral in its transition to a Supercar event, the Gold Coast 600, when IndyCar pulled out. Even as he was developing his local business, he took off for the States for a year or so to join the IndyCar fraternity simply because he had become passionate about it.

He worked for the Australasian-connected team PacWest—engineers John 'Ando' Anderson and Paul 'Ziggy' Harcus were legends; Kevin Kalkhoven ultimately bought it and changed its name; and Scott Dixon, whom Crusher called 'The Phantom' because of his failure to front on time, won his Indy Lights championship there. Crusher became a fixture in IndyCar, and a fixer in motorsport.

'I'd promised Jack Brabham a few years back that I'd keep an eye on young Matty and help him where I could,' Crusher told me. The words came so easily, but they masked something a lot deeper: the respect that he held for Jack's achievements and the connection he'd developed with the sport.

Crusher's home is a shrine to the gods of motor racing. Amongst his physical memorabilia he has the helmets of Formula One world champion Alan Jones and world speedway champion Jason Crump, and the helmet Ayrton Senna wore when he tested with Team Penske, signed by the Brazilian. He even has the winner's empty milk bottle from the Brickyard— the real deal, not the facsimile on sale in the gift shop. But they are 'things'—tradeable on eBay if the mood takes you. Deep down in his heart, Crusher is a true believer.

'I was sitting on a park bench in Sydney when the idea came to me—2016 would be the 100th Indianapolis 500, a big celebration. I'd enter it and get Matty Brabs to drive.' In the cab ride from the park bench to the airport, Crusher put a two-page business plan together and in the Virgin lounge he presented it to Glenn Duncan, second-generation owner of the incredibly successful hose and coupling manufacturer Pirtek. They'd just bought back their US franchise and Glenn, who was moving to Florida to run it, was looking for a means of putting it on the map. Motor racing and football had worked well for him with the trade in Australia. A few weeks later Glenn rang Crusher to tell him he was in.

'The whole thing would cost about $1.5 million and I could still lose my house if it went wrong,' Crusher said. It was only then that he told Matty. He hadn't wanted to get his hopes up. Geoff and Roseina cried when he told them. Shortly after, there were tears of a different kind.

'I had to tell Geoff to go f—k himself,' Crusher said bluntly. 'I'd chosen KV Racing—the old PacWest and his old alma mater—as the team to provide the car and infrastructure. Geoff wanted to go with Andretti.' Crusher had spoken to both operations and the choice came down simply to, 'With Andretti it would have been an Andretti car and every move we made, every communication, would have to be approved by them. Kevin Kalkhoven would let me run my own show. It would be Team Murray.' Crusher made the call his way and 'Geoff later apologised'.

Four years later, Matt sat back in his chair, looking past the photo of Jack on the wall, out to the lake and said, 'It was me pushing to go to Andretti. But it came down to a marketing decision for Crusher. It was his team, his decision. Doing it his way, he knew what he could do. My outlook was competitive, his was media.' It took a lot for Matt to make that statement. He's not one to cause offence.

The team creamed the media. Crusher is a PR master: he once dressed as flamboyant fight promoter Don King to promote an IndyCar battle between Juan Pablo Montoya and Dario Franchitti on the Gold Coast. Now, with his own team he went into overdrive. He arranged for Sir Jack's 1961 Cooper Climax and Geoffrey's 1985 top-ten finishing March to be brought to the Brickyard and he photographed them with the Team Murray car on the Yard of Bricks. He had a retro 1961 Jack Brabham race suit made for Matt so he could pose with his grandfather's car.

Each year the Indianapolis 500 runs an annual pit stop competition amongst the teams. It's a badge of honour for teams to win it. But Crusher kept his race crew working on the race car and arranged for ten US military veterans to enter the pit stop competition. They represented the US Navy Seal hero Chris Kyle who was murdered by a colleague in the grip of post-traumatic stress disorder. Hollywood made a movie about Kyle—*American Sniper*—and his widow Taya wholeheartedly endorsed Crusher's activity as a means of supporting her own charitable foundation. Team Murray didn't win the pit stop competition, but they annihilated the PR efforts of the other teams.

'It all went by so fast. I've never been so busy,' Matt told me. 'It was just a blur, and it was the best time of my life.' But, he added, 'I can see how you could get sick of it quickly if you just want to be there to race.'

The wheels fell off on the first lap.

There are two races at Indianapolis in the Month of May—the 500, and before that a road race around the grand prix circuit on the infield. The team considered Matty a chance for the GP, but it didn't start well. A rear wheel came off the car in the first lap of practice, just a fitment issue. But several laps later the car lost brakes as Matt pitched into Turn One. It was not a good look, and the team stopped and regrouped.

It was Matty's chance to step up. According to Crusher, Matty's calm and determination won the respect of the crew and when they took to the track again, they did so with Matty as their leader.

'I was lucky,' Matt told me. 'It was pretty scary.' But at the time he told no one that.

His recovery was sensational. Matt had not been able to practise on the team's soft qualifying tyres and he had nothing more than a theoretical idea of how they would react and how far he could push them. Yet he still put the car on thirteenth grid position, marginally missing the opportunity to participate in the top-ten shootout.

In the 219-mile (352-kilometre) race, the team's lack of practice showed. The crew member in charge of refuelling could not get the coupling to properly connect. Crusher took affirmative action. He marched down to Kalkhoven's other pit and commandeered their refuelling person. They lost a lot of time, and in the circumstances salvaging a sixteenth place was an act of genius. Brabham's stocks went up, not only in his own team but along pit row. People notice these things.

Two days later he was practising for the Indianapolis 500. 'We didn't have the car speed on the oval that we had on the road course,' Matt said. The average speed on the road course is around 110 mph (177 km/h). On the oval, it's double that. Teams use the same car for both, rebuilt for a different purpose. It's how the natural ability of the car translates to the oval that counts. Matt passed his Rookie Test and spent a week trimming out the car, taking track-hugging downforce off the aerodynamic package to gain more top-end speed. On Turn Two, it stepped out big-time, and was one of those moments that could have turned quickly to disaster. Instead Matthew Brabham, old head on young shoulders, saved it. Dario Franchitti, three-time Indy 500 winner and a mate of Crusher's, picked up his mobile phone and texted, 'Well held, Matty.' You'd frame an accolade like that.

Matt turned a 226.39 mph (364.26 km/h) to qualify 27th but it almost hadn't happened. The team manager had to wave the green flag to signify the start of the four-lap qualifying run. Crusher got so caught up in the moment, he came within a second of not doing it.

There's a science to winning Indianapolis. Neither Team Murray nor Matty Brabham knew it.

'We spent the race fighting tyre degradation and car vibration,' Matty said. 'At 220 mph [354 km/h] it intensified, and it got so bad I'd crash if I didn't get fresh tyres. We worked all race long, adding downforce. We were up and down in position like a yo-yo.'

In the first half of the race Matt stayed with eventual winner Alexander Rossi. 'I'd put on new tyres and I'd pass him—that was pretty cool,' Matt said. 'He was in the pit box ahead of us and it was obvious he was on a fuel-saving strategy [Rossi ran out of fuel on the slow-down lap] and we decided to do the same thing. But the car vibration got so bad I had to stop once more for tyres with just three laps to go.' Matt was classified 22nd.

Team Murray had finished the Indianapolis 500. It was a huge deal, a lifetime accomplishment for the knockabout journo who dared to dream. It was Crusher, not Matty, who was in tears. Crusher had his parents with him, his friends, and it was a massive moment. But above that, importantly, he'd brought Matty home safely. 'When you think what can go wrong, you feel so much responsibility for the young bloke,' Crusher said. 'Maybe, also, I set him up for an IndyCar career.'

But, so far, it hasn't happened. Matt is racing in Stadium Super Trucks, strange utility-like vehicles that blast over ramps placed around a road course. In pure motor-racing terms, it's a carnival sideshow. His talent is such that he was second in the series in each of his first two years and won it for the next two. He needs to win to earn. He can net around US$6000 a weekend, not a lot when you multiply it by only twenty race meetings in the year.

'My goal is still IndyCar,' he told me. 'But no one is going to take on a young guy without money. If I had US$ six million I could drive for any IndyCar team in the US. I've been offered deals as low as one or two million. If I could find a couple of million, I'd make something happen.'

His one consolation is that his stadium truck racing is at least an income: 'There are so many people as good as I am or even better who are not making it at all.'

There is still time. As we spoke, he had not yet celebrated his 26th birthday.

17

The Engine Room

Ando, Animal, Wombat, Mumbles, Ocka, Maori, Chip, Two Dot, Slugger, Squeak and Ziggy—to name just a few. Between them they've been the engine room for fifteen Indianapolis 500 wins—the Down Under team owners, engineers and mechanics who've made the Month of May their obsession. It's largely impossible to walk into an Indy pit garage without being assaulted by an Aussie drawl or the clipped vowel sounds of a Kiwi. They do stand out. At best count there have been more than 50 who have laid hands on the tools of the Indy trade, and two who've bet their house on running their own team. Happily, the risk-to-reward pendulum has swung in their favour.

Steve and Christine Horne, who ran Tasman Motorsport, now live back in New Zealand on beautiful Waiheke Island and keep their light aircraft and memorabilia in their own hangar at Ardmore Airport. Barry and Jeanne Green, who ran Team Green, live in Florida and sail boats, and Barry is restoring an old racing car. His brother Kim owns and promotes three IndyCar race circuits. None is mega wealthy. They leave that to Kevin Kalkhoven, an Adelaide-born, British-raised technology company innovator who owned a share of the KV Racing Team and became co-owner of Cosworth, the most successful racing-car engine maker of all time. Each has a Baby Borg on their mantelpiece, the miniature of the perpetual Borg-Warner Trophy upon which the face of every Indianapolis winner is engraved. The Down Under DNA trail weaves its way through the Indy 500 like an anthropological chromosome, joined by a common drive to succeed.

Motorsport has become rocket science. What used to be something blokes did on weekends—and, if they were lucky, turned into a day job—now requires formal university qualification. On the immaculately clean shop floor of Andretti Autosport on Zionsville Road, Indianapolis, Dave Meehan was screwing together the team's latest Indy Lights car the way he had always done it, meticulously and by hand. Dave, from Auckland, had been around awhile. He used to fettle a F5000 car for New Zealand legend Kenny Smith, pushing 80, one of the oldest active open-wheeler competitors in the world. Above Dave, upstairs in the design room, rows upon rows of earnest young men and women were punching code into computers—like an advertising agency or a bank: Mark Bryant from Hamilton, New Zealand, was booking time in the team's shared, 40-per-cent scale wind tunnel at US$30,000 a session. Mark holds a Masters in Motor Sport Engineering from Cranfield University in the UK.

Back on the floor, Ziggy Harcus, team manager and a Kiwi, in charge of a shop and road crew of more than 100 people, shook his head: 'We don't hang out as Kiwis, but we do see things differently. We're the first in and the last out. Upstairs it's a different world, more defined by regular office hours. They come in at seven and they're out by four.' Ziggy felt sorry for the new breed. He'd like them to be able to celebrate a win like he used to, but 'it's so intense—there's no time for a good night out'.

Steve Roby has been around long enough to be one of the godfathers of the Down Under contingent. He's never owned a team, but he's been mighty close to everyone else's. It's given him a unique perspective. The army brat whose dad rose to brigadier general in the Australian military, and who played fourth-grade rugby for Sydney's Easts alongside legendary commentator Gordon Bray, arrived in Indianapolis in 1976 just in time to join the McLaren team and bathe in the glory of Johnny Rutherford's win.

John 'Ando' Anderson arrived five years later and it took him another twenty to score his first Indy victory. He called the late Dan Wheldon over the line in 2005 to claim a first for them both. Two years later, he backed up for another win, this time with the Scotsman Dario Franchitti. 'It's like flying a model aircraft when you have him on a string,' Roby explained the role of the race strategist. 'If I get on the radio and say, "Get out of there", then he'd better do it.' If there's a situation the driver may not see from the cockpit, it's the strategist's call that could make or break him.

Ando, one of life's great larrikins, nicknamed Harcus 'Ziggy'. 'I had spiky hair back then,' the ever-smiling Ziggy said. 'He took one look at me and said, "You're Ziggy Stardust."' Try as he might, he couldn't shake it and his real name, Paul, sank without trace.

Ando and Ziggy were pretty much inseparable. Ziggy delighted in being recognised as Ando's wingman. They moved together from team to team—even went into management during the CART and IRL split when they took, predictably, the side of the rebel teams. They both for a few seasons worked for Barry Green, a boy from Busselton on the Margaret River in Western Australia.

The Greens were red-earth farmers, who owned some 320 hectares supporting English shorthorn cattle. Out there they raced hot-rods that they built themselves in tin sheds. Barry had harboured a desire to race pukka Formula cars, so he took the European trail and did alright, too—he spent a couple of years in Formula Three, which convinced him that 'you might be okay in Australia but in the UK you didn't see the way the guys went'.

His big opportunity came when Ron Tauranac, separated from Jack Brabham and at the time building Ralts, offered him a role as a test driver. Barry's young American wife Jeanne was given a clerical job in Ron's office—he called it office manager. They both lasted exactly one day before Tauranac's intensity got them: 'Ron was leaning over me, telling me how to use a file. I started to get a bad feeling. He had Jeanne running around the office at a crazy pace. We both agreed that night we couldn't do this.'

They went up the road to rival Chevron and stayed for two years. One of their clients was actor Paul Newman. 'You've heard of him?' Barry grinned.

Newman hired the Greens to run his Can-Am team in the United States. The actor was a successful amateur driver—he learned the craft while starring in the film *Winning*. Barry said: 'He just wanted to be one of the guys. Jeanne ran his office and his race-team budgets.' Green had been project manager on the Newman team for three years when the actor-racer merged with American race car importer Carl Haas.

'I couldn't see how I was going to fit in,' Barry said. So he moved again, taking '90 per cent' of Newman's team with him, this time to an IndyCar outfit owned by multi-millionaire Jerry Forsythe. That turned into Forsythe-Green Racing and then became Team Green when the partners fell out over the use of two promising young French-Canadian racing drivers. Barry's choice was Jacques Villeneuve, son of the late Gilles Villeneuve. Jerry wanted someone else.

Until then Jerry and Barry had been the best of buddies: 'He was an extremely good businessman; he could afford to do whatever we wanted and what he wanted to do was win and he let me do that. It was a dream come true.' Barry had even brought Ando and Ziggy on board to help set up his dream team. The split, over something as inconsequential as a driver choice, astounded the tight-knit Indianapolis motor-racing community.

Barry retained the core group for his own organisation. 'People are everything. We had 120 employees. A lot of people invested in me. I told them I'd work my ass off for them.'

In 1995 the rookie Team Green won the Indy 500 with Villeneuve. Jacques would go on to win the F1 World Championship, the title his dad had been chasing.

Team Green, Indianapolis 500 winners, had declared themselves open for business and for opportunity.

'Michael Andretti had seen what happened to his father, Mario, when he retired. He got bored very quickly. He didn't have anything after driving,' Barry told me. It was quite an insight into the mind of the world's most accomplished all-round champion. 'Michael said he wanted to be my partner, give himself a life after he retired from driving.' Barry didn't hesitate: 'I told Michael no one should ever be my partner. I'm a lone soldier.' Instead he sold the team to Michael and arranged for his brother Kim to become a minority shareholder. Barry became the team's consultant.

The Green brothers had been working together for only a relatively short time. 'My preference was not to work with Barry,' Kim said from his office in waterfront St. Petersburg, Florida, where, with partner Kevin Savoree, he runs three rounds of the IRL Series. St Pete is a quiet seaside town perfect for a life relatively free of stress. Once a year they close the streets and run the first round of the IndyCar Series. 'I wanted to build my own career and to a degree Barry [two years older] was setting my career path,' Kim said. Love interfered—a girl brought him to Indianapolis, and he joined the team just as Barry and Jerry were experiencing the first pangs of their divorce. 'Jerry was a tough old boy,' Kim said. 'Barry wanted to be his own boss and I'm not sure he thought Jerry's experience was good enough to make decisions.'

Same, it turned out, with Michael Andretti. Only this time it was Kim who was the put-out brother.

'I brought Dan Wheldon into Andretti-Green Racing and we won Indianapolis with him.' Two years on, the team brought on another UK driver, Scotsman Dario Franchitti, and they won again. 'By that time Michael wanted to take an active part in running the race team. I disagreed. I had 100 per cent respect for Michael in a race car,' he said. But today, 'I have no friendship with him.'

Just as people were confused by Barry splitting with Jerry Forsythe, Barry remains mystified by Kim's split with Michael Andretti. 'They were the best of mates,' he said. 'I sometimes wonder where the team would have gone, what we would have done, together, if Michael had not come along.'

In 2009 the name Green came off the hoarding, and the building Barry built—at the time the most outstanding race shop in all of Indianapolis—became Andretti Autosport. Ando was headhunted to be part of the start-up for the ill-fated US F1 Team, but he died suddenly of a heart attack following one of his regular racquetball games. Ziggy Harcus became the new team manager for Andretti.

Steve Horne's career path paralleled that of the Greens. He started out as a spanner man, followed by team management, then part team ownership, full team ownership, and, at the end, a well-founded judgement to get out while he was ahead. His dad was the Ferrari concessionaire in New Zealand. It wasn't as grand as it now sounds: 'He wrote to Enzo personally and said he'd like to sell his cars for him since no one else was,' Steve said. George Horne was big in New Zealand motorsport. He was on the organising committee of the first New Zealand F1 Grand Prix. In January 1957, young Steve was sitting in the wooden grandstand right opposite the control tower at the Ardmore Airport, home of the grand prix, when Englishman Ken Wharton flipped his

Ferrari Monza and died in front of him. 'People ask why I didn't become a racing driver,' he smiled ruefully.

Steve's grandmother had a shop opposite Les McLaren's garage, and Steve and his dad would visit. Stirling Moss was his hero. 'I always liked standing on corners; I learned at a young age the difference in lines, the skill in the application of brakes.' It made him an excellent judge of form. The big factor, though, was smell: 'We all have senses. The smell of Castrol R attracted me to engineering.' (Castrol R is pure mineral oil and an automotive aphrodisiac. At parties, true enthusiasts burn a little in a frying pan.)

Horne worked his way up through Kiwi motorsport, abandoning a good career as an accountant ('My mum got me to do that') to become part-time mechanic for Steve Millen ('the fastest Jag 3.8 in NZ') and then full-time for Reg Cook ('and win the NZ Touring Car Championship'). He'd been refused a job by Graham McRae ('he didn't want to know me') when in 1974 he got a telegram from an international team offering a job. Team VDS, the Belgian-based F5000 competitor owned by the quirky Count Rudi van der Straten, provided a conduit for Australians and New Zealanders to escape to the Northern Hemisphere. The count admired their work ethic—and paid in cash. 'My mum lent me $500 to buy an airfare and within a week I was at Brands Hatch in Britain with my toolbox as luggage,' Steve said.

Steve loved the international racing scene; loved Christine Gibson, too, whom he met in the UK where she worked in medical research. They married in Australia on a bet. 'I told the guys I'd marry her if we won four races of the 1978 Tasman Series in succession,' Steve said.

They lived in the US, and like so many of the husband-and-wife duos, Christine ran the team's finances while Steve took care of mechanical matters. The count's affairs were a little different to most: 'No credit cards—he'd arrive with a briefcase full of money,' Christine said.

When F5000 morphed into the closed-body Can-Am Series, it cleared a path for IndyCar to become America's true purist open-wheeler category.

The Hornes were asked by part-time team sponsor Jim Trueman to build a race team around aspiring American driver Bobby Rahal. Trueman owned motel chain Red Roof Inns, and he'd been a major financial supporter of Vern Schuppan's drive to third place in the previous year's Indianapolis 500. They called the team Truesports. It would take five years, but Rahal and Horne would win Indianapolis for Truesports in 1986, the year Jim Trueman died.

'The first thing I need is money,' Steve told Trueman when they began their Indy journey together. 'We spent US$50,000 in the first week on a shop and a trailer. I went back to Jim's secretary. She said he was skiing in Aspen. I said I need another $150,000 right now or I'm on the way back to the UK.' He got it. 'Money,' Steve said, 'is just another tool in the toolbox.'

For Steve, the IndyCar learning curve was steep. Just being around 'eye-watering methanol' was scary. 'At Phoenix in that first year we qualified second last and Bobby was yelling that the car was trying to kill him. We brought the car in for a pit stop and it caught fire.' Horne secured Lee Dykstra to help. The first thing was to convince Trueman to put a temporary stop to racing until they got the basics right: 'If we go to the next race we'll kill ourselves,' Horne told Trueman.

The race after that was Indianapolis—their first. 'You take a deep breath and you sense the heritage,' Steve said. We were sitting in the Supercar pits at Sandown in Melbourne where Steve had just resigned as the chairman of the Supercars Commission. It had been his life after active motor racing, a way of giving back.

'The sheer speed at Indianapolis is scary,' he said. 'The cars are designed to operate in a small band, and they are squirrelly. The wind swirls around the grandstands and you look to the control tower for the windsock. The fastest way around is to stay as high as you can get, minimum steering input, minimum tyre scrub. The driver has a listening tube in his helmet connected straight to the engine so he can monitor the *tick* ... *tick* ... *tick* of the turbocharger's pop-off valve. It's all about throttle control. If the pop-off valve blows, you can lose 30 horsepower [22 kilowatts].'

And then there's strategy. 'Jim Trueman owned the team, but he deferred to me,' Steve said. Though it wasn't a passive transfer.

'Jim had a strange way of empowering people,' Christine explained. 'He'd berate you, tell you to f—k off. It was his way of telling you to get on with it.'

In 1982, Rahal survived a massive first-lap melee when Kevin Cogan from the front row turned across the entire field at the start. Rahal finished eleventh. The next year he was twentieth, but in 1984 they were seventh. Truesports had become a 'works' March team. The British manufacturer was in the middle of its dominant period at Indianapolis. It won five 500s straight from 1982, three times with Team Penske. Young designer Adrian Newey arrived with the cars to help set them up. 'Bobby and I taught Adrian a lot,' Steve claimed with a grin. It's likely

Newey, renowned now as the best open-wheel car designer of the modern era, taught them a bit, too.

For a time, Enzo Ferrari wanted a piece of Truesports. The most powerful team owner in motor racing was locked in one of his many battles with Formula One over impending regulations, and he was threatening to leave that branch of the sport and head for IndyCar. Most likely it was a shock tactic, but he invited the principals of Truesports to Maranello, Italy, and had them bring their race car with them.

'I had two or three lunches with Enzo,' Steve said. 'He was intent—he wanted to win Indianapolis.' Bobby Rahal and Ferrari's driver Michele Alboreto both drove the Truesports March at the Fiorano test track opposite the factory. Then Ferrari reverse-engineered the March and built their own car— it was the Ferrari 637, designed, ostensibly, by Gustav Brunner, but inspired by Adrian Newey's March design.

In 1986 Jim Trueman was gravely ill with cancer. He arrived at the Brickyard on a mobility scooter. All race long he listened in on his headphones. Christine, as well as her lap-scoring duties, had charge of Jim's medications. It came down to four laps to go—Rahal leading, Kevin Cogan right behind.

'The fuel light is on,' Bobby shouted down the line.

'You can lift a little,' Steve told him.

But Cogan was so close, there was no opportunity. It was Steve's job to coax Bobby home except—'I was on the timing stand,' Christine said, 'and I looked down and Steve was on his knees, praying on the wall. Then Jim came across and put his arm around him.' With two laps to go, the fuel light went solid red—and it stayed like that until Bobby took the chequer.

Jim Trueman passed away ten days later. He left Steve Horne 25 per cent of his team. The Ferrari deal was off the table; perhaps it was never on it. Steve didn't pursue it. 'I just didn't feel inclined to start again,' he said.

The Hornes ran Truesports on behalf of Jim's widow Barbara and her family for five years. They started an ancilliary business, Truechoice, with New Zealand partner Phil Harris who had become IndyCar's go-to shock absorber expert. For a while Truechoice was the only place to consult if you wanted to make a car efficient. Steve and Phil were true innovators, always looking for a better way. A water-cooled brake system they designed remains a stand-out example. Phil still runs the skeleton of that business from his home on Lake Macquarie, just north of Sydney. It led to an even bigger project.

'I had a contrarian belief I could build a car made totally in the USA,' Steve said. It became the Made in America project. While other teams were relying on over-the-counter chassis, most of which, like March, were designed in the UK, Steve designed and built his own. The concept had potential but the money, and to a degree Barbara Trueman's enthusiasm, ran out before it came to fruition. 'It was always a three-year program and I was too emotionally attached to it,' Steve reflected.

Steve and Christine left Truesports in 1991. 'I left my soul behind,' he said.

The Hornes determined to spend their life savings, 'about $100,000', on establishing an Indy Lights team to foster young talent. They called it Tasman Motorsports Group—'because it sounded big'. Christine was like Mum to the mechanics.

At Truesports they'd had more than 100 people. Tasman had fewer than 50 and Steve had his own management style: 'At weekly meetings he wouldn't let them sit down,' Christine said. 'If they couldn't say it standing, it wasn't worth saying.' Australian touring-car driver and later ace commentator Neil Crompton gave Steve a five-minute egg timer to tightly control waffle.

'Indy Lights was a nursery; young drivers needed support, and so did their parents,' Steve said. 'I first used to push them away but then I realised it was better to include them in a positive way.' He'd done that with Bobby Rahal's dad Mike, back at Indianapolis. There was a lot of heart in Tasman Motorsports. They won the series four times over a period of six years and created a platform for the discovery of drivers of the calibre of Tony Kanaan.

Just like Ferrari had done, Honda came knocking on Steve's door. It's a big deal when an engine maker of world renown enters any motor-racing series; to be chosen as one of its partners was a huge fillip. Tasman stepped up to IndyCar racing. 'We'd bought two new Lola chassis but Honda wanted us to run Reynard,' Steve said. The Lola distributor Carl Haas wouldn't take his back, so Honda footed the bill for the lot. 'We were the rebels, we believed so strongly that Honda could win on debut.'

And they almost did. In 1995, with just ten laps to go, Tasman's veteran driver Scott Goodyear was leading, queued behind the pace car under a caution flag. Goodyear punched forward and in one of those split-second moments he was alleged to have passed the pace car in Turn Four. Officials gave him a black flag, ordering him to serve a drive-through penalty. Goodyear and Horne refused. They raced towards the finish, certain they could sort it out after the race but certain also they were not going to meekly give up their winning opportunity. On lap 195 they received notice of disqualification. 'It was like an arrow through my heart,' Steve said. 'But driving home that night we passed a hospital and Christine said, "There are people dying in there."' Perspective had been regained.

Steve and Christine had a firm policy not to get 'too close' to their drivers. Motor racing can be cruel—relationships can end instantly and tragically.

'Tony Kanaan was the only driver I ever got close to,' Steve said. 'When Jerry Forsythe tried to take him from us, I said I'd sue—me, sue billionaire Jerry Forsythe? Forsythe responded, "I'll buy the team." Christine and I gave him a silly number, and he took it. We stayed on for a year to help him run it, and then we quit.'

They went sailing in the Caribbean—Ando went along, naturally.

Steve Roby knows where the bodies are buried, and he won't tell. The former mechanic, team manager and head of product development for BorgWarner has knowledge of incidents that shaped and could have sunk IndyCar. Some of that knowledge will go with him to his grave. We chatted late into the night, in the vaulted lounge room of his stone-clad home in the Blue Ridge Mountains above Asheville in North Carolina, light snow falling outside, as he reflected on a remarkable career. He was happy to join the dots—connect the movements of the expat Australasians who had switched from team to team, supplier to supplier.

His early career was hitched to the driver they called 'Lone Star JR': Johnny Rutherford. JR drove with a single star in the middle of his helmet—a tribute to Texas, the Lone Star state. Roby was a mechanic on JR's McLaren when it won the Indy 500 in 1976.

He went with Rutherford to Texan Jim Hall's Chaparral team to win Indy again in 1980. 'It was the first time I was in charge,' Roby recalled. 'I said to Jim, "Let me tell you about JR. You'll need a spare car because he will crash. Don't ever wind him up, keep him calm, and trust him on engines."' McLaren and Chaparral had to build a special cockpit for Rutherford. He'd crashed a speed car and broken his arms so badly that his right arm was fixed at the elbow. 'It was why he was always better on ovals than road courses,' Roby explained.

Roby arrived at Indy via the UK. He worked with the F1 teams of Surtees, Brabham and Graham Hill. 'I was constructing the Hill F1 car and I told Graham, "I'm not going to build this car for some wanker." I talked him into using Australian Alan Jones.' Jones did four races with Hill. According to Steve, Hill invited Jones to test with him at Circuit Paul Ricard the day he had his fatal plane crash, 29 November 1975. With good fortune, Jones declined.

Roby left the Hill team at Watkins Glen in the US later that year. Without Graham, it wasn't the same. On a road trip across the States, he was hired by safety-equipment manufacturer and avid racer Bill Simpson to prepare his Indy 500 car, but it failed to qualify. 'Tyler Alexander, McLaren's team manager, grabbed me to work on the Rutherford car—and it won,' Steve said.

There was a float of Australasians in Indianapolis and Steve knew them all: 'Ocka', who wore flip-flops no matter what the weather and called them 'Maori working boots', fabricated a refuelling tank for the race pit painted as a Budweiser can. When officials told him to remove it, he carried it to Gasoline Alley and served real beer from it. Others included 'Mumbles', who arced up when food didn't arrive for the mechanics and downed tools, before having a massive blue with the team owner and driver; and Ron Baddeley, an Andretti mechanic, who invested vast amounts of money in his son's alternative career because there had to be something beyond motor racing— young Aaron became one of the world's best golfers.

For more than a decade Roby was the chairman of the Louis Schwitzer Award committee, a prize awarded in the name of the Swiss engineer and innovator who won the very first race at the Indianapolis Motor Speedway in 1909. The Schwitzer encourages and recognises safety advances. In 2002 it went to the group of medicos who developed SAFER, the energy-absorbing safety fence that now shields the speedway. In 2008 the award was given to a development of an Australian invention, the Bishop variable ratio rack and pinion steering system (a more efficient means of control and of damping vibration, a perennial Indianapolis problem), which recognised the work of Arthur Bishop, a Sydney engineering genius who had died in 2006. Engineering should be celebrated as the heartbeat of motor-racing success.

And then I asked about the Atlanta project, a source of controversy that's been swirling for decades. Roby went comparatively silent. It is important to emphasise he was not involved—the timing was wrong—but he knows what happened and he won't tell. Half a century on, the Atlanta project is still spoken of in whispers.

In 1971, the year after Bruce McLaren's death, the McLaren M16 shaped the future of IndyCar racing. It introduced aerodynamics unheard of in IndyCar—wings cunningly built into bodywork in such a way that they circumvented regulations; cooling systems so efficient that they promoted flat-out engine performance. Penske Racing's Mark Donohue took pole in the M16 and was romping away with the race when his transmission failed. The M16 was the class of the field and Donohue won in it the next year.

But by then a copy of the car had appeared on the grid— the Atlanta. It was the result, Steve Roby told me, of an internal 'issue' with McLaren team personnel. A deal had been struck whereby mechanics would receive a bonus if their car claimed pole and they'd get more if it won. The race mechanics believed the bonus applied only to them. Management, back in the UK, wanted to share it with all 44 team personnel including those at the McLaren factory. 'This did not sit well with the team at Indianapolis,' Steve said.

Indy was in the grip of a war between tyre companies. Firestone was under threat from Goodyear. 'The disgruntled McLaren group was approached by Gene White, the Firestone race tyre distributor, with funds to build a car,' Steve recalled. White was based in Atlanta, Georgia, hence the name.

The following year two Atlantas—M16 copies—were driven to fifth and tenth in the 1972 race. They didn't win because they weren't as good as the original. McLaren had designed the M16 chassis around the Offenhauser engine. The two Atlantas were fitted with Fords, which sat higher in the chassis and adversely affected the balance of the car. A designer could have fixed that but a pit crew member, less qualified and working from memory, most likely could not.

So it was simple: Atlanta had been the product of misplaced loyalties and slack IP regulations, nothing more. Except: 'What about the footprint in the paint, Steve?' I asked. He smiled but wouldn't speak.

The story that has swirled for so long is that the original design drawings for the M16 were kept in an office on the other side of a floor that had just been freshly painted. The only way in was to crawl over lathes and benches. But there was a slip and a single footprint was implanted in the paint. It was enough for McLaren to call in Scotland Yard. Imagine if that had gone public—allegations of industrial spying involving a major manufacturer and a winning race team, centred on the world's most important motor race. A lawsuit, it's said, was later settled, quietly and privately.

Later, in a more transparent age, motor racing was rocked by much larger cases of espionage. In 2004 two Ferrari employees were convicted of taking vital information with them when they joined Toyota. They were dismissed by Toyota. In 2007, McLaren Automotive was fined $100 million and stripped of its points in the Formula One World Constructors' Championship for 'illicitly collecting information from Ferrari'.

In the circumstances, the Atlanta project was a minor infraction, if at all. It's part of the legend of Indy and one day someone, just for the record, might come clean.

18

Aussie Heroes

'This is the greatest spectacle in racing and today one of these drivers will do something we will never, ever, forget.' Turn Four, 33 colourful cars in perfect formation, a quarter of a million fans at the track, an average of 5.4 million TV viewers, peaking at 6.7 million, and the voice full of measured excitement, not overhyped but not undermodulated, was calling the starters in the Indianapolis 500 down to the line. One chance to get it right. Timing—perfect. 'Green . . . Green . . . Green.' In 2019, Leigh Diffey became the first non-US-born commentator to call play-by-play for the world's greatest motor-racing spectacle. NBC Sports, America's Olympic Network, had won the rights to the Indy 500 from ABC, which had held them for 54 years. NBC had appointed Diffey as its anchor. It seemed like only yesterday he'd been a physical education teacher at Ipswich Grammar.

He had been at the Brickyard before dawn—not for the telecast but for the atmosphere. 'I wanted to hear the gun sound when the gates opened at 6 a.m., see the traffic stretching for a mile, listen to the music coming from the car radios.'

It was a crisp May morning and, as for most things that had happened in his life, Diffey was counting his earned blessings. He had also been appointed to call the track and field at the 2020 summer Tokyo Olympics (postponed because of the global health pandemic). There are few bigger gigs in live sport.

In motorsport, the NASCAR–IndyCar balance was being redressed. NBC had increased its audience by 11 per cent in that first year. NASCAR's Daytona 500 had dropped from 12 million to 9 million in two years. Diffey had hosted a NASCAR chat show for NBC and called two events as a standby, but 'they'd never let a foreign voice do it full-time'. Australian Supercar fans knew Diffey as 'Stiffy', a sobriquet given him by twice world motorcycle champion Barry Sheene, who'd moved to Australia because the metal in his shattered legs couldn't stand a Northern Hemisphere winter. Greg Rust, calling alongside Diffey, was 'Thruster'. Sheene, a first-class larrikin and amazingly well connected, encouraged Diffey to take his talent offshore.

Diffey had come up the classic way—his grandfather Clifton Dorset Diffey raced a Rudge Ulster with some success. His father, disappointed he was never allowed to do what Clifton had done, helped his boys Colin and Leigh when they went flat-track racing. Leigh picked up a microphone at Queensland's Tivoli motocross circuit ('we can pay you $60') and progressed to Supercross Masters under the tutelage of promoter

Phil Christensen, coincidentally an IndyCar tragic. Diffey bet his whole teaching career on crossing the border into New South Wales, ended up at Network Ten's *Sports Tonight* learning to be a reporter ('I'd never touched a typewriter') and went on air when Sports Director David White invested the station's flagging fortunes in V8 Supercar racing.

In 1999 Diffey was at the Le Mans 24 Hour race, co-hosting a documentary for Australian TV, his first offshore assignment. It was called 'as live'; as the cars came over the display ramp, he had one chance to nail the all-important intro. And he did it, his timing perfect. 'What are you doing in Australia when you could be doing it for the world?' the production crew needled him. Many others encouraged him, too, including British motorsport impresario Andrew Marriott; and his good friend 'Five Toes', motorcycle racer Daryl Beattie, second in the world champion-ship, who lost the toes on one foot to a hungry drive chain.

Diffey left Australia the next year—Network Ten was none too pleased—and worked for the BBC, on bikes and cars ('I called the CART race at the Lausitzring when Alex Zanardi lost his legs'), migrated to Speed Channel in the States and joined NBC in 2012. Most commentators are specialists in one branch of motorsport. Diffey does the lot. He has the widest repertoire of anyone in the business. He once called the Italian Grand Prix from NBC Sports' massive studio complex in Stamford, Connecticut, then drove to Watkins Glen to commentate the IndyCar GP later the same day.

He seems not to do his homework and yet he does. In his commentary position there's a one-pager on each of the teams. He calls it his 'wall of words'. He's renowned for his pre-dawn phone calls to his producers with helpful ideas. His co-commentators are friends: 'You must get on off-air to get on on-air' is his motto. At the Indy 500 he called with former racers Paul Tracy, 'who should have won in 2002 with Team Green', and Townsend Bell, who is still current in IMSA sports cars. 'They can speculate; it's not my job to tell an audience what an athlete is going through. My job is to build up the drama,' Leigh said. But never to overhype it. 'If a race is poor, you can't whip it into a frenzy. People know what they're seeing.' The Diffey style is casual and relaxed; if he's clearly having a good time, the audience will too.

Leigh took US citizenship when he joined NBC, and bought a home with its own (small) lake in historic Ridgefield, Connecticut, half an hour from the studio, where the Red Coats marched down the main street 250 years ago. He and his wife Michaela and their two sons eat at a restaurant run by the Citroën-owning brother-in-law of Keith Richards. 'Keith comes in spasmodically, but you never acknowledge his presence.'

Diffey once sat in the Indy stands with his father-in-law eating hot dogs and wearing their caps backwards. He rode in the IndyCar two-seater with Mario Andretti and when he called the 2019 race, it was 'the most exhilarating moment in my career'. Timing—perfect.

An IndyCar weighs 1590 pounds (721 kilograms) and at full boost puts out close to 700 horsepower (522 kilowatts). A fully enclosed NASCAR weighs double that, at 3450 pounds (1566 kilograms) and develops around 30 per cent more power, 1000 horsepower (746 kilowatts). The fastest NASCAR ever to go around the Indianapolis Motor Speedway was driven by Kevin Harvick; in 2014 he qualified his Chevrolet at 188.889 mph (303.922 km/h). On one magic day in 1996 Arie Luyendyk set the IndyCar dream lap: 237.498 mph (382.134 km/h). That's one reason why the NASCARs race the Brickyard '400', not a full '500'. Depending on race interruptions, the two classics take about the same time and require the same spectator attention span.

The inaugural Brickyard 400 was held in 1994, two years before the IRL split. NASCAR was about to explode into the psyche of race fans, and racing at the Brickyard gave it boasting rights. It also introduced NASCAR to Tony George. Australia's Geoff Brabham made his one and only NASCAR Winston Cup Series start in that race, driving for Mike Kranefuss, the former head of Ford's international racing efforts who retired to become a NASCAR team owner. The car was crashed by Robby Gordon in the previous race at Michigan's superspeedway and it crashed for Geoff, too, just after halfway. He was classified 38th. Ten Australians and New Zealanders have chanced their arm at NASCAR racing—amongst them Touring Car champions Dick Johnson and Jim Richards, and twice Bathurst 1000 winner Allan Grice. But only one has given it the commitment to carve a real career out of it.

Tasmanian Marcos Ambrose did nine seasons of NASCAR and won two NASCAR races, both on the Watkins Glen road course.

Ambrose won the Supercars Championship twice (2003, 2004) and might have done it again in 2005 if not for a now infamous clash with Kiwi Greg Murphy on the climb up to the Cutting at Mount Panorama in the Bathurst 1000 that put them both out. He'd already announced his intention to head for the USA at the end of that year.

Marcos was a product of open-wheeler racing. His dad Ross, a former racer, was a shareholder in Van Diemen Formula Ford cars. Marcos had taken his talent to the UK, raced Formula Three against Jenson Button, Kimi Räikkönen and Dan Wheldon, and returned to domestic sedan racing when the money ran out. He caught the NASCAR bug when he was on honeymoon with Sonja, naturally at Daytona. His Ford connections set him up with good—but not great—teams. In the closed shop of NASCAR, he made a name for himself as a good, hard runner, respectful of the heritage and the rules of engagement. When he won on the road course at Watkins Glen in 2008, he became one of only four non-US-born drivers to ever win a NASCAR Cup race (and one of those was Italian-born Mario Andretti).

There are few tracks that take your breath away, Marcos told me, sitting in his car with Ross, heading into the Tasmanian hinterland to inspect one of the family's wilderness lodge investments. 'Indianapolis is something special, so big, so daunting. You can feel the history, think about the winners, Foyt, the Unsers. And you think about those who didn't make it out. You'd be a fool not to.'

In 2008 he was at Indianapolis with the Wood Brothers and at the base of the learning curve. 'There's nowhere to hide. Anyone who thinks they can do an oval—any oval—needs to think again. Even in a straight line the cars don't handle that well. You need to find corner grip. Get too much slip angle and you can lose three seconds in 30 seconds. If you miss the line into a corner by a foot, you can be two metres too wide by the centre.'

Marcos's insight into the NASCAR experience is revealing, a lesson in taming the Brickyard. He separated Indy into two sequences—Turns One and Two, and then Turns Three and Four. Turn One was 'closed in, very narrow'. How fast he exited Turn Two dictated his entry into Three. 'You roll off the throttle early, soft on the brake, carry momentum. If you hit the brake too hard, the front spoiler can hit the ground. The tyre is the biggest suspension component on the car and the right rear wheel holds the whole car up. You apply the half-and-half rule—a half toe out on the right, a half toe in on the left. As soon as you get it mid-corner, you hammer the throttle.'

The first time he went to Indy he was stymied by tyre wear: 'They'd just groomed the track and it shredded the tyres. We allowed for three to four sets in practice. We did five. I was thinking we're either going to qualify or bin it. In the race they were just delaminating. It was hard to do more than ten laps. We were relying on a caution every few laps to reduce wear. We just weren't dialled into the track at all. Some teams were, others weren't. Indy is like that.'

History records Marcos as a good, consistent mid-field finisher at Indianapolis—his best result a sixteenth in 2013, his lowest a 34th in 2011, his average a 22nd. You had to be born to ovals. 'I had the opportunity to run better than I did,' he mused. 'In road racing I was able to steer the team in the direction I wanted. I couldn't engineer the oval car with the same authority.'

Marcos almost did a decade in the States. He could have stayed on, but it was punishing. The NASCAR series criss-crosses the country—a minimum of 36 races a year. 'Jimmie Johnson had twelve employees, a private plane, a fitness coach, a nanny. I was doing it myself.' He and Sonja had two growing daughters,

Adelaide and Tabitha, and he missed his folks at home. He returned to Australia to take up his Supercars career for Roger Penske's new team—'You don't say no to Roger Penske,' he grinned—but development within the series had moved on, and Marcos pulled the pin.

'He was very gracious in the way he handled it,' Penske told the media. 'Quite honestly, I respect him.'

Marcos has built his own simulator motion rig at home and races 'socially' against Scott McLaughlin and Shane van Gisbergen. He drives in international sim-racing series under an alias.

Australian fighter pilot Matt Hall could not get Turn Three right. Not ever. In three years of contesting the Red Bull Air Race just marginally overhead the Brickyard, he clipped the 25-metre-tall air gate each time, incurring a penalty. 'I cannot explain it, it became a standing frustration.' Turn Three is a chicane set up above the Indianapolis Motor Speedway infield, near the golf course opposite the Pagoda. It needed to be taken at a huge angle. 'Maybe I was being overaggressive,' he surmised. There's a lot of similarity between an aerobatic aircraft and an IndyCar. It's best not to overdrive either of them.

The Red Bull Air Race was another of the great diversification ideas of the Indianapolis Motor Speedway to maximise the full potential of its venue. The extreme lifestyle energy-drink maker had inaugurated the global air race series in 2003, taking Formula One to the skies. It never reached the proportions of F1, but it was an exciting spectacle. When it shut down in 2020,

Hall, the only Australian ever to fly the series, was its champion. 'I guess that makes me unbeaten and perpetual,' he joked.

Hall flew a Zivko Edge 540, an American-built, specialised single-seat competition machine about the same length as an IndyCar. Its six-cylinder Lycoming engine developed less than half an IndyCar's power, 308 horsepower (230 kilowatts); it weighed a little less, 1169 pounds (531 kilograms) dry weight; and its manufacturer imposed a maximum 230-knot (425-km/h) airspeed on its frame. But it could roll through 420 degrees in a second and withstand forces of plus or minus twelve times the force of gravity.

'From the time it breaks loose to when it falls out of the sky takes about 0.6 seconds,' Matt said. That happened to him just the once, thankfully over water, and he pulled it back from a semi-submersed position to land safely. Part of the skill is the pilot's ability to find the horizon and hold the aircraft to it. 'It's not something you can learn in a sim,' he said. 'It's muscle memory on the stick.' In other words, practised intuition. A racing driver's skill.

Matt was a third-generation pilot; his grandfather served in World War II. Matt's theatre was Iraq in 2003, where in 'an eight-second event' he fought for his life as three ground-to-air missiles homed in on him and he rolled his USAF F15 fighter out of the last one's way with so little room to spare that all other options had been exhausted. Matt was an eighteen-year veteran of the RAAF, had clocked up 1500 F/A-18 Hornet hours and was a fighter combat instructor when the mood took him to go air racing. He talked it over with his wife Pedita. 'These guys are crazy,' he said. 'It's got you all over it,' she replied. He resigned his commission and underwent Red Bull's stringent qualification procedures. Not even a fighter pilot earned automatic inclusion.

Red Bull modified its racecourse to fit into spectacular venues: over Perth's Swan River, landing on Langley Park where the World Rally Championship used to run; over the Thames in the heart of London; at Interlaken; and past the Chain Bridge in Budapest. Surprisingly, it doesn't take much space.

At Indianapolis it fit into the infield, overflying the grandstands at Turns Three and Four to the north, landing and taking off on 500 metres of access road near Hulman Boulevard down the middle of the course, and slightly overflying the golf course to the east. The course had ten gates, each 10 metres wide. With a wingspan of close to 8 metres, there was not a great margin for error.

'Crosswind was a major issue,' Matt recalled. The same challenge that beset IndyCar drivers affected the air racers too. 'The wind generated within the grandstand created huge turbulence that could push you into a gate—20 knots [37 km/h] of crosswind equalled 10 metres of sideways movement for the aircraft.'

Red Bull Racing was not pylon racing, where multiple aircraft race together. Red Bull was more like rallying—one at a time—or like a blindingly committed qualifying run for the Indy 500. The pilots would walk the course beforehand, finding visual reference points to guide their turn-in and acceleration cues. Each race was two and a half laps over a 3.1-mile (5-kilometre) course and at Indy it took around 1 minute 4 seconds.

Matt Hall is built like a racing driver—slight of frame and compact in the cockpit. Fully kitted with helmet and suit, he weighs 75 kilograms. But when he hit maximum g, the forces of gravity compressed him, and he would for an instant weigh

900 kilograms. The Zivko could take him from zero to 10 g's in 3/100ths of a second. His body could sustain that force for only 2–2.5 seconds—'how long it took for the blood to drain from my brain'. Yet through it all his hands had to remain soft and fluid on the stick. 'Adrenaline is not your friend,' he told me. 'It means you're pushing too hard.' Matt spoke of a phenomenon called temporal distortion, known to racing drivers as well. It's when time slows down so the pilot or driver can make conscious decisions in an instant. 'I have one and a half hours of memory from the 0.6 seconds it took me to hit the water,' he laughed.

Forty-five thousand people watched the final day of the last Indianapolis Red Bull Air Race and Matt would love to go back to complete unfinished business. Meanwhile he is biding his time at the airfield he bought at Lake Macquarie, in New South Wales, running a charter operation, taking joy rides and waiting for his son Mitchell to be old enough to follow in the family tradition.

The Indianapolis Motor Speedway hosted a round of the World MotoGP from 2008 to 2015. Australia's twice world champion Casey Stoner scored the perfect triple there in 2011—pole, fastest lap, win—and it set him up for his second world title. 'I thought we could do it again in 2012,' he said. Stoner, just 26, had already announced that it would be his last year in the sport and a third world title would be a nice way to bow out. It wasn't to be, but his ride at Indianapolis that year went down as one of the bravest the sport has known.

Casey Stoner subscribed to the code of top riders injured in the most unforgiving and precarious branch of all motorsport: 'Suck it up and get on with it.' In qualifying at Indianapolis in 2012 the electronic traction control of his Honda RC213V malfunctioned and high-sided him on Turn Thirteen, the tight left-hander that skirts the Brickyard's IndyCar Turn Four. 'As soon as I tried to stand up and put weight on my right leg I felt a clunk like the tibia and fibula had broken—and that meant out for the season. But it turned out my ankle was still attached to my leg and I thought, "I can get points out of this,"' Stoner said from his acreage in the Gold Coast hinterland where he lives with his wife Adriana (she was once a young fan) and two daughters.

'The Indianapolis road course was not fantastic as a bike track,' he explained. 'It ran clockwise for the IndyCar GP and Formula One [there were eight F1 races at the Brickyard from 2000] but they reversed the direction for the bikes. They were concerned about safety, speeds too high and not enough runoff. But the corners in that direction were always closing on you, getting tighter, and you were forever braking on the side of the tyre, putting traction at risk.'

Of all the riders in MotoGP, Casey Stoner was the master of the big, controlled power drift. On an opening radius bend, he could initiate and hold a power slide like no one else. But such corners were in short supply at Indy. He crashed in 2010, chasing Valentino Rossi, when the front end of his ill-handling Ducati washed away on one of the closing radius turns. Stoner had won Ducati's only world title for them in 2007; no one rode Ducati to its full potential like him, but even he ultimately called it quits. He moved to Honda and won his second world title in their first year together. 'Most riders at the time complained about the Honda,' he said. 'I quietly thought to myself: *They haven't ridden the Ducati.*'

Stoner had not grown up following cars. He left Australia when he was just fourteen and with his parents chased the European dream, living in caravans and maintaining focus on their motorcycle grand prix ambition. He knew little about the Indianapolis 500 or its heritage. 'I was overwhelmed when I first went there—just the sheer scale of it—and it could hold so many spectators.' It disappointed him, though, that most of the motorcycle action occurred behind Gasoline Alley away from the grandstands. 'It wasn't like Europe where spectators could get right around the track.'

To a degree, the track suited him—not its direction, but its surface: 'The Europeans liked grip, a circuit that felt good under them. Coming from a dirt-track background, I was more comfortable when the circuit was a bit dirty and slippery.' Indianapolis delivered. There were three changes of surface over every lap and 'the changes were on big joins right in the middle of a corner'.

He was accelerating hard on the Honda in 2012 when the electronic traction control was caught out by the surface. 'I was trying to get on the gas while it was shutting down, slowing the wheel.' He was flipped over the bars and slid chest-down along the track while the bike pirouetted in the air behind him. He ended up in the 'cat-stretch' position and when he tried to stand, his right leg wouldn't take the weight. 'Indianapolis has a really good medical system,' he said. 'They determined it wasn't a tib-fib and by midnight they'd completed all the scans.'

Next morning he woke to an ankle that was so swollen 'it went straight from calf to foot and there were no longer any visible toes'. He swallowed Aspalgin—pain relief then readily available and now only by prescription—had his boot maker modify a boot to be four times larger than his normal size, and went out to race. 'Most people have spot injections for the pain,' he said, explaining with great nonchalance the need for pain alleviation, which is a constant in a motorcycle rider's life. 'But spot relief only holds up for maybe twenty minutes and I need it for the full 45 minutes of a grand prix. The pain never goes away. It gets to a point where your body collapses on it.'

Casey started from fourth grid position. He'd done only one flying lap before the crash to achieve that. 'The race was a bit of a blur. I spent most of it trying not have people run into me.' Casey liked a lot of rear brake to set the bike up for corners. Not that day. He locked his leg in position on the peg and relied almost entirely on front brake alone. 'I got to within three laps of the end before the pain really got to me,' he said. He let Yamaha rider Andrea Dovizioso through into third and coasted over the line in fourth to where his crutches were waiting. 'The scans had come back and I needed corrective surgery. If I'd crashed in that race, I probably would never have walked straight again.'

Despite missing three rounds, he still claimed third in the world title and in the last race of his career won the Australian Grand Prix for the sixth successive time.

Three Australian Formula One drivers flirted, briefly, with the idea of racing at Indianapolis.

Mark Webber, nine-time F1 winner, entered early negotiations with Indy team owner Jerry Forsythe two years before he entered F1. Webber was part of Mercedes-Benz sports-car team—a huge and coveted contract for a young driver—but after his car crashed twice in the 1999 Le Mans 24 Hour, flying through the air because of a major aerodynamic flaw, Webber was keen to extricate himself from that very dangerous space.

Forsythe was using Mercedes engines so the transition was logical and could have been factory supported. Webber and his wife Ann had drawn up three parallel paths to achieve Mark's goal of reaching F1 by 2001. IndyCars was one of them, but by then Webber was well advanced on his European campaign.

Mark raced at Indianapolis five times when the World F1 Championship went to the Indianapolis Motor Speedway between 2000 and 2007. It would have been six, but he was part of the 2006 debacle when Michelin could not guarantee the safety of the tyres it brought to the US Grand Prix, especially on the speedway's high-speed Turn One banking, which the F1 cars drove in the opposite direction. Michelin's teams, of which Webber's Williams was one, completed only the formation lap before pulling permanently to the pits. Just six cars, the Bridgestone runners, contested that grand prix, won by Michael Schumacher. Indianapolis was not kind to Webber. His best—in fact only—race finish on the speedway's grand prix circuit was seventh in 2007, his first points for his new Red Bull team and the last time the F1 grand prix ran at Indianapolis after Tony George found the cost of F1 untenable.

Australia's 1980 World Formula One Champion Alan Jones tried oval racing just the once. It was 1976 and he was keen to break the F1 contract he had with John Surtees, the only man ever to win the world title on two wheels and four, but also one of the hardest, most demanding and most frustrating of team owners. The money on offer in IndyCar racing had big appeal. 'Teddy Yip financed a test for me in Bill Simpson's McLaren at Ontario Motor Speedway,' Jones recalled from his Gold Coast home, but the test did not go well. 'I was taking lines like an F1 driver—up high on the banking and then diving down to the apex on the white line. A.J. Foyt walked up to me and said, "Boy—we don't take lines here, we just go around."' Foyt's message was clear—the only way to survive on the high-speed ovals was to maintain a predictable discipline.

The forthright Jones was unimpressed. 'I saw it all as a bit like rollerball,' he said. 'You could be driving around in seventh place, minding your own business, when the guy in second would have a monumental crash and suddenly you'd be part of it. I'm not decrying it. Driving the ovals is a black art. But it's not for me.' Jones went back to Formula One and won his world title for Williams four years later. In 1984 he was called up to drive for Newman/Haas in an IndyCar road race at Elkhart Lake, Wisconsin, subbing for the injured Mario Andretti. He brought it home third.

Australian and New Zealand Grands Prix winner Warwick Brown, who drove in F1 just the once—the 1976 US Grand Prix at Watkins Glen where he finished fourteenth after losing third and fifth gears—thought the IndyCar drivers were heroes. Brown was the bravest of the brave—the first driver to get a F5000 car through the right-hand sweeper under the bridge at Surfers Paradise without lifting the throttle. 'There's two or three occasions in your life that stick with you as something special,' he said. 'For me, the standout was Turn One at Indianapolis—three cars abreast at something like 240 mph

[386 km/h]. People don't realise how violent motor racing can be . . . 10,000 horsepower [7460 kilowatts] all trying to get into the same piece of real estate at the same moment. There's technique involved, but it's more about balls.'

Brown tested an IndyCar just the once: 'But it was a start-up team, and they had no idea what they were doing. The test was terrible. I just sat there, thinking, "I've got a good contract in F5000 [he was with Team VDS] and I don't need to take this risk." If it had been a good team, I would have loved to race Indy.'

In late 2017, twice sports-car World Endurance Champion Brendon Hartley faced the dilemma every racer wished they had. The Palmerston North racer was to sign a contract to contest the 2018 Indianapolis Racing League series with Chip Ganassi alongside countryman Scott Dixon—a Kiwi dream team. But Red Bull Racing stepped up with an offer to join their Scuderia Torro Rosso Formula One team. Hartley had been a Red Bull Junior team member before being passed over. Now they wanted him back, and F1 had been his personal dream. 'It gave me many sleepless nights,' Hartley told Greg Rust's popular podcast *Rusty's Garage*. Fast and furious negotiations extracted him from IndyCar and installed him in F1. But Hartley only drove the one season and his best results were two tenths and a ninth. Red Bull removed him from their Formula One roster, and he moved on to Formula E.

By 2008, Australians and New Zealanders had won world titles on two wheels and four, even in the air. They'd won at Monaco and Le Mans. Indianapolis, though, had evaded them. A wave was building, you could feel it.

19

The Winner Is . . . Dixon

'I don't think I knew it was the last lap. I went through Turn One flat out. Then the team came on the radio and said, "You've just won the Indianapolis 500."' Even now, sitting in the immaculate family room of his immaculate home with his immaculate wife Emma at his side, Scott Dixon, the first of two Australasians ever to win at the Brickyard, just could not find the words to explain the feeling.

'There were no tears, no cries of elation—I just wanted to get back to the pits fast, to see the team, to see Emma.'

It had been the perfect year. In 2008 he had won Indy from pole position, won the American Championship and married English Commonwealth Games athlete Emma Davies in the Yellow Drawing Room of the Duke of Richmond's Goodwood House.

Later, he became the most successful driver in the Indy Racing League Series (five championships) and with Emma had earned admiration as the most understated power couple in all contemporary motor racing. They had added three children—Poppy, Tilly and, after a bit of a wait, Kit—to their accomplishments. The kids were the most important of all. Scott and Emma's future vision included England for the girls' middle school (because of Emma they have a home there) and New Zealand for college. Their spectacular Cotswold-influenced Indianapolis home, designed by Emma, would have been the end game for most high achievers but for them it was lovely, wonderful, but saleable. 'I like to keep it minimalist,' Scott told me without a hint of irony or insincerity. 'I'm quite happy to travel coach. I could think of doing a lot more with the money.'

So much achieved. He would soon turn 40. Time to stop? 'It's just a number. I'm driving much better than I was ten years ago and I'm still improving. TK [Tony Kanaan, fellow Indy 500 winner and friend] is 46.'

The media call Scott Dixon the 'Iceman', the same as Formula One's Kimi Räikkönen, but the name is all they share. Räikkönen is a known tearaway who uses silence as a shield. Dixon is genuinely quiet and shy—humble is not too big a stretch—and in a car his attitude is more one of balanced determination than unbridled risk. Like Räikkönen, he recognises his natural environment is the cockpit, not a press conference: 'I tell [team owner] Chip Ganassi that he pays me to do media. I do the driving for free.'

Scott Dixon was the world's first crowd-funded racing driver. In the late 1990s when Scott had to break free from New Zealand before it stifled his ambition, his fundraiser was a novel concept, initiated by his father Ron, refined by businessmen Craig Harris and Chris Wingate, supported by Auckland motor dealer and massive enthusiast Peter 'PJ' Johnston, and endorsed by rich-lister Sir Colin Giltrap. Twenty-five shareholders invested in a Dixon-specific company, all but one with no more ambition than to see him succeed and get their money back. 'I had a chat with that person and they've now all been paid back,' said Kenny Smith, five-time New Zealand Gold Star champion, three-time New Zealand Grand Prix winner and a Dixon devotee.

Smith, the elder statesman of New Zealand motor racing, had been approached by Ron and Glenys Dixon to mentor their precocious son. They had spent ten years in Australia, running a restaurant in Rockhampton, working the Far North Queensland gem fields, driving effluent pump-out trucks, racing speedway (Ron broke his back in a stock-car crash), and managing Townsville's Bohle Speedway on the edge of the city. They lived in a house on the track. Scott, born in Brisbane, shared a bedroom with his two sisters. Their parents bought them 50cc PeeWee motorcycles.

Back in New Zealand, Scott went go-karting with his sister Adelle when he was seven. Glenys became a karting mum with all that implies. They're at every club sporting event—the mums with the hearts of gold—organising, directing, time keeping, judging, cajoling, disciplining, mostly all at once. Inevitably they're controversial: 'You get so much flak from parents—"who do they think they are?",' Glenys told me. But kids' sport can't live without them. On the day we spoke, Glenys turned up at her neat two-storey townhouse in Dannemora, east of the Auckland CBD, fresh from netball, driving the Honda Scott had got her from the local distributor with the numberplate INDMUM. She had become a netball and cheerleading grand-mum, with a side interest in helping Honda run New Zealand's 2-litre touring-car series. 'I've been at Pukekohe all weekend and at Western Springs Speedway on Saturday night,' she said breathlessly.

When Scott cracked it big in the States, Ron and Glenys spent eight years with him, driving his RV so that he would have some form of comfort at the racetracks. They weren't on their own. Danica Patrick's folks and Dario Franchitti's dad were part of the parental support caravan. For the Dixons, it wasn't a new experience. Karting in New Zealand, at Scott's level, demanded constant travel. They bought a campervan but were just as happy in a tent. 'We always camped, no hotels, we didn't have money to spend,' Scott said. His obvious pride in home and family is like a badge of honour he wears even now.

Enthusiasm drove them. They secured Scott a special licence to race cars at thirteen. When he rolled a Nissan Sentra at Pukekohe Raceway, south of Auckland, TV cameras caught him leaving the upturned car with a pillow strapped to his back so he could reach the pedals. 'He was the youngest in the world to race a single-seater,' Glenys proudly proclaimed. In 1994, he won the New Zealand Formula Vee Championship at fourteen and the national Formula Ford title at fifteen. By then Kenny Smith had stepped in.

'He was just a kid,' Kenny said. 'He had a TV in his tent so he could watch cartoons between races.' Kenny helped the Dixons set up the car and helped Scott learn how to use it.

In Australia, Kenny introduced Scott to New Zealand expat

Graham Watson who had the agency for Ralt racing cars. He claimed Rookie of the Year in the Australian Gold Star title then won it the next year in Simon Hardwidge's Reynard, engineered by his flatmate Trevor Schumack. The Holden Racing Team offered him a test at the short Calder circuit in Victoria. The plan was to integrate him into their Young Lions program—a stairway to Supercars. He was sensational, but he gave the car low marks on brakes and handling. Perhaps because of that youthful honesty, the test went nowhere. Instead, he turned to the United States. He was just eighteen.

'There were a lot of people in the USA I knew that I didn't know I knew,' Kenny Smith joked. In 1998 he and Scott had flown to Laguna Seca Raceway in California on an exploratory mission. It was hard to keep the kid focused. 'He wouldn't get eye contact with anyone; he'd rather go back to the hotel for a swim,' Kenny said. Smith had done a lot of legwork already by telephone. He had a three-way conversation going—with two Australians and a New Zealander, all in Indianapolis.

'Vern Schuppan didn't want to know me,' he said. Schuppan had joined fellow Le Mans 24 Hour winner Stefan Johansson in an Indy Lights and management company. With twenty or so young prospects pushing for a test with the team, the prospect of trialling a seemingly disinterested youngster from Down Under was not appealing. 'I knew how hard it was for an Australian or New Zealander to get traction in the States,' Vern had told me. But Kenny persevered. He not only talked Vern into a test, but got it at half price—US$10,000.

'Ando [John Anderson, who was running PacWest] agreed to slot Scott into a car the day before Vern's formal test,' Kenny said. 'It was an opportunity for him to learn what an Indy Lights car felt like.' At Laguna Seca, Steve Horne from Tasman Motorsports joined in the fun. 'He let it be known up and down pit row that he was keen to talk to Scott and me.' It was a red herring. Steve didn't have the capacity to take Scott on. He knew what he was doing—sparking additional interest in the young Kiwi.

They arrived at Sebring, the flat, featureless airport circuit upstate from Miami, Florida. PacWest went first on day one. 'He was so good in a comparatively poor car that they were tempted to sign him then,' Kenny said.

The Johansson test was even better. 'We'd gathered twenty drivers that day,' Schuppan said. 'It was a big test. I was over the back of the track when one of the good guys, an Italian, arrived. Scott had baulked him on his out lap and the guy had fist-waved him as he went past. Next lap Scott out-braked him and drove away.' Dixon was flat-lining the esses, one gear up on the rest of the test field.

Schuppan called Johansson and said, 'We have to have this guy.' It's usual for young drivers to pay but Schuppan had a career-long policy: 'I've never run a pay-driver in my team. If they're good enough, we should pay them.' Schuppan flew to New Zealand and extracted a US$100,000 commitment from Scott's backers to cover his test activities throughout the year. 'Fair enough they should do that,' he said. The racing would be covered by sponsorship from an IT company Schuppan and Johansson had secured. 'It costs about US$800,000 to run an Indy Lights team.'

It was new territory for them all. Vern had joined Stefan only that year expecting to move quickly from Indy Lights to Champ Car. Dixon was their big hope—a driver so good in Schuppan's opinion that he could 'go all the way to Formula One', and they had him under a five-plus-five-year contract. They took him to Dijon for an F1 test with the Prost team: 'I couldn't believe the sheer pace of the cars, how nimble they were,' Scott said. He tested later, too, with Williams—but his eyes were always on Indianapolis.

No one was making money. Dixon wasn't being paid except for a stipend from home, Schuppan had agreed to exist on subsistence wages to help fund the team's first year, the IT sponsor was having the vapours, and Scott's New Zealand backers weren't paying their bills on time. 'At Long Beach, California, Stefan said Scott couldn't get in the car unless money arrived,' Vern said. Vern countermanded the order. They'd bet heavily on Scott. There was no pulling out.

Scott was in major contention for Indy Lights' Rookie of the Year. Schuppan recalled: 'By the last round, the only way he could be beaten was if Northern Ireland's Jonny Kane, driving for Barry Green's team, started from pole, won outright and Scott finished out of the points.' But that's what happened. A puncture had dropped Scott back through the field. He finished second to Kane in the title by a single point.

Under huge financial pressure, the Johansson–Schuppan partnership dissolved. Scott's management was taken up by Stefan Johansson along with Kenny Smith. Scott, their primary—in fact only—asset, was in demand. Two teams, both run by Australians, wanted him: PacWest Racing run by John Anderson, and Team Green run by Barry Green. 'Ando said he'd take Scott to Champ Car if he drove a season of Indy Lights for them and finished in the top five,' Kenny said. The youngster did better than that. He won and in 2001 moved up to the main game.

The first time Scott Dixon raced a Champ Car on an oval, he also won. He was driving for PacWest, a team owned by one of America's wealthiest telecommunications operators. The close finish, by just 0.3 second, on the 1-mile (1.6-kilometre) Nazareth Speedway, won on a fuel-conservation strategy, made him at the time the youngest winner ever in professional US open-wheeler competition—twenty years, nine months and fourteen days. He won the Rookie of the Year title and eighth outright in the series. What could go wrong?

In 2002 the telecommunications sector crashed. Half a million people in the US industry were made redundant, twenty-three telcos went bankrupt; 5 trillion dollars was wiped out of the market. Bruce McCaw's PacWest Racing closed its doors early into the 2002 season.

Never underestimate the power that major automotive companies exert on motor racing. Holden versus Ford at Mount Panorama was, for many years, the living example of the rule of 'win on Sunday, sell on Monday'. But it's not necessary to have the brand wrapped in a sedan car body. An engine is enough.

With the closure of PacWest, Toyota moved swiftly to place Scott Dixon with Chip Ganassi Racing. 'Toyota were the brokers,' Scott told me. 'They were already paying for me at PacWest, and they'd made a commitment to me.' It was good money, too—upwards of US$10,000 a race plus prize money. Toyota was in a battle with Honda in the series' engine manu-facturers' cup. It needed to shore up its title opportunities.

'When we first sat down with Chip, you could tell he was making a big statement, going out of his way to help,' Scott said.

Scott's crowd-funding contract was a stumbling block. Kenny Smith recalled that Ganassi said he had people who could tear the contract apart: 'But I wouldn't do that. They were all friends.'

Scott intervened: 'I asked if I could do a quick payback at a premium', and according to Kenny that's what happened.

'Everyone got their money back, three times over,' Kenny said.

Dixon drove the last half of the 2002 Champ Car season for Ganassi. He was in a third car, hastily grafted onto Ganassi's two major entries. The strategy took Toyota to championship victory on 332 points ahead of Honda on 283. Ganassi had broken the dam wall in 2002 and joined the IRL with a partial program. In 2003 he committed completely and took Scott Dixon with him. The season would be held exclusively on ovals and Dixon won it.

'I'd first seen Indianapolis as a spectator in 2002,' Scott said. 'It was staggering. Indy was like nothing else. I went through a real love of oval racing. For someone who'd grown up on road courses, this was special.'

He failed to finish his first Indianapolis 500 in 2003 but was classified seventeenth: under a course yellow flag he'd been weaving aggressively to keep heat in his tyres and he brushed the wall. The car was too badly damaged to continue. His teammate Tomas Scheckter, son of world F1 champion Jody, was fourth but from Ganassi's point of view an erratic seventh in the series. Chip had already decided to replace Scheckter with the team's new test driver, Tony Renna.

'I recommended Tony for the job,' Scott said. The pair had been Indy Lights teammates at PacWest and they shared very similar backgrounds and ambitions. Tony started speedway racing at six and before he was fifteen, he'd won 252 races and two national quarter-midget championships. He was four years older than Scott and helped Scott find his feet in the US while still a teenager. Californian born and Florida raised, Renna could do handy things—like securing a rental car, still forbidden to Scott because he was too young.

They went to the gym together—not just any gym but a specialised facility called PitFit, where owner Jim Leo custom-designed equipment for racing drivers and limited his clientele so he could provide specialised support. Dixon has been his star client, coming up twenty years.

Renna had looks, style, talent. The missing ingredient was money. The Ganassi opportunity, to be teammate to Scott in the IRL-winning team, was his big break.

In October 2003, the Ganassi team went tyre testing at Indianapolis. They'd just won the IRL title and the prize-giving banquet was due to be held in Orlando, Florida, the same week. But testing for the season ahead was important. It was cold at Indianapolis and a fresh breeze accentuated the wind chill. Scott completed his test schedule, up to 228 mph (366 km/h), and then left to fly to the prize-giving.

Overnight the team fitted Tony's sculpted seat to Scott's car. At around 9 a.m. Tony pulled out of the pits in the early morning chill for his first sequence of flying laps as a Ganassi driver. On the fourth lap, the car spun on entry to Turn Three. It flew high, above the SAFER barrier, and impacted with the catch fencing where it disintegrated. Debris, including the gearbox clip, flew into the empty spectator area. It was reported that the driver capsule with Tony within it was impaled on the fencing.

Scott learned of his friend's death when he landed in Orlando. He is today as equivocal as he was then: 'Those catch fences are cheese graters. Something has to be done.'

Blair Julian had Scott's back since he first raced in the United States. The Taranaki-born carpenter and his older brother Anton raced speedway in New Zealand and headed for the USA only after Blair had finished his apprenticeship. 'They're solid,' Leigh Diffey told me in admiration. 'Blair is the sort of bloke who'd carry a log over the hill into battle if you asked him.'

Both brothers picked up work with an early iteration of Stefan Johansson Motorsport—Anton on tools, Blair running the team's hospitality. When Scott arrived, Blair was assigned to his car. 'We hadn't met in New Zealand. I knew of him, of course,' Blair said. Dixon kind of adopted the Julian brothers. 'We couldn't get rid of him,' Blair smiled. 'He spent a lot of time sleeping on our couch. Stefan had an indoor kart track and we'd all go there and try to keep up with him. We all approached it a bit casually. Scott wasn't super focused.' There were a few parties, a rugby bar: 'We tried to look out for him.'

Scott and Blair have now been together for two decades. He was Scott's chief mechanic and is now his crew chief, responsible for overview of race preparation and running in each event. In pit stops, he's the one on the front right-hand tyre of the car, choreographing the fuel and tyre ballet: 'I take ownership [of his car and his safety],' Blair told me. 'I need to make sure it's safe for Emma and the kids. If something happened and I hadn't been there to help him, I'd never forgive myself.' It's a statement powerful in its intensity. It's the Anzac spirit—brother for brother, mate for mate. Yet for all the safety precautions, the risks in this branch of motor racing, the high-speed, high-impact ovals, remain huge.

In the Indianapolis 500 of 2017, Dixon had the biggest crash of his career. It was lap 57 and he'd taken an early lead from pole position. British driver Jay Howard went high and his car smacked the wall hard enough to remove the right front suspension and wheel assembly, still tethered to the tub. The car drifted down into the lanes. Dixon was two behind. 'He was quite a way ahead, up in the grey,' Scott said. 'I expected him to stay up there.' Dixon said his own car had been running loose, not pin-sharp perfect. 'Decelerating in an unstable car was difficult. I got on the brakes, tried to slow down and move around the accident.' But it wasn't possible.

The TV showed Scott's double movement, a turn down the track and then a last-millisecond dive up. He ran up the back of Howard and was launched: 'I was higher than I'd ever been, and I thought, *This is going to hurt*. In crashes it feels like a couple of minutes. You hope for the best, but you take precautions: get your hands off the wheel, and you still feel like you can control it.'

The crash was catastrophic. He was vertical, pointing downwards and heading for the inside catch fencing. 'If I'd just been a couple of feet to the left, I would have been in it,' he said, a bit horrified. As it was, his nose cone kissed the wire and then he smashed back to Earth, the car deconstructing around him and the tub sliding back out onto the circuit. 'You get the wind knocked out of you and the adrenaline kicks in. When I got out of the car, I looked back at it for a moment and I thought, "I hope that person is okay."' He didn't register it was his own car.

Emma was in Gasoline Alley. She saw it all on the big screen. She was at the medical centre when doctors put an orthopaedic walker boot on him and gave him relief for a painful ankle. 'I didn't think he was coming home,' she said.

Blair Julian was running the pit. 'It shook me up a bit,' he said in that typically understated bloke's way after the danger has passed. 'I didn't see it, but I heard the spotter call it.' When the wreckage was brought back to the pit, Blair thought, 'What are we doing here?' Once more he referenced Scott's beautiful wife and children: 'But you don't understand how competitive he is. He's prepared to risk it all.'

'Every time you go to Indianapolis you feel it's going to be your year,' Scott said. 'But there are 32 others who feel the same way.' He is an articulate, considered person, but that's as close as he can come to explaining why he continues to go back. When we spoke in 2020, it had been twelve years since he last won the 500, and that was getting close to the all-time record. Juan Pablo Montoya had gone fifteen years between his first and second victory, but he had not been a full-time driver in between. Scott had. Gordon Johncock took nine years between his two victories; Arie Luyendyk seven; the late Dan Wheldon, six. Montoya's record was not one Scott wants to break. He was keen to score his second win on his next attempt.

'Indianapolis is globally important, it's gravitational,' said Mike Hull, long-time team manager of Chip Ganassi Racing. We'd just been on a tour of the Ganassi Indianapolis facility— half race shop, half Hollywood. The main assembly area sits behind a huge glass wall, three storeys high, on view to all. Visitors walk into a reception area crowded with race-winning cars—from IndyCar, to the Ford GT40 sports car to, naturally, the Corvette pace car given to the winner of the Indianapolis 500. Ganassi had won the 500 four times, twice with Dario Franchitti, once with Juan Pablo Montoya and once with Scott. 'We always introduce Scott as the winner of the Indianapolis 500, not as five-time Indy Series winner,' Hull said.

By rights there should be a waxworks likeness of Dixon in the Ganassi foyer along with their other trophies. He has anchored the team for eighteen years, the longest tenure of any IndyCar driver in any team. He has faced off against eighteen teammates in the IndyCar Series and only two have had his measure. Dario Franchitti took three championships from him. Starting in 2009, the New Zealander and the Scotsman formed a powerful alliance, battling each other for the title, fighting Australian Will Power who was driving for rival Penske. Extraordinarily, Dixon and Franchitti remained friends through it all. In 2017 they were even victims of an armed hold-up together, late at night in a Taco Bell drive-through, a mile from the Brickyard, celebrating Scott's pole position that day. Two teenagers escaped with their wallets but not their prized Rolex watches. 'And we got a free meal,' Scott quipped, 'because we no longer had money.'

Dixon considered himself fortunate to have stayed the distance: 'Back in 2005, Ganassi was a revolving door. I had five or six different teammates. So many cars were crashed [a tally indicated the team went through 28 tubs in the season]. Lots of blame was being laid everywhere. Chip asked Steve Horne, then freelance, to try and determine what the issue was. Both Ryan Briscoe and Darren Manning left the team. My contract rolled over into 2006—otherwise Chip could have gotten rid of me, too.'

The big turnaround came in 2006 from Dan Wheldon who'd just won the Indianapolis 500 and the IndyCar Series for Barry Green's team. Ganassi stole him away. 'Dan and I didn't see eye to eye at all,' Scott mused. 'He was a typical Brit, talked a lot, flashy, in your face. We didn't vibe. We were doing stupid shit, not helping each other.' Teammate tension can be good for a team—just ask F1—or it can be debilitating. Scott had a typical Kiwi response: 'We went out for a few beers and sorted each other out.' Dan had just come fourth, Scott sixth, in the 500. They both knew they could do better than that. 'Dan was super intense,' Scott said. 'I've never known anyone to write a debrief as well as him. He was OCD, always looking for something better.'

Wheldon finished the IndyCar Series ahead of Scott the first year. Scott reversed the order in the next two and won the series outright in the third. It's fair to say that Scott wore Wheldon down, who, with his form lowered, moved on. It takes a special person to work inside Ganassi. 'Chip is fiery. He's a racer, just loves to win,' Scott said. 'If you have a similar personality, it could be very different to my own experience. For the most part I just get on with it.' Scott and his new teammate Franchitti were following Wheldon closely when he had his fatal crash at Las Vegas. 'We both moved to the bottom of the track. We knew something was going to happen.'

Consistency has been Dixon's hallmark. There had been just one season, 2004, in which he had not claimed at least one victory, and even then he was tenth in the series. But the Indianapolis 500 remained elusive. 'What's different with Indy is that the strategy changes quite a bit,' he said. 'In Formula One there might be an A strategy or a B strategy. For us it's C and ongoing. It's tough to get three and half hours of racing right, let alone have a whole month go your way. And when it does, you think, "It can't go this well, it's going to implode."'

Would he swap some of his championships for another Indy 500 win? 'The year I finished second [by 3/100ths of a second to teammate Franchitti] it really sucked, man. I'd rather have crashed out than finish so close to the front.' He paused: 'You know, I'm really privileged to have been one of the 70 who have won it at all.'

There is no sign of a trophy in Scott and Emma Dixon's home. That would be a bit showy. There's no indication that he has been recognised twice by the Queen's honours list with a Member of the New Zealand Order of Merit in 2009 and a Companion of the Order of Merit in 2019. Only a knighthood remains. You need to dig to discover that he has been twice named New Zealand's Sportsman of the Year, that the mayor of Indianapolis proclaimed Scott Dixon Day to honour his fifth win of the IndyCar Series. ('We love Scott and Emma here in Indianapolis,' Indianapolis Motor Speedway CEO Doug Boles said. 'They're part of the community and big in charity work.') And it's a deep dive to confirm that he had been named as one of the top 50 drivers in the world never to race in Formula One, a backhanded compliment because his achievements have been at least comparable. For that matter there are none of Emma's trophies, either, to show that she'd been Welsh and British 800-metre track and field champion.

The only overt display of any kind is a matching, tiny, six-pointed star tattoo they both wear. It seems so ... 'cute', not totally out of character with Scott's proposal to Emma when he held up a huge banner in Auckland airport that read 'Marry Me'. With attention to detail, he'd lettered it in Welsh as well as English. 'I actually got my tattoo when I was eighteen and on a night out with the girls. It hurt like crazy but I went through with it,' Emma said. 'Scott got his here in Indianapolis—a six-beer bet.' Love is grand.

20

The Winner Is . . . Power

'Do you know what it's like growing up with a brother named Will Power? Dad's like, this is [softly] Damien, and this is WILLPOWER!!!'

Stand-up comedian Damien Power has a schtick he does on his older brother. He delivered it, with impeccable comedic timing, for the first time at the Sydney Opera House after Will won the IndyCar World Series for Team Penske, and before he won the Indianapolis 500. It was funny, but poignant:

'He's now officially the world's best at driving really fast in a circle. You take your car out into the car park, mate, and start driving in a circle—my brother will lap you. When he won, he got to spray a woman with champagne, which is what he always wanted to do. He didn't want to race. He just went racing to spray women with champagne.

'He risks his life to drive really fast in a circle, that's not a joke, that's serious. He actually said something to me after he won the championship and it's changed my perspective on everything: He said, "You know what, Bro? Everything I've ever dreamed of having I have right now, and it doesn't make you any happier, it can make you sadder . . . what we don't get is that success is being content with what you have and being in the moment with your friends and family." And he looked me right in the eye, and I'll never forget that, as if he saw right through me, and then he just started up his Ferrari [laughter] and he flicked me a small diamond, he carries a pouch of them, and he started doing circles and then went home and sprayed Mum with champagne.'

On 27 May 2018, three hours before Will Power became the first Australian to win the Indianapolis 500, Daniel Ricciardo became the third Australian to win the Monaco Grand Prix. Both drivers deserved their time in the spotlight. But to do it simultaneously was a unique accomplishment, a red-letter day for Australian sport, let alone motor racing. The Australian media, more attuned to European motorsport, initially leaned towards the ever-smiling Danny Ric. He was arguably better known, even though he'd raced less in his homeland. By that evening, the enormity of Will Power's achievement had swung the pendulum towards him. It wasn't until the following morning—24 hours is a long time in a news cycle—that both drivers were acclaimed equally as Aussie heroes. Power's achievement gained real traction. He was welcomed by Prime Minister Scott Morrison at Parliament House in Canberra, and by US Vice President Mike

Pence at the White House. (Pence had been a representative for Indiana.) Australia's US Ambassador Joe Hockey threw a party for him in Washington.

Power had four years earlier won the American Championship, the US equivalent of the World Formula One title. Australian enthusiasts had been waiting with increasing anticipation for a new world champion since Alan Jones last won it in 1980. They could have looked to the States. The IndyCar Series fielded drivers from twelve nations that year, only two fewer than F1, and it was ferociously fought over road and street courses, short ovals and superspeedways with skill levels bordering on superhuman.

Power was four years into his IndyCar career before he won on an oval. It was ten years before he claimed the Indy 500. At the end of 2019 his win rate on ovals in IRL competition was just over one in three: nine ovals to 26 road course victories, with another two in the earlier Champ Car series. 'The oval is very much about driver feel,' he told me. 'You can't get it from data. Indianapolis is so finicky. You can't make a mistake or you're into the wall. It's hard to achieve the discipline.'

Power undersold himself. Yes, the ratio could have been more balanced, but his number of road course victories was phenomenal. At the start of the 2020 season Power was the most successful road course winner in IndyCar, ahead of Scott Dixon. And he had claimed 58 pole positions, only nine short of Mario Andretti's record.

Arguably, Power came to the ovals too late. He'd followed the traditional route from Australia—tilting at windmills in Europe. He was already 24 the first time he saw the Brickyard—and that was from the side window of a tourist bus. He paid US$10 at the

Indianapolis Museum for the ride. The first time he raced there was 2008, the year Scott Dixon won. Dixon is just seven months older than Power but because of his career path, he'd spent seven more seasons in oval racing before Power arrived. By the close of 2019 his win ratio was roughly 50:50 oval to track—21 oval, 23 road course—but comparison with another driver's efforts is a bit meaningless. It's what happens on the day that counts. 'Dixon is a legend in my eyes,' Power said.

There's something about Will Power's eyes that defy you to take a step closer. Everyone talks about them. 'Fans are drawn to him,' Terry Lingner, veteran TV producer, told me. 'The intensity in his eyes is compelling. Anytime we shoot him we magnify his eyes. That's our best shot.'

Veteran journalist Robin Miller is a bit more descriptive: 'He's like a dingo—like a crazy dog.' He meant it kindly.

'I'm not supposed to show bias,' Doug Boles, president of the speedway, said, 'but in 2015 when Will was battling Juan Pablo Montoya in the last four laps for the Indy 500 win, I was rooting for Will. He gets it. I knew he'd celebrate so well.'

Power is a hero among those who count.

Bob Power, Will's dad, has the eyes. We were standing in 37-degree Celsius heat on high bushfire alert on the compressed red-dirt surface of the Millmerran short track circuit on Queensland's Darling Downs, 200 kilometres west of Brisbane. Almost every Australian country town has a speedway. This one was special. It was the scene of Will's first big win, a 100-lap butcher's picnic in 1998, his small four-cylinder Datsun pitted against six- and eight-cylinder cars. 'He just worked his way through the field, one by one, nothing desperate.' Bob smiled with pride and as he removed his sunglasses he didn't squint; there was a defiant catch-me-if-you-can hardness in his eyes.

'Let's get his name out of the way,' Bob said.

Will's great-grandfather William Steven Power was a pioneer motorcycle racer. In the same era when Rupert Jeffkins was attacking the Indianapolis 500, William was setting hill climb and distance records across south-east Queensland. He set a cross-country record from Brisbane to Toowoomba and back in 1915 on his 7-horsepower (5-kilowatt) Indian. Bob and Margrett Power named their third-born son after the family's original speed king. 'He was always William,' Margrett said. 'Will Power was just too much.'

Speed is a family tradition. Will's great-uncle Brian raced the Lotus 39 in which Jim Clark won the 1966 Warwick Farm international round of the Tasman Series. The car passed to local Lotus concessionaire Leo Geoghegan, who won the Japanese Grand Prix, then Brian put a 1.5-litre Ford in it and contested Formula Two.

Will's grandfather Douglas, a WWII pilot, delighted in taking his family to race meetings at Lowood, Strathpine and nearby Leyburn, and at the Australian Grand Prix at Southport. Douglas's wife banned him from competing, especially while he was building the family's awning business in Toowoomba. Bob Power was banned, too, but he bought a speedway car on the quiet and when his dad discovered it, the bans were lifted. By the time Will came along, in 1981, Bob was racing in the Australian F2 Championship. He had two businesses going and motor racing served as stress relief. 'Looking back on it, I shouldn't have motor raced. It takes too much out of your family life,' he said. Margrett didn't go to the races.

The four Power boys—Will was number three—grew up in the shade of a magnificent Moreton Bay fig tree dominating the front garden of their home, perched on the escarpment of the Great Dividing Range overlooking the Lockyer Valley. They were a wild bunch—there was the incident of the water bombing of a police car: 'They didn't catch them,' Bob grinned. They had their 50cc motorcycles and were told by their parents to restrict them to paddock bashing. Will was sent to boarding school for six months to learn some manners then Bob pulled him from school to become his apprentice in the canvas business.

Bob always thought Nick, his second son, was the motor-racing natural. But Nick went breakdancing instead. Today he is a highly respected b*boy, a rapper, choreographer and producer. Youngest brother Damien is the stand-up comedian and writer. Both perform globally. Only the eldest, Kenny, has a day job. He is an accountant on the Gold Coast.

It helped to have a motor-racing father. Bob owned a Spectrum Formula Ford, which Will tested for the first time, aged sixteen, at the small but fast Lakeside circuit north of Brisbane. He was quick right out of the box. Bob helped him understand technique. Will's room in the family home is a testament to his dedication to going fast. It's as he left it: dust-covered early trophies, former helmets, a couple of trophy-surfboards he'd won early in his career at the Gold Coast 300 and 600 races. The room is where he used to go to think about going quicker. His brothers might have been up for a night out, but if it was the night before a race—even if it was at Millmerran—he'd be in his room, visualising.

Bob estimates he's invested 'about A$1 million in Will's motor racing'. Bob not only knew how to motor race, he also knew which doors to knock on and who the good guys were. When Will won the Queensland Formula Ford title in his father's eight-year-old car, he was also contesting the national championship for a southern states team. He claimed a close, frustrating second to Will Davison in the 2001 National Formula Ford title, with seven-time Supercars champion Jamie Whincup third, then backed up the next year to win the Australian Driver's Championship in Formula Holden with a dominant seven wins out of twelve races.

Will started to attract backers. 'Tony Quinn asked me at Lakeside what he could do to help,' Will recalled. Quinn, who built and sold a huge pet food business in Queensland, was a motor-racing tragic. He raced sports cars, developed two race-tracks in New Zealand, and offered philanthropic assistance to young racers with the right attitude. 'I gave him a number, then realised it wasn't enough and went back with a second request,' Will said. Quinn, like others, came through.

'A lot of people have a plan, but we didn't,' Bob Power said. 'Our attitude was, let's keep going and see what door opens.'

The Gold Coast 300 IndyCar race provided a strong pointer. Will was a kid, pre–Formula Ford, when Alex Zanardi won for Chip Ganassi Racing at Surfers Paradise in 1998. 'I'd never been to an F1 race as a kid, but the Champ Cars so impressed me. They blew me away,' Will said. 'I went down to watch Zanardi in the braking zone—cool.' And then, thoughtfully, he added, 'It was a world I thought might be possible for me.'

But his backers looked to Great Britain. 'I'd always wanted to race F1—Senna, Prost, Mansell were my heroes when Dad was racing Formula Two,' Will said. The backers lined him up with a cut-price F3 drive in the British championship. Halfway through the season, he'd crashed it twice trying too hard to make a poor car perform and he'd made the decision to stop throwing money at it.

It wasn't a call he made in isolation. He'd met Mark Webber and Mark's now wife Ann at Silverstone. Mark was only five years Will's senior, but he was in his second year of F1, with Jaguar, and he and Ann could empathise with what Will and his then girlfriend Kerry Fenwick were going through. Webber is admired now for his support of up-and-coming prospects. It was even more extraordinary back then: he was on his own F1 launch-pad, yet he took on Will as a project.

In two years, Mark introduced Will into a decent F3 drive with Australian Alan Docking's team—for which Webber had driven when he was starting—and then underwrote his entry in the World Series by Renault. Ann gave Kerry a job as the couple's PA. Power even tested a F1 Minardi, the team owned by Australian aeroplane broker Paul Stoddart, which had given Webber his first F1 season. After arriving in 2003, Power spent three seasons in Europe. Experience like that is never really wasted.

Craig Gore was an enigma in Australian motor racing. He was, for sure, an enthusiast. His property-developer father Mike had raced massive sports sedans including a Holden Monaro GTS, which he kept towards the front of the field. Craig used motorsport as a vehicle to promote his companies—a financial services organisation called Wright Patton Shakespeare and a wine export business called Aussie Vineyards. He could have chosen golf or tennis. Instead his active and enthusiastic support of motor racing directly assisted the careers of several drivers, among them Marcos Ambrose, Supercar driver David Besnard and Will Power.

Gore was the money behind Team Australia, an ambitious Champ Car project undertaken by former Brabham and Penske engineer-turned-team-owner Derrick Walker, who reasoned that the Gold Coast round of the Champ Car series needed a local flag bearer. He painted his cars green and gold and put an Australian in them—first Besnard, then Marcus Marshall, and finally Power. Power stayed the distance the longest, and even moved with Gore's sponsorship when he took his bank roll from Walker's Champ Car operation and gave it to Kevin Kalkhoven's IndyCar team.

There is an etiquette in motor racing. Derrick Walker had kept a keen eye on European racing. Many of the Indy stars of tomorrow were over there, learning their trade. Walker asked Trevor Carlin, owner of the World Series by Renault team that Will drove for, if it would be okay if he tested the young fellow in his Champ Car.

Will flew to Portland, Ohio, and tested with his eyes on stalks: 'Brakes and steering were comparable to what I was driving, but the horsepower was awesome.' Moving to the US would be the end of his F1 ambitions but 'with everything I'd done in Europe, I knew I could beat those guys'.

It was the first time in his motor-racing career that Will, his father or their backers did not have to pay. 'I wasn't happy with Will going to Champ Car—you can get hurt,' Bob told me. 'But the Craig Gore deal was paid.' He seemed to be still celebrating.

Will Power claimed sixth outright in his first Champ Car series in 2006 and Rookie of the Year.

Champ Cars raced almost exclusively on the road and street circuits. Will saw an oval only once in two years—the Milwaukee Mile—and he came eleventh. Robin Miller told me: 'Will hated ovals when he first started. If only he'd had the confidence he has now.'

When Craig Gore took his cash to Kevin Kalkhoven's IRL team in 2008, Will Power went oval racing in earnest. It was like going to university. Eleven of the eighteen venues were ovals, each with their own character. His teammate, Catalonian Oriol Servià, tried to help but Power was cautious, a bit suspicious: 'When you're working your ass off to be successful, you're not going to help someone else, too.' In his first attempt at the Indy 500, he claimed thirteenth, 30 seconds behind the winner—Scott Dixon. Servià was eleventh. In the series Servià was ninth, Power twelfth.

The last race of the season, non-points scoring because of the IRL–Champ Car conflict, was an Australian promoter's delight. In qualifying for the Gold Coast 300, Will Power for Team Australia was on pole. Scott Dixon for Ganassi was second. Ryan Briscoe for Penske was third. The Australian flag, and Gore's banner, both flew proudly over the street circuit on the beach. Briscoe won; Dixon was half a second behind. Power, who'd seized the lead from the start, made a marginal misjudgement off the back straight and kissed the right-hand wall with the steer wheel of the green and gold car. On lap seventeen, he was out. Worse still, he was out of a job. Gore's support had come to an end.

Bob Power said: 'With blokes like Gore, when they get successful, they keep pushing and pushing until there's nothing there. It's like with the share market—they didn't know when to get out.' But without doubt, Craig Gore helped to 'make' Will Power.

Will Power had arrived in the United States solo. Kerry had stayed in the UK, their relationship behind them. He was bouncing off the walls in a tiny flat in Indianapolis. 'I said to Derrick Walker, "Who is this guy?"' recounts Robin Miller. (Miller has since become one of Power's biggest fans.) 'He was quiet, bashful, long hair, he had no self-confidence. And yet when you spoke to him, he was so self-deprecating, so funny. Who was to know he'd become the fastest guy in Indy for a decade?'

Walker got the message. He asked his PR operator, a recent graduate of Indianapolis's Purdue University, Liz Cannon, to keep an eye on the young Australian. Will and Liz remain a bit coy about it. There are certain lines in business you don't cross, and they didn't, at least not immediately. They would marry in 2010.

The bond between driver and engineer is just as sacrosanct. Derrick Walker brought in Dave Faustino in Will's second year with the team. Equipped with a Bachelor of Science in Mechanical Engineering from upmarket Rutgers University in New Jersey, Faustino had developed a reputation for working well with rookies. Power's growing confidence and Faustino's guidance netted them two wins, importantly five poles and fourth outright in the championship. When Power moved to KV Racing in 2008, Faustino went as well. They talked in shorthand to each other, sharing data at lightning speed. One didn't function without the other.

But what would they do next? Will had been offered a seat at A1GP, a global one-make open-wheeler series in which teams raced under the flag of their country. Alan Jones was the chairman of Team Australia; Alan Docking ran the team. Liz begged him not to do it. It was obvious to her and most observers that the ambitious idea was doomed. 'What happens if Roger Penske or Chip Ganassi call you?' Liz challenged. As if.

The US legal system was brutal to Team Penske's dual Indianapolis 500 winner Hélio Castroneves. The Internal Revenue Service hit him with six charges of tax evasion for failing to report around US$5.5 million in earnings over a five-year period. Each count carried a five-year prison term. Sheriffs arrested him on the eve of a Petit Le Mans car race and he was arraigned and bound in handcuffs and leg chains as practice began. But when he was released on $10 million bail, he returned to Road Atlanta to win the race with co-driver Ryan Briscoe.

Castroneves would not be available to Penske for the first IndyCar round of the 2009 series—his trial preparation was paramount. A replacement driver was essential. Maybe, Penske reasoned, it would be for just the one race, maybe longer.

'Derrick Walker went to Roger Penske and said, "You've got to have this guy."' Robin Miller was getting agitated just in recounting what went down.

Walker was persuasive: 'If he wins just one race with you, he'll be unstoppable.'

Tim Cindric, president of Penske Racing, made the call to Power—asked him in for a meeting, nothing more.

'Roger Penske thanked me for crashing out at Surfers Paradise, making it easier for Briscoe to win,' Will said. It was a test. Penske was looking for honesty and Power admitted the crash was driver error.

'Will came across the highest of all we spoke to. He had no other interests in his life. He wasn't married and he would race for food.' In that casual manner Tim Cindric summed up the key requirement of the Penske Way—absolute commitment. Other drivers he interviewed had been looking for commitment in return. 'Most wanted to talk long-term,' Cindric said. 'The clincher with Will was that he said, "I don't care if it's a one-off deal. I just want to race for you. I'll take my chances."'

Will got the call-up.

In that one race at St. Petersburg, for the first and only time, the most successful team in IndyCar would be represented solely by two Australians. Ryan Briscoe won for Penske and Power came home a safe sixth, rammed up the gearbox of Tony Kanaan. It was an immaculate drive in a new team and he'd displayed his ability without showing off. 'There are a lot of talented people who wouldn't succeed at Penske,' Cindric said. 'Our philosophy is that if it's good for the team then it will be good for you.'

Castroneves was still in limbo; his trial determination had been set for the Friday of the next round, the Long Beach Grand Prix. Penske invited Will to join them, knowing Hélio might be clear to race. 'Will was so excited I'm sure he slept in his race suit,' Cindric said. Power had won at Long Beach the previous year for Kevin Kalkhoven and the win gave him immense confidence. With a massive last-moment lunge, he put his Team Penske Dallara Honda on pole position. Cindric was on his radio and told Power, 'I have good news and bad news— The good news is you're P1 [pole], the bad news is that Hélio has been acquitted.'

Cindric was playing with him. Castroneves would drive but the team also had a car for Will. They transferred all the set-up data he'd gathered and his race seat to that car. 'He would have won, too, if it wasn't for a breakdown in radio communications,' Cindric asserted. Uncertain of his fuel position, Power coasted in second to Dario Franchitti. After two races, the substitute driver was lying second in the championship. Penske gave him a drive in the Indy 500 as a reward. Even Power, focused on one step at a time, recognised it as another test.

For the full Month of May he got a tutorial from three-time Indy winner Rick Mears. 'Rick taught me about the feel of the car. He could predict its footprint on the track before it became apparent by any other means. And he taught me about experience—look at the guys doing well, they're the ones with twenty years of racing behind them.' Power qualified ninth—a sensational result, so far above expectation that the team wouldn't let him out on the track again to try to go faster; no need to take a risk. In the race he got as high as second before a rear wheel issue dropped him to fifth.

Penske gave him another five races. It was all a bit piece-meal with a makeshift crew—one of Penske's sports-car teams on their weekend off. Power won at Edmonton, leading home Castroneves. Briscoe won on the Kentucky Oval; Power was ninth: 'You just get white-knuckled on the wheel. You can screw yourself out of a position by trying too hard.'

At Sonoma, 100 kilometres north of San Francisco, he crashed. In practice a car spun over a blind rise and stopped near the middle of the road. One car scraped by but Will, close behind, was unsighted and slammed head-on into the stalled vehicle. 'I broke my back and I thought: *That's the end of my career*.' He'd compressed two vertebrae and required intense recuperation. Roger Penske sent his private plane to bring him home and in November he announced Power as a full-time member of his team for 2010.

'Maybe if Hélio hadn't had his tax problem, Will wouldn't be in IndyCar today,' Tim Cindric surmised. 'It was all circumstantial.'

Will and Liz, not yet Mrs Power, were within the Penske bubble. It's another world, bordering on corporate. Insiders are looked after very well. 'We were on Roger's yacht,' Liz told me. 'It's one room short of being a cruise ship, all white and cream. Nicole Briscoe missed a step and there was red wine everywhere. Roger and his wife Kathy were very good about it. But the rest of us never forgot—"Don't do a Nicole".' Liz is a good corporate wife, outgoing, intelligent, supportive but a little guarded: 'I keep my distance.'

Will agreed. 'You want to be the guy no one knows much about.' He's skilled at the nuance of motor racing's body language: 'You know you're in trouble when your competitors start saying nice things about you. The real compliment is when they don't want to hang with you.'

We were chatting on the U-shaped lounge of their rumpus room, on the shoreline of Lake Norman, about twenty minutes north of Team Penske's motor-racing headquarters in Moores-ville, North Carolina. Upstairs, their four-year-old Beau, named for Liz's late dad, was in the care of Liz's mother Kathy, who is also the couple's PA. It's a racer's room—trophies nicely displayed, a collection of other people's helmets on shelves (helmet swap is an obsession of IndyCar competitors), and off in a side room is a drum kit and a newly arrived guitar. Behind the door is something special, an electrically driven gimballed race car cockpit rig in which Will sits and is moved through 75 degrees as if on a rotisserie. He designed it himself and a nearby race car fabricator built it. It helps develop his core.

'You want to make it hard for the team to get rid of you,' Will said. It sounded strangely paranoid coming from the driver who had ticked the boxes. We had been discussing Ryan Briscoe's departure from Penske at the end of 2012. 'Ryan was the nicest teammate I ever had. He pushed me to beat him and he made me better. I felt bad about Ryan leaving.'

Will had just celebrated a decade with Team Penske: 'Roger is very loyal. Tim will always do his best for the team.' Then Will added, 'He's very fair.' So corporately, it paid to stay on his toes? 'I'm as good as I've ever been. I'm looking forward to my best season ever,' Will said.

Roger Penske is the busiest billionaire in motorsport. He had given me some time in his trailer at Mount Panorama during his Australian team's successful assault on the 2019 Bathurst 1000, and set me up with his people. A month later he'd bought the Indianapolis Motor Speedway and the Indy Racing League, the whole thing. It was massive news for American motor racing. The Hulman-George era was over. The Penske era, welcomed by the entire sport, was about to begin.

Our ongoing correspondence, funnelled through his staff, provided insight into the Penske Way: 'We really focus on a few key areas when we consider if a driver will be a good fit for our team. The first is performance and have they been able to win and perform consistently in the series where they have raced. We look at communication—with engineers, mechanics and the crew, so we can all work together to improve our performance. The other important element is how drivers engage with our partners. It is so important in racing today to have a good connection with the people and companies that support our programs. In many cases our drivers are a direct representation of our partners' brands so being a good ambassador is very beneficial to our team and our relationship with our sponsors.'

Will, according to Roger, had met the criteria. He'd 'continued to win consistently and was an IndyCar Series championship contender for us and Verizon [the team's corporate partner] every season'. He had 'come close at Indianapolis a few times and then had a great win'. He had 'that ability to dig deep and find that extra speed'.

In 2010 Will took the IndyCar series by storm. Team Penske hired Dave Faustino to reconnect the winning combination. The previous year Power had struggled with an engineer who communicated differently to Faustino. He wasn't wrong, just different. Will would be handed a print-out of his telemetry traces and left to work them out for himself. Faustino would give him a brain dump, verbal and succinct. The pair delivered Penske five victories and eight pole positions, and won the Mario Andretti

Road Course Championship for the first of three consecutive and five total years. In December, Will married Liz in Hawaii.

Will Power epitomises passion. In a world where sport as much as any public endeavour is homogenised, contained by carefully crafted public statements, it's a rarity to find a champion whose emotions are truly on display.

In 2011 Will earned himself a US$30,000 fine for displaying not one but two fingers—one from each hand—to the IndyCar race director, captured on international television. He'd been disadvantaged in a race restart, botched by officials, and nothing could contain his anger. It's likely he won a lot of fans that day. He won the next two races and was still in title contention when they went to Las Vegas. Dan Wheldon died in front of him, their two cars facing each other; Power was in terrible pain, and looking directly into Wheldon's eyes in that moment. James Davison was there: 'When we got in the course car to go back to the medical centre, Will was screaming. There was no consoling him or talking to him. He was enraged, wild.'

First-intervention teams brought Wheldon into triage and worked on him in front of the other drivers. 'You can't unsee that stuff,' Will said. He heard Liz crying outside the door and he went to her. It wasn't until later that night that his own injuries were detected—he'd suffered another vertebral compression fracture, and he needed surgery.

It was surreal, sitting with this perfectly rational young couple in the lounge of their frankly beautiful home with the jet skis on the dock at the end of the garden and Kathy upstairs supervising tradesmen as they prepared for the summer, and we were talking about the ever-present potential of violent death.

They talked of the good times—when Will won the IndyCar Championship Series in 2014 and he cried with emotion on the victory podium. There'd been eleven drivers who'd won races that year, tied with the most ever, and Will had gone into the final race with a slender lead over teammate Castroneves. The championship was his to lose and he didn't. A calmly measured ninth brought home the title; his emotion was hard to control, though, when the helmet came off.

And then there was 2018, when he won the Indy 500 on his eleventh attempt and Liz stalked the pit lane chewing on an empty water bottle, collapsing to the ground when he won; the look on Will's face when he took off his helmet—the raw animal response of the gladiator standing over his kill changed to one of beaming delight when he saw her running to him in the lucky red top she always wore when he raced.

He'd won the Indianapolis Grand Prix on the road circuit earlier that year to score a unique double. And he'd won the A.J. Foyt Trophy for best performance on ovals.

And then there was his response when he threw away his 2019 Indy 500 defence when he marginally missed his pit box entry, so the refueller had to reposition to attach the coupling. The heavy fuel rigs are flung at the car in a wide, balanced arc. A miss can be dangerous. Officials assessed it as such and penalised Power back to 21st position, enraging him: 'I didn't hit the guy. Wait until I see them. What a disgrace,' he said over his radio. It's amazing that he wasn't fined for that but by the time we spoke, he'd mellowed: 'Yeah I missed the box,' he conceded. He spent the rest of the race working his way back to fifth, only 1.5 seconds behind the winner, teammate Simon Pagenaud.

For the new 2020 season Power had invested a lot of time helping to develop the new wraparound safety windshields that would be compulsory for IndyCar going forward. They'd been designed to provide additional security in high-speed crashes—the sort experienced on the superspeedways. That season it was planned there would be only two superspeedways employed—one of them, naturally, was Indianapolis. The odds were swinging in favour of the driver, and Power had become enthusiastic about the prospects. It led him to tell media that he wished he had another ten years in the sport, to take full advantage of the improvements. His comments had been misinterpreted as a veiled hint of impending retirement and he was filthy on himself for letting his guard down, especially as it appeared likely there'd be a new teammate—a Kiwi-born Australian, twelve years his junior—coming on strength.

'It would be such a waste to stop now,' Will said.

21

The Future Is McLaughlin

Scott McLaughlin had been offered a fast track to racing in the US. Team Penske, the most successful team in IndyCar, had invited him on board. There would be no junior category, no hand-to-mouth existence, no waiting for the phone to ring. He would be in at the top. 'I would race a wheelbarrow if Roger Penske asked me,' McLaughlin quipped.

It was early 2020, and the 26-year-old New Zealand–born Australian resident had won the Australian Supercar Championship in two consecutive years for DJR Team Penske, and he had won the Bathurst 1000. Team Penske had responded by offering him a test in their IndyCar program and then confirmed his entry in the Indianapolis Grand Prix, for six years the exclusive domain of Team Penske drivers Will Power and Simon

Pagenaud. Each had won three (Frenchman Pagenaud was with another team the first time he won).

McLaughlin had flown to the United States twice—first to test the Penske IndyCar at Sebring, and once more to drive in the IndyCar program's official test session at the Circuit of The Americas. Both were road courses. At the end of the COTA test, he moved to Texas World Speedway, one of only seven super-speedways in the United States, and had driven on an oval for the first time. 'I saw 222 mph [357 km/h]—that's 50 km/h faster than I've ever been,' he said, wide eyed. 'My out lap was the fastest lap I've ever driven on any racetrack, anywhere.'

Scott's open-wheeler experience was scant. Ten years before he had driven three rounds of the Victorian Formula Ford championship. The sixteen-year-old had won once, and claimed three podiums, a pole position and a fastest lap.

'We call this the Mason–Dixon line,' Team Penske president Tim Cindric said as we strode down the massive concrete corridor, wide and high enough for a semi-trailer, which divided Team Penske's race car operations in Mooresville, North Carolina. In America's Civil War, the Mason–Dixon Line separated the northern and the southern states. At Penske, one side was the team's NASCAR operation, dedicated to the deep south, populated by a brightly coloured confusion of stock cars. There was a gallery above, leading off the gift shop, and most fans wanted nothing more than a selfie from the balcony. If they got lucky, they could take in Roger Penske's original stock car in the background.

On the other side, hidden from public view, was the IndyCar shop and the Acura sports-car program, both philosophically northern. There, waiting for us, were Scott McLaughlin and Will Power. Will was a bit of a surprise. He'd been at home when I left him just an hour before, but here he was in the workshop. There was a sense of the alpha male guarding his territory. Doug Boles, president of the Indianapolis Motor Speedway, had joked about it: 'We had Scott Dixon do some track development work for us,' Doug had said. 'There was a small bump out of Turn Three and we'd asked Scott to do a few laps to make sure we'd fixed it properly. Within hours I had Will on the phone asking what was going on. This was his track [he'd just won on it] and he didn't want any changes made without his knowledge or consent.'

In their own way Scott McLaughlin's eyes were as expressive as Will Power's, wide open and eager. He was a day away from his test at the Circuit of The Americas and if the team had told him about the superspeedway test to follow, no one was letting on.

It's not fair to say that he hadn't done the hard yards, but his career path had been more linear than that of many others. He hadn't endured three years in the European wilderness, living hand-to-mouth, like Will Power. He'd not suffered the unjustified indignity of Formula One rejection, like Ryan Briscoe. He'd not been given a taste of the big time and then languished, like Matthew Brabham. He'd not had to crowd-fund like Scott Dixon. He'd had ambition and with some good fortune thrown in—because that counts for a lot—every step so far had been in the right direction. He'd even met his dream girl, Karly, in Las Vegas and on 14 December 2019, the day they were married in

California, Team Penske had announced his first IndyCar test at Sebring.

'I always followed Scott Dixon,' McLaughlin said. 'I was ten, getting up in the very early morning because of the time difference, recording all the IndyCar races. A lot of kids fell in love with Formula One—not me.' The two Scotts met for the first time five years later. 'It was at a charity kart race supporting Canteen, the kids' cancer organisation.' McLaughlin had been karting with success since he was six. 'He was so welcoming, like he knew who I was. I just couldn't get over the stutters,' he said, still bashful.

McLaughlin was in Year 10 at St Stephen's College on the Gold Coast when he knocked on the door of Supercar champion team Stone Brothers Racing (New Zealander Jimmy Stone had been with Bruce McLaren on the day he died, in 1970) and asked to do school work-experience with them. 'I never told them I raced, I just wanted to see how the team worked.' The encounter established his career path.

The logical progression from go-karts was still open-wheeler race cars: 'My parents were really nervous about that.' Wayne and Diane McLaughlin had built a successful transport business in Australia—six trucks to begin with, 70 when they sold it. 'Dad arranged for me to test for Stone Brothers at Queensland Raceway,' Scott said. 'I didn't know it, Dad had come to an arrangement that if I hit a certain lap time, he'd find funding for a year in the development series.' The target lap time was 1 minute 13.8 seconds. Scott was in the 1 minute 12s. His folks let him leave school early to apprentice in sheet-metal fabrication—a handy skill for a race driver—and he won the development series at nineteen. A year later, driving for veteran team owner and talent spotter Garry Rogers, he became the youngest-ever

THE FUTURE IS McLAUGHLIN

winner in the Supercar Championship, at nineteen years, ten months and three days.

The Penske organisation—trucks, leasing, machinery—established a business foothold in Australia in 2014. It would mirror its mammoth operation in the US. A race team would provide the brand awareness, so they bought 51 per cent of Dick Johnson Racing, the country's oldest continuously operating race shop, and DJR Team Penske was born. 'We sent people over there who know our culture,' Tim Cindric said. 'It took us two years to be successful.' Scott McLaughlin set out to make himself part of their success.

'Through Marcos Ambrose, I texted Tim. I thought they'd never consider me.' But McLaughlin undersold himself. He was becoming Australia's Next Big Thing. In 2016 Penske invited him to the centenary running of the Indianapolis 500 as their guest. 'I went straight to the museum where there was a Penske 50th anniversary display, watched from their suite in Turn One, went to the pit stop challenge, met Rick Mears in the garage, and met Roger and Kathy. I got so comfortable I started calling them by their first names.'

McLaughlin joined DJR Team Penske the next year, delivered a second in the championship and won the title the next two years in succession. Over 89 closely contested races, he claimed 49 per cent of all pole positions and 38 per cent of all wins.

'We're taking him slowly, one step at a time,' Tim Cindric said. 'He's got to feel right.' Cindric knew: his own son Austin, five years younger than Scott, was a Penske protégé in the NASCAR feeder series: 'Austin and Scott work out together.'

The team had wisely arranged for Scott to complete his superspeedway Rookie Test at Texas World Speedway. It qualified him to move to the oval, but no one, least of all McLaughlin, would talk that up. 'I had to average 185 mph [297 km/h]; that was very slow [in Indy terms] but it felt so fast, faster than I'd ever been,' Scott said. Penske started him on high downforce then trimmed the car out just a little: 'The faster you go the more comfortable you get.' They gave him 140 laps and he worked up to 222 mph (357 km/h).

Rick Mears counselled him: 'Trust your backside.'

'In a Supercar you feel it more through the wheel,' Scott had replied. 'My arms and hands were stiff at the end of the test.' He was in no doubt of the steepness of the learning curve. But 2020 was shaping up as a very good year.

Roger Penske's purchase of the Brickyard guaranteed that. It was much more than a business decision. 'Once we were presented with the opportunity to become just the fourth owner in the history of the Indianapolis Motor Speedway, it simply became a matter of how do we get this done,' Penske wrote to me. 'The Speedway and this sport have meant so much to me in my life and in my career. It is where my love of racing began, when I first came to the Indianapolis 500 with my dad in 1951.' Team Penske had won the Indy 500 eighteen times. 'It's where we've enjoyed some of our finest moments and learned some of our most valuable lessons,' he said. Penske was brimful of ideas: 'We are getting on a train that is already moving forward. We have so many opportunities to connect with a new audience—online content, streaming and social media. We can bring our fans closer to the sport so they can experience what happens in the garage and inside the cockpit.'

His opportunity to do all that arrived sooner than he expected. In the first quarter of 2020, the COVID-19 pandemic shut down the world. The Indianapolis 500 was one of the last global sports to move its date, later even than the Tokyo Olympic Games. The Indy Racing League was forced to postpone or cancel races on its schedule. The plans to enter McLaughlin in the Indy GP were abandoned. The race went ahead in early July 2020 without him—he was trapped in Australia due to COVID-19 travel restrictions—and Scott Dixon won. Penske and the teams intent on keeping Indy racing at the forefront of public awareness sought alternatives.

In the last weekend of March 2020, the Indy Racing League endorsed its first simulator race series—live-streamed across the world. Most of the drivers from the real world competed, using their home sim-rigs or more complex professional units, driving the actual liveries of their 2020 race cars. Leigh Diffey called the races.

In the first race, Will Power, driving from his home in North Carolina, claimed third and Scott McLaughlin in a Penske car, from his home in Brisbane, came fourth ahead of some of the biggest names in the sport. The last of the six-race series was held on the Indianapolis Motor Speedway and McLaughlin, a highly skilled gamer, won the Indianapolis 175, a shortened version of the 500.

It was a sensational victory. McLaughlin had positively showcased himself to US audiences without ever turning a wheel on a real racetrack.

'Roger Penske will not give up,' Diffey said in a phone call from his home in Ridgefield where he'd been calling the virtual races. 'Indianapolis is a big deal for him. He won't let it down.'

On 23 August 2020, Roger Penske locked the gates of the Indianapolis Motor Speedway to spectators and ran the 104th Indianapolis 500.

By then the global pandemic had claimed more than 800,000 lives, with at least 174,200 of those in the United States and 794 in Marion County, Indiana, home to the great race. Penske had planned to limit attendance to 50 per cent capacity and then reduced it to 25 per cent, but when it became clear that transmission of COVID-19 was an ever-present risk, he ran the race with zero spectators. It was important to him that he keep faith with his sponsors, and with the fans who watched it on TV.

From the front row, Scott Dixon dominated and led for a total of 111 laps but finished second to Takuma Sato. Both were behind a pace car after a crash only five laps from the chequered flag—a crash that had, coincidentally, involved Sato's teammate Spencer Pigot. It was Dixon's third second place, each time completed under a caution: 'It's hard when it slips away like that,' Dixon told Leigh Diffey's NBC commentary team. 'You can see it, taste it, but you can't do anything about it.'

Will Power led for one lap but finished fourteenth. James Davison retired in flames on lap five when his right front wheel exploded. Scott McLaughlin, his giant leap into US racing on hold, watched the race from isolation in Darwin where he was defending his Australian Supercar Championship title.

It's important, always, to look for a positive. The remarkably consistent Dixon had amassed the third-highest number of leading laps in Indianapolis 500 history—563 of them over his career. The highest achiever was four-time winner Al Unser on 644. The second-highest, from a century ago, was Ralph De Palma on 612. De Palma shared 198 of those laps with Rupert Jeffkins.

Acknowledgements

Rupert Jeffkins started it all. I first heard of him from my grand-father Charlie, who owned Woolgar's Garage in the basement of a bond store on Circular Quay near the Royal Automobile Club. Long before they became classics, old Lagondas and Bentleys would rattle down the steeply angled, wooden-slatted rampway into Charlie's dark cavern and there seemed no hurry for them to be serviced.

Charlie, a 'gentle-man', as attested on his gravestone, would treat them with reverence. He never seemed to make much money from working on them. Charlie and my father, his stepson, John Arthur Henry, were stalwarts of the Olympia Speedway in Sydney's Maroubra sand dunes. Charlie most likely was an occasional riding mechanic.

They filled my young head with stories of the greats—
A.V. Turner, Hope Bartlett, Phil Garlick and, just occasionally,
they would mention Jeffkins, although he was a mystery to
them. That was Rupert—for all his bluster, he was an enigma.
It's taken previously unrelated efforts by a group of enthusiasts, principal amongst them Brian Lear, to piece together his
remarkable story. Motoring editors Peter Robinson and the late
Eoin Young discovered him in the 1970s and wrote a piece for
Wheels magazine, lauding his achievements but sceptical of his
claims. The late Barry Lake pursued him for a decade but, like
so many of Barry's projects, frustratingly never quite got over
the line. Speedway historian Jim Shepherd had him in his grasp
at the Melbourne Motordrome, but he slipped through Jim's
fingers. The president of the Liverpool Historical Society, Glen
op den Brouw, took a giant leap when he started the Facebook
page 'Friends of Rupert Jeffkins' to bring context to the simple
gravestone in his local cemetery. That brought Greg Fitzgerald
forward. Greg is a sound-mixing genius on films like *Mad Max*.
He's also Rupert's great-grandson from his first marriage. Rupert,
Greg explained, had left Greg's great-grandmother pregnant
and unmarried and had become something of a dark part of
his family's past. Brian Lear was able to produce the marriage
certificate that at least proved legitimacy. Rupert's pivotal role
in *Speed Kings* is a compilation of all their efforts and to Brian,
especially, thanks for so willingly sharing.

The American racing obsession runs deep in Australia. Phil
Christensen, journalist and promoter, has curated ten speed cars,
sprint cars, midgets and quarter-midgets including the Genesee
Beer Wagon of three-time USAC champion Sheldon Kinser,
cousin of World of Outlaws sprint-car king Steve Kinser. Phil has

stopped short of the massive investment required for an Indy roadster. New South Wales Central Coast bus and coach proprietor Aaron Lewis has 'contented' himself with buying, restoring, racing and trading no fewer than seven rear-engine IndyCars ranging from Jack Brabham's BT25 through to Graham McRae's actual Rookie of the Year Eagle. Aaron got to drive one of his Eagles on the Brickyard during the Indy 500 Centenary celebrations in 2016. To both Phil and Aaron, thanks for your insight.

Family and friends of drivers in Australia and New Zealand embraced the Speed Kings project. Greeta Hulme and her daughter Adele; Jan McLaren and the curator of the McLaren Heritage Centre, David Rhodes; Kiwi racing legend Kenny Smith; Garry Pedersen; and especially Brian Lawrence (who opened so many doors, including that of Graham McRae); Jann Tauranac, who took me to her father, Ron; Damien Power, who allowed me to use his material; and Neil Crompton, who arranged entree to Roger Penske and Steve Horne, all took delight in contributing. And then there were the parents—Glenys Dixon, Bob and Margrett Power, Geoff and Marion Briscoe, and Bob Cunningham, who freely shared family recollections. Michal Barton of Automoto Bookshop made his library available to me.

There must be someone in Marion County, Indiana, not touched by the Indianapolis 500, but you'd be hard-pressed to find them. The race is part of their DNA. Becky Stamatkin is the third generation of her family to have run the Workingman's Friend diner since 1918. Robin Miller has been eating there for half a century. To them both, thanks for the best damned double cheeseburger in the Midwest, and to Robin, an Indy-media legend, for the revelations. Indianapolis Motor Speedway historian Donald Davidson and his co-author Rick Shaffer literally

339

wrote the book on the race. They are both human encyclopae-
dias and their willingness to talk across unfriendly time zones
was golden. J. Douglas Boles, president of the Speedway, and his
colleagues Alex Damron, Suzi Elliott, Wes Johnson and particularly photographers and archivists Chris Owens and Joe Skibinski
opened the vault, a motorsport record like no other in the world.
Terry Lingner crosses the streams—part-TV producer, part-
team owner, and a tapped-in member of Indianapolis racing
society. He's an invaluable resource, a fact recognised by NBC
Sports, which has made him their Hoosier on the ground. The
teams, Ganassi and Andretti in Indianapolis and Penske in North
Carolina; the chassis-maker, Dallara, on Main Street, Speedway,
right opposite A.J. Foyt's satellite operation; and Jim Leo's PitFit
gymnasium are all professional purveyors of their craft. To them,
their drivers, engineers and team management, and to all those
who paved the way—all of you covered in this book—thank you
for your participation and congratulations on your achievements.

Speed Kings is the fourth in what has become a motorsport
series published by Allen & Unwin and my deep appreciation goes
to publishing director Tom Gilliatt; senior editor Samantha Kent,
who is never content to leave well enough alone; copy editor Susin
Chow; proofreader and all-round genius Emma Driver and cover
designer Luke Causby for continuing the grand partnership.

Speed Kings was the most consuming of all four titles. To my
family, Jenny, Andrew, Karen, Kate, Dan, Cameron and Matilda,
thank you for letting me steal our summer. And to my part-
time American family the Diffeys—Leigh, Michaela, Myles and
Reeve, thanks for your support and encouragement. Leigh is a
true Aussie success story and for all of us in media who think
maybe we could have or should have, he's living our dream.

Bibliography

Books

Bloemaker, A., *500 Miles to Go*, London: Frederick Muller Limited, 1962

Borgeson, G., *The Golden Age of the American Racing Car*, New York: W. W. Norton and Co., 1966

Burgess Wise, D., Boddy, W., Laban, B., *The Automobile: The first century*, London: Orbis Publishing, 1983

Carnegie, T., *Indy 500: More than a race*, New York: McGraw Hill, 1987

Clark, M., *Denny Hulme: A celebration of a Kiwi icon*, Auckland: Bruce McLaren Trust, 2012

Clark, M., *The Kenny Smith Scrapbook*, Albany, NZ: Bateman, 2016

Court, W., *Grand Prix Requiem*, Stamford, UK: Patrick Stephens Limited, 1992

Davidson, D., Shaffer, R., *Official History of the Indianapolis 500*, Malvern, UK: Icon Publishing Limited, 2013

Davis, P., *Australians on the Road*, Sydney: Rigby, 1979

Davis, T., Armont, A., *Brabham: The untold story of Formula One*, Sydney: Harper Collins, 2019

De Paolo, P., *Wall Smacker: The saga of the speedway*, Ancarano, Italy: Edizioni Savine, 2017

Doyle, G., *Ralph de Palma: Gentleman champion*, Oceanside, CA: Golden Age Books, 2005

Gabbard, A., *Indy's Wildest Decade*, North Branch, MN: CarTech Auto Books, 2004

Garner, A., Spiegel, M., *Indy 500 Memories*, USA: self-published, 2016

Greenhalgh, D., Floyd, T., Tuckey, W., *Australia's Greatest Motor Race 1960–1999: The first 40 years*, Sydney: Chevron Publishing, 2000

Hartnett, L., *Big Wheels, Little Wheels*, Melbourne: Lansdowne Press, 1964

Henry, A., *Brabham: The Grand Prix Cars*, Richmond, UK: Hazleton Publishing, 1985

Howard, G., *Lex Davison: Larger than life*, Sydney: Turton & Armstrong, 2004

Jones, A., Clarke, A., *AJ: How Alan Jones climbed to the top of Formula One*, Sydney: Penguin Random House, 2017

Kerr, P., *To Finish First*, Auckland: Random House NZ, 2007

Ludvigsen, K., *Indy Cars of the 1940s*, Hudson, WI: Iconografix, 2004

Ludvigsen, K., *Indy Cars 1911–1939*, Hudson, WI: Iconografix, 2005

Lurani, G., Hodges, D. (ed.), *A History of Motor Racing*, Feltham, UK: Hamlyn Publishing, 1972

McKay, C., *This Is the Life*, Sydney: Angus & Robertson, 1961

Macknight, N., *Technology of the Champ Car*, Richmond, UK: Hazleton Publishing, 1998

Malsher, D., *The Sheer Force of Will Power*, Sydney: HarperCollins, 2015

Mansell, N., *The Official 2001–2002 Formula One Record Book*, London: Virgin Publishing, 2001

Murray, B., *Crusher*, Brisbane: BAM Media, 2017

Myrhe, S., *Scott Dixon: Indy to Indy*, Auckland: Hodder Moa, 2006

Nunn, J., *Khaki Town*, Sydney: William Heinemann, 2019

Nye, D., *The Jack Brabham Story*, Windsor, NSW: Minidi, 2004

Nye, D., *McLaren: The Grand Prix, Can-Am and Indy Cars*, Richmond, UK: Hazleton Publishing, 1984

Penske, T., *Team Penske: 50th Anniversary at the Indianapolis 500*, New York: Rizzoli Publishing, 2019

Phipps, D., *Autocourse: The review of international motor sport 1966–1967*, London: Haymarket Press, 1967

Pollard, J., *One for the Road*, Sydney: Jack Pollard, 1974

Reinhardt, J., *The Indianapolis 500*, Bloomington, IN: Red Lightning Books, 2019

Roberts, M., *Casey Stoner: Pushing the limits*, Sydney: Hachette, 2013

Shaffer, R., *CART: The first 20 years*, Richmond, UK: Hazleton Publishing, 1999

Shaw, J., *Autocourse Indy Car 1995–96*, Richmond, UK: Hazleton Publishing, 1997

Shaw, J., *Autocourse Indy Car 1996–97*, Richmond, UK: Hazleton Publishing, 1998

Shepherd, J., *Big Rev Kev*, Sydney: Lansdowne Press, 1983

Shepherd, J., *A History of Australian Speedway*, Sydney: Frew Publications, 2003

Simpson, S., *Wizard Smith*, Sydney: Murray Book Distributors, 1977

Tibballs, G., *Motor Racing's Strangest Races*, London: Robson Books, 2001

Tremayne, D., *Jochen Rindt: Uncrowned king*, Sparkford, UK: Haynes Publishing, 2010

White, G., *Indianapolis Racing Cars of Frank Kurtis*, Hudson, WI: Iconografix, 2000

Woods, B., *Legends of Speed*, Sydney: HarperSports, 2004

Young, E., *Forza Amon*, Newbury Park, CA: Haynes Publishing, 2003

Young, E., *It Beats Working*, Stamford, UK: Patrick Stephens Limited, 1996

Interviews

Ambrose, Marcos: Tasmania, January 2020

Bartlett, Kevin: Maleny, Qld, January 2020

Bogle, Kimberly: USA, February 2020

Boles, Doug: USA, February 2020

Brabham, Geoff and Roseina: Gold Coast, Qld, November 2019

Brabham, Matthew: January 2020; USA, February 2020

Briscoe, Geoff and Marion: Sydney, February–April 2020

Briscoe, Ryan and Nicole: USA, February 2020
Christensen, Phil: Southern Highlands, NSW, August 2019
Cindric, Tim: USA, February 2020
Cunningham, Bob: New Zealand, December 2019
Cunningham, Wade: USA, February–April 2020
Davidson, Donald: December 2019; USA, February 2020
Davison, James: Melbourne, January 2020
de Ponti, Stefano: USA, February–April 2020
Diffey, Leigh and Michaela: USA, February 2020
Dixon, Emma: USA, February 2020
Dixon, Glenys: New Zealand, December 2019
Dixon, Scott: January 2020; USA, February 2020
Dykstra, Lee and Pauline: USA, February 2020
Elliott, Suzi: USA, February 2020
Firestone, Dennis: USA January 2020
George, Tony: USA, February 2020
Green, Barry: USA, January 2020
Green, Kim: USA. January 2020
Hall, Matt: Newcastle, NSW, February–April 2020
Harcus, Paul 'Ziggy': January 2020; USA, February 2020
Harris, Phil: Lake Macquarie, NSW, December 2019
Horne, Christine: New Zealand, December 2019
Horne, Steve: November 2019; New Zealand, December 2019
Hull, Mike: USA, February 2020
Hulme, Greeta: New Zealand, December 2019
Jones, Alan: Gold Coast, Qld, February–April 2020
Julian, Blair: USA, January 2020
Leo, Jim: USA, February 2020
Lewis, Aaron: Central Coast, NSW, January 2020
Lingner, Terry: USA, February 2020
McLaren, Jan: New Zealand, December 2019
McLaughlin, Scott: Brisbane, Qld, February–April 2020
McRae, Graham: New Zealand, December 2019
Miller, Robin: USA, February 2020
Murray, Brett: Gold Coast, Qld, August 2019

BIBLIOGRAPHY

Penske, Roger: correspondence, February 2020
Power, Bob and Margrett: Toowoomba, Qld, November 2019
Power, Will: Australia, August 2019
Power, Will and Liz: USA, February 2020
Roby, Steve and Kathy: USA, February 2020
Schuppan, Jenny: Adelaide, November 2019
Schuppan, Vern: Adelaide, August 2019, November 2019
Smith, Jim: Bondi, NSW, January 2020
Smith, Kenny: New Zealand, December 2019
Stoner, Casey: Gold Coast, Qld, February–April 2020
Tauranac, Ron: Buderim, Qld, January 2020
Wilson, Rob: UK, February–April 2020

Index

INDEX

INDEX